Macmillan Computer Science Series

Consulting Editor
Professor F.H. Sumner, University of Manchester

S.T. Allworth and R.N. Zobel, *Introduction to Real-time Software Design, second edition*
Ian O. Angell and Gareth Griffith, *High-resolution Computer Graphics Using FORTRAN 77*
Ian O. Angell and Gareth Griffith, *High-resolution Computer Graphics Using Pascal*
M. Azmoodeh, *Abstract Data Types and Algorithms*
C. Bamford and P. Curran, *Data Structures, Files and Databases*
Philip Barker, *Author Languages for CAL*
A.N. Barrett and A.L. Mackay, *Spatial Structure and the Microcomputer*
R.E. Berry, B.A.E. Meekings and M.D. Soren, *A Book on C, second edition*
P. Beynon-Davies, *Information Systems Development*
G.M. Birtwistle, *Discrete Event Modelling on Simula*
B.G. Blundell and C.N. Daskalakis, *Using and Administering an Apollo Network*
B.G. Blundell, C.N. Daskalakis, N.A.E. Heyes and T.P. Hopkins, *An Introductory Guide to Silvar Lisco and HILO Simulators*
T.B. Boffey, *Graph Theory in Operations Research*
Richard Bornat, *Understanding and Writing Compilers*
Linda E.M. Brackenbury, *Design of VLSI Systems — A Practical Introduction*
G.R. Brookes and A.J. Stewart, *Introduction to occam 2 on the Transputer*
J.K. Buckle, *Software Configuration Management*
W.D. Burnham and A.R. Hall, *Prolog Programming and Applications*
P.C. Capon and P.J. Jinks, *Compiler Engineering Using Pascal*
J.C. Cluley, *Interfacing to Microprocessors*
J.C. Cluley, *Introduction to Low Level Programming for Microprocessors*
Robert Cole, *Computer Communications, second edition*
Derek Coleman, *A Structured Programming Approach to Data*
Andrew J.T. Colin, *Fundamentals of Computer Science*
Andrew J.T. Colin, *Programming and Problem-solving in Algol 68*
S.M. Deen, *Fundamentals of Database Systems*
S.M. Deen, *Principles and Practice of Database Systems*
C. Delannoy, *Turbo Pascal Programming*
Tim Denvir, *Introduction to Discrete Mathematics for Software Engineering*
P.M. Dew and K.R. James, *Introduction to Numerical Computation in Pascal*
D. England et al., *A Sun User's Guide*
A.B. Fontaine and F. Barrand, *80286 and 80386 Microprocessors*
K.C.E. Gee, *Introduction to Local Area Computer Networks*
J.B. Gosling, *Design of Arithmetic Units for Digital Computers*
M.G. Hartley, M. Healey and P.G. Depledge, *Mini and Microcomputer Systems*
Roger Hutty, *Z80 Assembly Language Programming for Students*
Roland N. Ibbett and Nigel P. Topham, *Architecture of High Performance Computers, Volume I*
Roland N. Ibbett and Nigel P. Topham, *Architecture of High Performance Computers, Volume II*
Patrick Jaulent, *The 68000 – Hardware and Software*
P. Jaulent, L. Baticle and P. Pillot, *68020-30 Microprocessors and their Coprocessors*
J.M. King and J.P. Pardoe, *Program Design Using JSP — A Practical Introduction*
E.V. Krishnamurthy, *Introductory Theory of Computer Science*
V.P. Lane, *Security of Computer Based Information Systems*
Graham Lee, *From Hardware to Software — an introduction to computers*
A.M. Lister and R.D. Eager, *Fundamentals of Operating Systems, fourth edition*

Continued overleaf

Tom Manns and Michael Coleman, *Software Quality Assurance*
Brian Meek, *Fortran, PL/1 and the Algols*
A. Mével and T. Guéguen, *Smalltalk-80*
Y. Nishinuma and R. Espesser, *UNIX — First Contact*
Pim Oets, *MS-DOS and PC-DOS — A Practical Guide, second edition*
A.I. Pilavakis, *UNIX Workshop*
Christian Queinnec, *LISP*
E.J. Redfern, *Introduction to Pascal for Computational Mathematics*
Gordon Reece, *Microcomputer Modelling by Finite Differences*
W.P. Salman, O. Tisserand and B. Toulout, *FORTH*
L.E. Scales, *Introduction to Non-Linear Optimization*
Peter S. Sell, *Expert Systems — A Practical Introduction*
A.G. Sutcliffe, *Human-Computer Interface Design*
Colin J. Theaker and Graham R. Brookes, *A Practical Course on Operating Systems*
M.R. Tolhurst *et al.*, *Open Systems Interconnection*
J-M. Trio, *8086-8088 Architecture and Programming*
A.J. Tyrrell, *COBOL from Pascal*
M.J. Usher, *Information Theory for Information Technologists*
B.S. Walker, *Understanding Microprocessors*
Colin Walls, *Programming Dedicated Microprocessors*
I.R. Wilson and A.M. Addyman, *A Practical Introduction to Pascal — with BS6192, second edition*

Non-series
Roy Anderson, *Management, Information Systems and Computers*
I.O. Angell, *Advanced Graphics with the IBM Personal Computer*
J.E. Bingham and G.W.P. Davies, *Planning for Data Communications*
B.V. Cordingley and D. Chamund, *Advanced BASIC Scientific Subroutines*
N. Frude, *A Guide to SPSS/PC+*
Barry Thomas, *A PostScript Cookbook*

Introduction to Real-time Software Design

S.T. Allworth

R.N. Zobel

Second Edition

First published 1987
Reprinted 1988, 1989

Published by
MACMILLAN EDUCATION LTD
Houndmills, Basingstoke, Hampshire RG21 2XS
and London
Companies and representatives
throughout the world

Typeset by TecSet Ltd, Wallington, Surrey

Printed in Hong Kong

British Library Cataloguing in Publication Data
Allworth S. T.
Introduction to real-time software design
—2nd ed.—(Macmillan computer science
series).
1. Real-time data processing   2. Programming
(Electronic computers)
I. Title   II. Zobel, R. N.
005.3   QA76.54

ISBN 0-333-41793-3
ISBN 0-333-41792-5 Pbk

*to Leyla
and Lesley*

Contents

Preface

The first edition of this book (by Steve Allworth) was based on a series
of lectures written to introduce the design of real-time software to
undergraduate electrical engineers at the University of Essex. At that
time the advent of microprocessors was causing a minor revolution in
the computer industry, resulting among other effects in a mushrooming
of the number of real-time applications being attempted. At the time of
writing this second edition, this revolution has increased dramatically;
more sophisticated microprocessors of higher power have appeared,
along with support chips and large capacity memories at ever-decreasing
system cost. Many of these applications are conducted by electrical and
electronic engineers after only a restricted study of software design, or
by computer scientists familiar only with large software systems, and
neither group is therefore well acquainted with many of the software
aspects of real-time systems. This trend is continuing, often because of
the difficulty of fitting many diverse topics into the curriculum or
because other aspects of the course are seen to be more pressing. A
suitable text on which to base a concise course of lectures was
developed from the scattered literature quoted in the first edition.

This second edition updates and expands the original material, adding
further topics such as interfaces, real-time languages, distributed systems
and signal processing. The book presents the design of real-time
software in a structured way, concentrating on the basic principles rather
than particular realisations. It is our belief that by applying a strong
structural discipline to the design of real-time software it can be made a
relatively straightforward task. Indeed, the increasing cost and diversity
of real-time software makes simplification of the task an imperative. It
has been felt desirable to relate, in a small way, the design principles to
other disciplines concerned with real-time systems outside software
design, to avoid the 'water-tight box' syndrome, and thus attempt to
show how the software design integrates with the overall system.

Chapter 1 introduces the topic in general, and puts forward the virtual
machine concept as a fundamental design tool. Part I looks at how such
a machine can be constructed: chapter 2 describes the machine, and
chapters 3, 4 and 5 discuss the nucleus of the machine, scheduling and
reliability considerations. Part II is concerned with the design of the

processes that make up a real-time system, and with some of the software tools necessary for their construction: chapter 6 discusses the general design philosophy and introduces a number of process virtual machines; chapter 7 considers interfaces and the low-level processes associated with them; chapter 8 discusses design and development tools, and chapter 9 looks at the real-time features of some high-level languages. Part III considers the special problems of real-time signal processing in chapter 10 and of performance prediction, measurement, and evaluation in chapter 11.

This book is intended to be a concise introduction to the subject of real-time software. It does not claim to offer total coverage of the topic. We do not attempt to give other than a mention of areas that are currently the basis for research; rather we try to outline general principles.

The computer scientist and engineer increasingly find that their job involves not only applications programming but the design of real-time software for mini and microprocessor systems. We hope that the following chapters will provide a clear introductory framework of the techniques used in this area of software design.

STEVE ALLWORTH
DICK ZOBEL

Acknowledgements

Steve Allworth would like to thank Frank Coakley, his colleague on many real-time software courses, for his advice and criticism; Kevin Cox, Mick Langfield and Ian Witten for their patience and helpful comments; and the University of Essex, the Cable and Wireless Ltd, and the Canberra College of Advanced Education for their generous assistance in preparing the first edition. To friends and family go particular thanks: to Jane, for diligently typing and weathering the storms, and to Margot Tolmer and the Irvings of Mill Farm, for providing understanding, shelter and support.

Dick Zobel would like to thank Lesley and his family for tolerating his absence while typing the second edition on the BBC Microcomputer upstairs; Steve Allworth and Macmillan Education for their sorely tried patience; Frank Sumner, Sheila and Margaret for prompting and understanding; and the Computer Science Department at the University of Manchester.

This book contains many important points and practical hints and tips. These are indicated by the ● symbol at the beginning of the paragraph in which they appear.

1 Introduction

Over the past few years the dramatic decrease in the cost of computing hardware has led to a proliferation of real-time systems in a wide range of applications. Most of the systems now being introduced are used to control commercial, industrial and communications systems. Even domestic devices and automobiles are incorporating real-time systems. The facilities required of the software in these applications vary as widely as the style of application. As a result it has become necessary to develop a set of generalised real-time software design techniques that are useful in the full range of applications. However, before this can be attempted it is necessary to define the properties that such systems have in common.

1.1 WHAT ARE REAL-TIME SYSTEMS?

Many attempts have been made to define a 'real-time' system. At best these definitions are incomplete and do not encompass all the characteristics of such a system. Rather than attempt an accurate definition, we shall discuss the properties and facilities that are commonly regarded as making up a real-time system.

1.1.1 Control Systems

A real-time system reacts so as to affect the environment in which it is operating. It is a collection of devices, controlled by a stored program of instructions. This program acts as the regulating element in a feedback loop, which then forms part of a commercial or industrial system.

For convenience, we shall divide the entire real-time system into two parts — the *controlled system* and the *controlling system*. The controlled system consists of the hardware devices which go to make up the part of the system that interfaces with the environment. The controlling system consists of the software element together with its associated processing hardware.

The configuration and behaviour of the components that constitute the controlled system vary with the purpose of the system. In a data-processing environment the devices may be terminals, disc drives, line printers and card readers; they may be multiplexers, line drivers and teleprinters in a telecommunications environment; or indeed, they may be valves, relays or hoppers in a process-control environment. Normally, the various devices do not function completely independently of one another. In an air-conditioning system, for instance, the heating element will usually have some knowledge of the action of the fan, so that an even temperature of ducted air can be maintained.

It must be noted that many computer-controlled devices and elements now themselves include microprocessors. Important consequences of this are that such devices and elements are programmable and hence may have a sophisticated interface through which instructions, data and status information may be communicated, and that their actions are not fixed.

A definition of a real-time system, then, must include the fact that it is a control system. The design of the controlled system is very much system-dependent. However, the design of the controlling software can, hopefully, be generalised. This book will attempt to define a set of design techniques and guidelines that will be of use in producing such software.

1.1.2 Software Systems

Perhaps, if we analyse a range of software systems, we will be able to derive a closer definition of the software controlling a real-time system.

Batch Accounting Systems

Most computers are used in the control of accounting and administrative systems. The computer system does not normally control the business system directly. Rather, it processes the data which are used for administrative control. A commercial computing system is a collection of applications programs: data verification, payroll, database management and other financial calculations. These programs manipulate data and thus assist indirectly in the control of the business system. In a conventional 'batch' system, these programs are run in batches, selected in such a way as to optimise the use of computing facilities. Because the computer system does not exercise immediate control over the business system, and therefore the programs do not have to be run with stringent time constraints, we will not consider this collection of batch applications programs as being a real-time system.

On-line Systems

Most modern business computer systems are based on fully on-line
operation. An on-line system acts so as to maintain continuous control
of a business system. It does this by ensuring that, as each transaction
occurs, the relevant files and reports are updated before the next
transaction affecting these files is handled. This implies that the
applications programs are not always run at times dictated by the
optimum use of computing resources. Instead they are run at times
imposed by requests from an environment of enquiry terminals,
point-of-sale terminals and other devices that are designed to input
individual queries or transactions.

The software controlling an on-line system is therefore extremely
time-critical. It is this *time-critical* aspect that differentiates an on-line
system from a batch system, and qualifies it as a real-time system. The
large number of on-line systems currently in operation constitutes the
bulk of all real-time systems. Many on-line systems require a large
number of terminals and consequently extra facilities are needed to
service the traffic.

Operating Systems

Most modern computer installations have a collection of programs which
control the computing system itself. These programs, making up the
operating system, are designed to (1) control the devices that make up
the hardware of the system; (2) ensure that the hardware resources of
the system are employed optimally; (3) provide utility programs such as
editors and file-organisation facilities; and (4) provide a multi-access
environment for a number of simultaneous users. The device-control
programs, interrupt handling routines and other software at the nucleus
of a multiprocessing operating system can be regarded as a real-time
system. The controlled system in this case consists of the disc drives,
printers and similar devices that make up the computer system itself.

Process-control and Communications Systems

Process-control systems include embedded computers for controlling
chemical plants, missile systems, manufacturing machinery and,
nowadays, individual automobiles. Communication systems include
computer-controlled telephone exchanges and computer networks. The
fact that a real-time system is working as a controlling element in a *time-critical* environment becomes very evident when viewing these
applications. Another aspect that emerges when considering this area of
application is that the software must be *reliable*. Large sums of money,

valuable equipment and often human lives depend on the correct and reliable operation of the software controlling these systems.

1.1.3 General Properties

From the discussion to date, we can see that real-time software must be that which works in a time-critical environment to control some system of devices. However, since real-time systems are usually created to be part of marketable products, it is necessary to extend our description still further.

Responsiveness

In order to control its environment successfully, a real-time system must be *responsive* to changes in its environment. It is this responsiveness that forms the fundamental property of a real-time system. Unless the system reacts sufficiently rapidly, it cannot be considered to be operating in real-time. This property is usually quantified as the system's *response time*. The response time of a system is the time that the system will take to react to a change in, or stimulus from, its environment. The response time must be such that the system appears to react 'instantaneously'. What is regarded as an 'instantaneous' reaction will vary with the device. For a power-station boiler, 'instantaneous' may mean reaction to a temperature change within thirty minutes. For the system controlling a missile, the reaction to a course change must occur within a few milliseconds.

Correctness and Completeness

● A real-time system should accurately and totally control an aspect of the environment. To be effective, then, the system must be *correct* and *complete*. It must be complete in the sense that it has catered for all possible eventualities and situations that may arise in the environment or in the controlling software itself. It must be correct in that suitable decisions are made when the different situations arise (even if the decision is to do nothing at all). A wide range of situations and conditions occur in a real-world environment, and so it is extremely difficult completely and correctly to specify the requirements of a system designed to influence or control a portion of the real world. Before a real-time system can be designed, a requirement specification must be produced. Ideally the requirement specification must rigorously describe the action to be taken for every situation that the system will face. This is often the most difficult aspect of the project, and much of the final correctness of the system will depend on its success. To ease this problem it is appropriate to add defensive programming as a tool for providing for recovery from error conditions and exceptions. This should be viewed alongside correctness and completeness as a method of improving system integrity and hence reliability.

Reliability

● A real-time system must be *reliable*. It must be able to provide a service that can be closely defined in terms of guaranteed minimum mean time between failure and mean time to repair. The system must 'fail softly' — it must provide a useful degraded service in the face of hardware failure. An example of the stringent reliability requirements imposed upon real-time systems is a stored-program-controlled telephone exchange. It may be expected to operate over a forty-year period with no more than a total of two hours out of service, depending on the degree of degradation of service.

Economy

The *cost* of instantaneous response, completeness, total correctness and absolute reliability must be taken into account when considering these ideals. As with any product, the designer will be constrained in his pursuit of an ideal design by economic considerations. An on-line system that guarantees a maximum response time of half a second may not be able to compete with a system that only offers a response time of two seconds, but sells at half the price!
● In order to maintain its commercial viability, a real-time system must be as inexpensive to produce, run and maintain as possible. The following section will discuss this aspect in more detail.

1.2 SOFTWARE COSTS

● The continuing reduction in the cost of computer hardware has not been paralleled by a corresponding drop in the cost of software. When attempting to analyse the factors behind this situation it is important to remember that real-time software is a *commercial product*. The form of the design of any product will influence the cost of manufacture, and the cost of maintaining the product over its lifetime. One purpose of this book is to discuss techniques that can be applied when designing real-time software, such that the overall cost of the product is reduced. As a first step, we shall attempt to define the causes of high cost in software. This will point the way toward techniques which produce more economical designs. Recent developments in tools to speed up software development, reduce its cost and make it more reliable have given rise to an integrated project support environment (IPSE) approach. However, the underlying reasons for high costs remain.

1.2.1 Life-cycle Costs

When calculating the cost of any product it is necessary to analyse the costs throughout the *entire* life cycle of the product — not just the initial cost of production.

Hardware

Tracing the life cycle of a hardware product is reasonably elementary. A need (or market) is established, and the product is designed and manufactured. After being commissioned, the product enters a maintenance phase where worn parts are replaced and the product is serviced to ensure reliable operation. At a certain point in the product's life, the maintenance costs start to increase.

This occurs as the product nears the end of its useful life. At a certain point it is scrapped. The cost of the product *versus* time, over its lifetime, is shown in figure 1.1.

Software

The software element of a real-time system has similar phases in its life cycle, but note, from figure 1.2, that the curve displays a radically

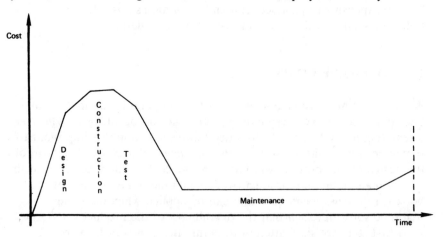

Figure 1.1 Hardware life cycle costs

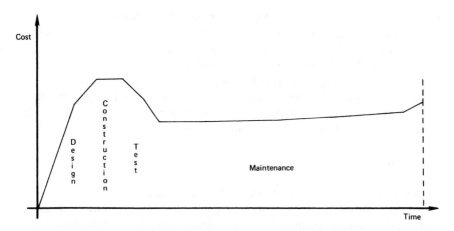

Figure 1.2 Software life cycle costs

different picture. The maintenance phase is a much greater factor in the product's lifetime cost. Software is far easier to change than hardware; it can be readily adapted to suit changing conditions and requirements. It is for this reason that the maintenance aspect will always dominate software costs.

Conventionally, maintaining a system means replacing parts that no longer carry out their function. By its very nature, software cannot 'wear out', but it can malfunction, or the functions required of it can change as time goes by. Maintenance in software terms means *changing* the software to repair shortcomings or modify its behaviour. Only in software that is not changed and is totally stable throughout its lifetime will the curve in figure 1.2 follow that of a hardware product.

So, if we can reduce the cost of maintenance, we should be able to reduce the overall cost of the product. Now, what causes high maintenance costs? As a result of studying the behaviour of a number of large software systems over their life cycle, Belady and Lehman (1976) proposed six 'laws', two of which are the following

- *The law of continuing change*: a system that is used undergoes continuing change until it is judged more cost-effective to freeze and recreate it.
- *The law of increasing unstructuredness*: the entropy (disorder) of a system increases with time unless specific work is executed to maintain or reduce it.

In other words the product becomes more and more disordered as time goes by. This is reflected in the gradually rising cost curve shown in

figure 1.2. It eventually becomes so complex that it becomes
unacceptably difficult to maintain. It is the complexity inherent in the
product that results in the high cost of maintenance and, at the
beginning of the life cycle, in the high cost of production.

The continuing rapid development of hardware has given rise to
modular hardware design and manufacture in an attempt to prolong the
life of a product. As we shall see, a similar argument applies to software
development and brings other advantages too.

Complexity

A major contributing factor to the high cost of software is its
complexity. Consider for a moment a mechanical analogy. Mechanical
contrivances vary in complexity. If the contrivance is a simple device
with one or two moving parts, then its production and maintenance are
reasonably straightforward tasks. However, as the device becomes more
intricate, with a great number of moving parts, production and
maintenance become more difficult. If all the moving parts are
interconnected in different ways, then the situation becomes even more
complicated.

The creators of mechanical systems attempt to alleviate these
problems by developing highly modular designs. The device is designed
as a number of subassemblies, each subassembly being broken down
into smaller units. The designer attempts to make each of these
subassemblies as independent as possible, so that the installation of a
new part requires as little work and causes as little disruption as
possible. Modern technology abounds with plug-in pull-out disposable,
sealed subassemblies — for sound economic reasons!

Turning once again to the software environment, it requires a
surprisingly small amount of program code before a piece of software
becomes incomprehensible to the human mind. A mechanical engineer
would blanch at the prospect of constructing a contrivance consisting of
one hundred thousand individual pieces. However, a software system of
one hundred thousand instructions is considered medium sized. The
potential complexity inherent in even a small software system is
immense. If it is to be constructed economically, and economically
maintained, then complexity must be minimised.

Structure

● The way to reduce this complexity is to impose a strong modular
structure on software design. Unless a structure is imposed at the design
and construction stage, it may well prove impossible to manage the
building of the system in the first place. If software is not constructed in

a highly structured manner, then its complexity will result in errors difficult to detect during the testing phase. These errors will appear gradually as time goes by and will demand constant maintenance. In non-structured software, the very act of correcting one error may propagate other errors — a function of the intricate interconnection of all the system's parts.

In order to lower maintenance costs a software system may be 'frozen', but this is not always a solution. Inevitably inaccuracies and shortcomings are discovered in the requirement specification and changes must be made. The stringent reliability requirements imposed upon real-time systems imply that the software should contain minimum errors when delivered, and that any enhancements to the system should introduce a minimum of new errors. Strongly structured software has been shown to be the most powerful means of reducing such errors.

In the ensuing chapters we will see that it is possible to enforce the necessary structure on real-time software, from the overall design right down to the individual lines of program code.

1.3 VIRTUAL MACHINES

The design of real-time software appears, at first sight, to be an extremely difficult task. On the one hand, we have a complex and often hazily defined problem area and, on the other, a hardware processor that is only capable of carrying out simple instructions. The designer must create a design for a large program of simple instructions which will satisfy the requirements of an ill-defined problem area. Fortunately, tools and techniques are available to assist this mapping of problem to machine.

1.3.1 Defining the Problem

Before the construction of a software system can commence, the designer must be completely clear as to what is required of the system. Formalised requirement specification and documentation techniques have been developed to assist in defining the problem. Examples include structured analysis and design technique (SADT) (Ross, 1977) and specification and design language (SDL) (CCITT, 1976). All such techniques are aimed at producing a highly structured document which precisely and completely defines the system to be built. They are often in graphical form and include a rigid set of rules aimed at highlighting areas where the specification is vague or incomplete.

1.3.2 Implementing the Solution

Designers represent their designs as symbolic models. An architect uses
a scaled drawing to describe what will eventually be a three-dimensional
structure. Electrical engineers use circuit diagrams to represent what will
be a complex of electrical components. Physicists use mathematical
formulae.

Software designs are expressed as data structures which model items
in the problem area, and the actions which will manipulate this data.
When implemented, the design will result in a program made up of the
simple instructions and data items necessary for currently available
computer hardware.

To assist with the modelling problem there are a number of powerful
software development support systems — for example, Modular
Approach to Software Construction Operation and Test (MASCOT 3)
(MASCOT 3, 1986), and Integrated Project Support Environments
(IPSEs) (McDermid, 1985). This is further discussed in section 8.3.

If there were available a machine that could use, as its basic software,
the requirement specification document, then the software design
problem would be solved. It would be necessary to describe accurately
the system to be built and then this description would serve as the
software model.

● Unfortunately, such a machine does not exist as physical hardware.
Currently available computer hardware cannot use, as its basic software,
the forms of symbolic model that would best represent the application
areas. We can, however, create such a machine. This machine, a *virtual
machine*, is created by placing layers of software between the user and
the hardware. The layers of software create successive virtual machines
or *levels of abstraction*, each successive layer forming a more
sophisticated machine whose attributes are more closely tailored to the
designer's requirements. The software comprising each virtual machine
layer automatically translates the data and actions which define the
machine at that layer into the simpler data structures and actions which
define the previous layer.

● This automatic translation of higher-level abstractions into detailed
lower-level operations achieves a significant reduction in overall system
complexity. If no virtual machine exists, then the designer must be
aware of the detailed operation of the physical hardware. In this case
the final design specification will be extremely complex, since it must
closely specify a physical machine level program. In many ways the
designer will be creating a solution to hardware idiosyncrasies, rather
than a solution to the problem at hand.

Consider figure 1.3. From the direction of the problem, or system to
be designed, formalised specification and design techniques provide the

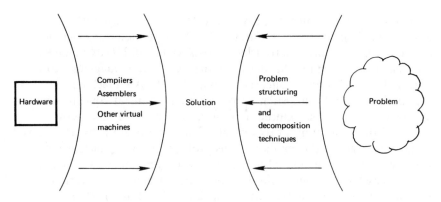

Figure 1.3 Problem vs *hardware*

designer with a more structured and well-defined description of the problem.

From the direction of the hardware, successive layers of software provide the designer with a more and more convenient virtual machine.

It remains for the designer to create a mapping between the requirement specification and the data and actions required for the virtual machine. This job is not easy. However, it is certainly less complex than trying to map the problem directly onto the physical hardware.

Example

Imagine the situation where a scientist wishes to create a simple program to carry out some calculations. His problem is to design the software to solve a series of equations and formulae. With no support software to provide a convenient virtual machine, he must concentrate on translating the equations into a large number of machine instructions. A problem that can be expressed conveniently as a few lines of mathematical formulae becomes a complex problem in machine code.

If, however, the scientist was presented with a machine that would accept and implement his problem, stated not as machine instructions but as a mathematical formula, then his task would be greatly simplified. He would not need to become involved in the detailed machine operation, and the likelihood of error is thus reduced. More importantly, he is free to concentrate on the problem itself, rather than the implementation of its software solution. In order that he may interface with a virtual machine, as opposed to a real machine, a translating program must be provided to translate the scientist's description of the problem solution into a form suitable for machine execution. Commonly this translator exists as a FORTRAN compiler. The scientist can express his design in the FORTRAN language, to be executed, as far as he is concerned, on a 'FORTRAN machine'.

A designer in a business data-processing environment conceives his problem in terms of structured data files, movement of data between files, and the generation of reports. The basic hardware is by no means an ideal vehicle for the solution of his problem. (Nor, in fact, is the scientist's virtual machine, although it may go some of the way.) The data-processing designer requires a 'business' machine. This form of virtual machine is conventionally provided by a COBOL or RPG language translator. Figure 1.4 shows the layers of software providing virtual machines in a commercial environment.

If we consider the area of real-time software, it is clear that the designer of a real-time system would be able to utilise a virtual machine

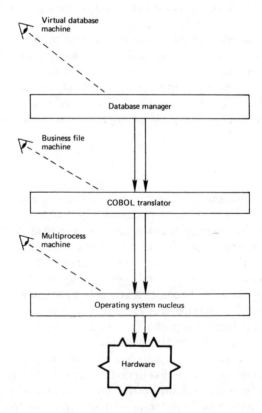

Figure 1.4 Levels of business-orientated virtual machines

tailored to *his* environment. A major benefit would be the reduction in complexity and, therefore, cost of the final design. The virtual machine, not the designer, would take care of the detailed translation into machine code.

1.4 SUMMARY

Most descriptions of real-time software emphasise the need for a rapid response to the environment. In many early systems, this was possibly the sole design criterion. However, as with any product, real-time software must be as correct, complete, reliable and economical as possible. A design that results in fast responsive software is not completely useful unless it employs a strong structure to reduce complexity. Some of the tools and techniques discussed in the following chapters are by no means specific to real-time software, but they must be included in our discussion as they are vital for successful design.

We have already introduced the first of these tools — the virtual machine. Chapters 2 to 5 will discuss a virtual machine designed for use in a real-time environment.

Concepts

Real-time; controlled system; controlling system; batch; on-line; life-cycle cost; maintenance; complexity; structure; virtual machine.

PART I: THE REAL-TIME VIRTUAL MACHINE

2 The Real-time Virtual Machine — its Properties

We may think of a real-time system as carrying out a set of activities or tasks. Controlling a device could be one activity; keeping a record of the overall performance of the system may be another. All the activities in the system are interrelated and interact with one another. Some activities may be more vital than others, dependent upon the environmental conditions affecting the controlled system at any one time. Continuous variations in the nature of the environment make it difficult to predict which activities, from a set of possible activities, a real-time system will be required to carry out next. Clearly, a real-time system is multifaceted and exhibits enormous complexity. We are faced with a set of interdependent activities, all jostling to be carried out within strict time limits. Unless some form of abstraction is applied, the design process becomes almost impossible.

A method of attaining this abstraction is to design, create and use a suitable virtual machine. If such a machine can be developed for a real-time environment, then the design problem can be reduced to manageable proportions. This chapter will discuss a virtual machine which provides a useful basis for the design of a real-time system. The form of the machine to be used is strongly influenced by ideas developed in the MASCOT 3 (1979) development system and the UNIX (see Ritchie and Thompson, 1978) operating system.

We have already seen that the existence of a virtual machine enables a designer to attain a degree of abstraction from the computer hardware. However, the virtual machine must do more than simply reduce programming complexity. It must be adapted to suit the needs of its environment and area of application. It must be designed in such a way that it facilitates and encourages the creation of clear, logical and easily implemented designs. More, it must promote the design of systems that are as simple as possible.

It is with these criteria in mind that we shall discuss the design of a real-time virtual machine. We shall proceed by considering what facilities a real-time machine would require, and systematically include them in our model. At each stage we shall attempt to ensure that the form of the machine will encourage clean designs of minimum complexity.

2.1 PROCESSES

A real-time system can be seen as one that carries out a set of activities. The most elementary real-time system would, therefore, be one which carried out one, and only one activity. An example of this would be a system that ensures, by controlling a valve, an even flow of fluid in a pipe; note figure 2.1. Without control the flow is likely to change as a result of fluctuations in input pressure, and also independently because of variations in demand at the output. The activity to be performed by this controlling system is quite straightforward, as is evident in figure 2.2.

In order to build such a controlling system it would be necessary to provide a suitable program of instructions, together with the processing hardware on which it could run. We shall call the combination of a simple free-standing program and its processing hardware, which together implement one activity, a *process*. As we refine our virtual machine, so we may need to extend the definition of a process. For the moment we shall retain the correspondence between an activity that needs to be carried out and the process that carries it out. The simple flow-control system that we have been discussing would consist of one process, as it only carries out one activity. We shall represent a process graphically in the manner used by the MASCOT system, as shown in

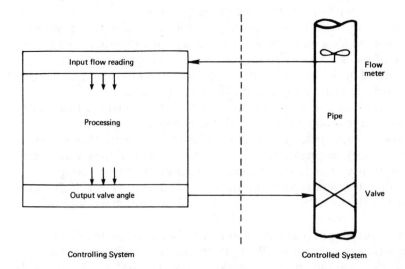

Figure 2.1 Fluid flow control system

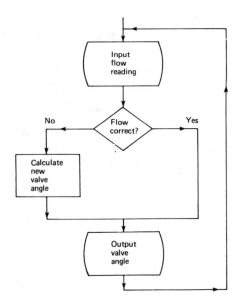

Figure 2.2 Fluid flow processing

figure 2.3. In order to specify the process completely, we would need to define precisely what activity the process must carry out, and also its interaction with the outside world.

● Our simple virtual machine will support the existence of a single process. To extend our model further, the real-time system could be asked to perform a number of unrelated activities. Expanding our previous example we could look at a system that controls the flow of fluid in a pipe, the level of grain in a bin, the temperature of a furnace and the level of fluid in a tank.

Here, the pipe, bin, furnace and tank are all part of separate, unrelated machinery, and therefore the activities controlling them will have no effect on one another. As in the previous system, the controlling activities can be implemented as individual processes. The

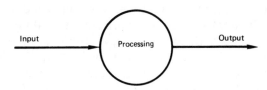

Figure 2.3 Process symbol

situation is shown in figure 2.4. Since the devices they control are independent, the processes themselves are independent. Since no process depends upon another, they need not co-operate with one another or synchronise their activities in any way. The system design task would simply be that of designing the programs for each process, and providing suitable processing hardware. But our virtual machine must be extended to support as many processes as the designer may require. Not surprisingly, this will bring some problems such as whether the machine can cope with all the processes it is asked to perform with respect to the total processing time and storage required, and how the processes communicate with each other.

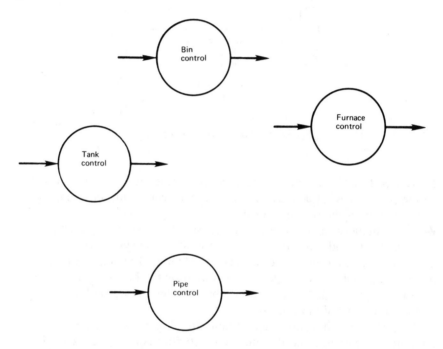

Figure 2.4 Multiple independent processes

● It is unlikely that a real-time system would be asked to control a number of totally unrelated devices. Normally, it would be required to control an environment where the devices, and therefore the processes controlling them, are interrelated in some way. Figure 2.5 depicts a hypothetical grain-roasting plant. Now, if the pipe, bin, furnace and tank described in the previous paragraphs were in fact the devices in the grain-roasting plant, then they would form parts of an interrelated system. In this situation the action of one device must take into account

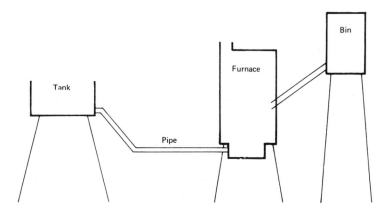

Figure 2.5 Grain-roasting plant

the action of the other devices. We are no longer faced with a set of independent processes, and the virtual machine that supports multiple but independent processes is no longer adequate. It must be extended to include *interaction between processes*. In a graphical representation we could illustrate this interaction with arrows. Where one process wishes to interact with another, we will draw an arrow between the two processes. If each process wishes to interact with all the others, then we have a situation as shown in figure 2.6. Clearly, with more than three or

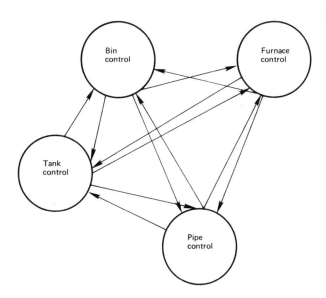

Figure 2.6 Potential process interconnection

four processes the situation becomes extremely complex, as can be seen from the confused nature of the diagram.

● If we are to design a worthwhile virtual machine, we must control this complexity. Fortunately, if we give some thought to the way that devices, and therefore processes, wish to interact, we can make a number of abstractions. These abstractions, if applied to the virtual machine, will achieve considerable reduction of the potential complexity.

The interaction of processes will reflect the interaction of the devices they control. This interaction may be direct or immediate, in that the action of one device will cause the starting or stopping of another device's activity. Alternatively, the interaction may be indirect where a device may receive information about the status or actions of another device and be obliged to modify its actions accordingly. The corresponding processes will need to interact in a similar manner. They will need to be able to synchronise their activities, so that the action of one process can cause the activation or suspension of other processes. Also, they will need to be able to send information to one another and to access information that reflects the status of the system as a whole. In order to include the necessary facilities in our virtual machine model, we shall have to discuss process interaction in more detail. We shall also have to involve the process engineer and the control system designer in our discussions. The following paragraphs deal with the topics of communication and synchronisation, both vital for successful operation of our virtual machine.

2.2   COMMUNICATION

● Information may be communicated between processes in two ways. First, a direct transfer of information may occur from one process to another. Second, each process may access or update pieces of shared information. This shared information is available to some or all of the processes in the system. Recall the grain-roasting system. The process controlling the furnace will send an indication of the required fuel flow rate directly to the process controlling the fuel pipe valve. Meanwhile, both processes may require a knowledge of the current ambient air temperature in order to modify the behaviour of their devices. In the first case we have a direct transfer of information between processes. In the second case, both processes will wish to access a common pool of information.

2.2.1 Channels

● In order to provide direct communication between processes in the virtual machine we need to introduce the concept of a *channel*. The graphical representation for a channel used in the MASCOT system is shown in figure 2.7. A channel provides the medium for items of information to be passed between one process and another. A channel has a certain elasticity. More than one item of information can pass through a channel at any one time. Items passing through the channel will usually be ordered so that the first item passed into the channel will be the first item removed at the other end. The virtual machine is unconcerned as to precisely how the transfer of information is effected. It is sufficient in our virtual machine design to say that, where a channel exists between two processes, items of information may flow through that channel from one process to another.

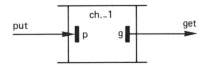

Figure 2.7 The channel

2.2.2 Pools

● To provide system-wide information we must introduce another concept to our virtual machine — a *pool*. Items of information in a pool are available for reading and/or writing by a number of processes in the system. Information does not flow within a pool. A pool acts as a repository of information; any item in it will be available to processes using the pool. The virtual machine provides no indication as to how the pool will be set up; it simply provides the facility for specifying that a pool of information does exist. Figure 2.8 illustrates the MASCOT symbol for a pool.

Pools are as important an element in the virtual machine as processes. Whereas processes are software models of the activities that a real-time system must perform, pools form the software models of *items* in the system. These items include physical devices and mechanisms in the controlled system, and conceptual items such as logical files. In many applications the pool has information written into it endlessly, but the storage allocated to the pool does not need to be infinite, since eventually old information ceases to be of any practical use and can be discarded.

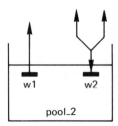

Figure 2.8 The pool

2.2.3 Intercommunication Data Areas

The ideas just introduced stem from earlier work on MASCOT. The version currently being standardised (MASCOT 3) develops these ideas further, particularly for large systems and multiprocessor target systems. The basic communication model of MASCOT 3 is shown in figure 2.9a, in which the two types illustrated are *activities*, referred to earlier as processes, and *Intercommunication Data Areas* (IDAs) which combine the channel and pool concepts. It is useful at this point to introduce some definitions of these and to add some additional concepts of MASCOT 3.

(i) Activity

● This is a basic processing element having a single thread of program execution. An *activity* does not have right of access to either data or code outside of itself; all external communication must be through an IDA.

(ii) IDA

● This is a basic element through which activities communicate with each other. An *IDA* may provide just communication or just a pool, but typically contains both a data or information area and associated access procedures. The latter relate only to the activity which invokes them. The consequence of this is that an IDA may exhibit active concurrency with respect to more than one activity, and consequential upon this is a requirement to provide synchronisation and mutual exclusion, concepts which are discussed in both the next section and in section 9.1.

(iii) Path

A *path* provides the means for interaction between activities and IDAs.

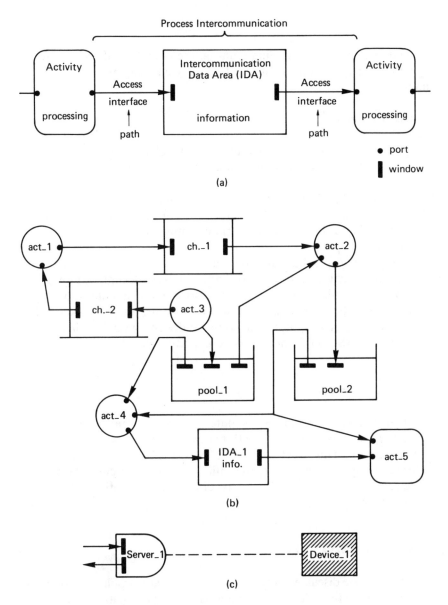

Figure 2.9 (a) Basic communication model for MASCOT 3.
(b) Activities, IDAs and pools. (c) External device server

(iv) Port

An activity may have a number of *ports* on its boundary, to each of which a path is connected as required by the activity. The type of port is determined by an access interface specification.

(v) Window

The *window* is the corresponding point on the boundary of an IDA to which a path may be connected. An IDA may have any number of windows.

(vi) Access Interface

This specifies a set of interactions that can take place on a path, implying common constraints on both activity and IDA.

The channels and pools discussed earlier are alternative forms of IDA with slightly modified graphical symbolism. Figure 2.9b shows a simple system consisting of five activities communicating via an IDA, two channels and two pools.

The simple concepts illustrated here are inadequate for complex systems, particularly with respect to the hierarchical decomposition of the problem into subsystems from both process and communication points of view. These topics are developed in subsection 6.1.5. Related to this is an integrated approach to software design and development supported in MASCOT 3 and discussed in section 8.3.

2.2.4 External Devices

Many real-time systems employ computers 'embedded' in larger systems. There is a need to communicate with hardware devices external to the computer system. This is achieved in MASCOT 3 by a *server*, shown graphically in figure 2.9c, and representing the only elements which include handlers and low-level code for direct communication with external hardware devices.

2.3   SYNCHRONISATION

● So far we have discussed only half of the complexity problem introduced by process interaction. As well as communicating information to one another, processes may wish to synchronise their activities. This synchronisation involves the ability of one process to stimulate or inhibit its own action or that of other processes. In other words, in order to carry out the activities required of it, a process may need to have the ability to say STOP or GO or WAIT A MOMENT to itself, or other processes.

If each process has the power to stop or start the activity of any other process in the system, the complexity shown in the interaction diagram (figure 2.6) will still apply. It is important that a process must *not* be allowed to have this direct power over other processes. Fortunately, we can design simple procedures which fulfil all the requirements of interprocess synchronisation and, at the same time, limit the process-activation and suspension powers of the process using them.

2.3.1 Significant Events

● Interprocess synchronisation centres around the occurrence of significant events in the system. Consider an example. One process in a system may need to suspend its activities at a certain point until such time as a valve is closed. Another process in the system will be the one which controls the valve and causes it to close. Synchronisation between these two processes centres around the significant event of the valve closing. The first process must *wait* for the event to occur; the second process will *signal* that the event has occurred.

Synchronisation is based upon communication of a piece of information between processes. This information is simply: 'the event has occurred.'

If two procedures — WAIT(event) and SIGNAL(event) — exist, they can be used to implement all necessary synchronisation.

WAIT(event) causes the process using it to suspend activity as soon as the WAIT operation is executed, and it will remain suspended until such time as notification of the occurrence of an event is received. Should the event have already occurred, the process will resume immediately. A waiting process can be thought of as being in the act of reading event information from a channel or pool. Once this information appears, it can continue.

The SIGNAL operation broadcasts the fact that an event has occurred. Its action is to place event information in a channel or pool. This in turn may enable a waiting process to continue.

● The designer, when using the virtual machine, need not be concerned with how the WAIT and SIGNAL operations are implemented. He is nevertheless in a position to base the design of process synchronisation on the occurrence of significant events. He can display process interdependency diagrammatically by showing the channels and pools through which knowledge of the event is transmitted.

2.3.2 Interrupts

● It must be mentioned at this stage that the signalling of an event is
not necessarily performed solely by processes within the system. In the
previous example, the valve-control process presumably monitored the
state of the valve until such time as it closed. At this point, the process
signalled the event. The designer may, however, prefer the valve to
signal the event directly. We shall display sources of events, external to
the software, as squares, shown in figure 2.10. This feature is, in fact, a
hardware interrupt mechanism, described in more detail in section 4.1.
However, the user of the virtual machine need not concern himself with
the physical implementation of the mechanism.

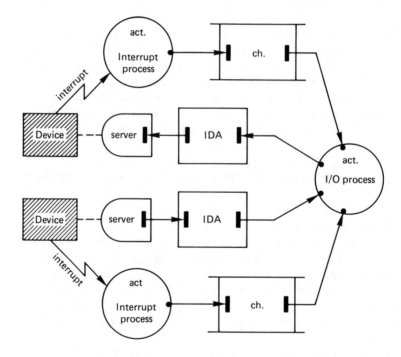

Figure 2.10 External signals — interrupts

2.4   EXAMPLE

In order to illustrate our ideas more clearly, it may be useful to analyse
a very simple example. We shall look at a small information system. A
number of terminals are attached to a computer system. By using a
terminal, a person may interrogate and possibly update information in a

set of files held on the computer's backing store. The person must first make himself known to the system by typing in a password. He can then, using a set of one-line commands, read from and, if he is eligible, write to the system files. This arrangement is, of course, a very simple basis for a management information system, stock-control system, airline booking scheme or similar. To start the design for the software needed to control this system we shall identify first the *items* in the system, and then the *activities* that must be carried out.

2.4.1 Items

2.4.1.1 The Users

Each user of the system will have a password, and some security code that indicates to which files he may read and/or write.

2.4.1.2 The Terminals

In this simple system we will assume that each terminal is allocated a unique location in the computer's main storage, in which it can place a character as it is typed. Similarly, there is a unique location where it accesses the next character to be sent to the terminal.

2.4.1.3 The Commands

Each command to the system will take the form of a line of text and represents one action. Such actions would include 'read a file record', or 'write a file record', or 'move to the next record'.

2.4.1.4 The Responses

These will be strings of text, displayed at the terminals as responses to commands.

2.4.1.5 The Files

These are the information files that the users wish to manipulate.

2.4.2 Activities

2.4.2.1 Handle Terminal Input

The system must move characters out of each terminal's input location fast enough to ensure that no character is overwritten by the next incoming character. The characters make up commands. Each command consists of a string of characters terminated by an end-of-line indication. The activity-handling terminal input will send in characters until an end-of-line character is received, at which point it will signal that a command has been read.

2.4.2.2 Handle Terminal Output

The system will build responses to the user in the form of strings of characters. We must provide an activity that will place these responses, character by character, into the terminal's output location.

2.4.2.3 File Handler

We need to include an activity to control the organisation and access to the information in the system files.

2.4.2.4 Carry Out Commands

Finally we will interpret the user commands. We must ensure that the user and/or the command is valid and legal, then take action on the command and provide a response to the user.

2.4.3 The Design

Every *item* in the system will be modelled as a *pool*. Every *activity* will be modelled as a *process*. One possible design is shown in figure 2.11. A terminal is in fact two devices, the keyboard for input and the screen or printer for output.

The IN process builds up commands, character by character, in the COMMAND pool. When it receives an end-of-line indicator, it sends a message down c1, indicating that a command has been received. When the OUT process receives a message down c2, it transfers the response specified by the message to the terminal output location. When signalled

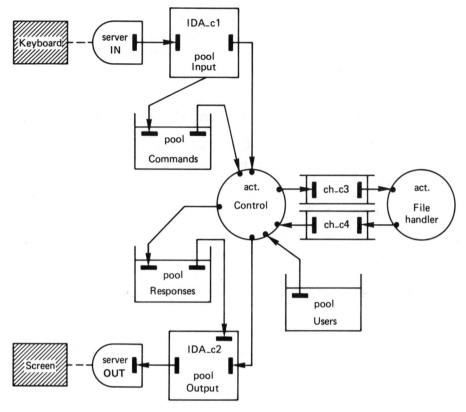

Figure 2.11 Possible design for information system

by IN, the control process checks the validity of the command by referring to the USERS pool to check user passwords and security codes. It then sends a request for action by the file handler down c3. It receives an acknowledgement to this request on c4. It then places the response to the command in RESPONSES and signals OUT.

● Thus, we build up an initial, broad software design, modelling the items as pools, activities as processes and communication synchronisation as channels.

2.5 SUMMARY

At this stage the virtual machine is sufficiently well-defined to be used as a system design tool. The system of co-operating processes closely parallels the system of interrelated activities that must be performed by a real-time system. At the top level of his design, the designer produces:

(1)   a description of the system pools;
(2)   a description of the basic process activities;
(3)   a chart of the interrelationship between the system elements showing channel and pool access indicators.

Next he tackles the internal design of the processes themselves. The current form of the real-time virtual machine simplifies this task. Each process can be designed as if it were the only process in the system. Its interfaces with the outside world are defined in terms of channels and pools. It can therefore be designed as if it were a free-standing 'batch' type of program.

In the following three chapters, we shall discuss how the real-time virtual machine can be created.

Concepts

Activities; processes; channels; pools; synchronisation; significant event; WAIT; SIGNAL; interrupt.

3 Implementing the Real-time Machine

It would appear that the real-time virtual machine described in chapter 2 should provide the software designer with a useful working environment. This chapter will describe the software and hardware necessary to support the existence of such a virtual machine. It will be necessary to implement processes, and to provide communication and synchronisation facilities between the processes.

● A *process* consists of a processor, program code and sufficient memory to accommodate this program code. We must produce a machine that provides these resources for as many processes as the designer sees fit. Each process must, as far as the process itself is concerned, have its own processor (CPU), program and memory. We can provide these resources by either dedicating unique resources to each process, as in a distributed system, or by sharing the available resources between the processes.

3.1 IMPLEMENTING PROCESSES — DEDICATED RESOURCES

The recent availability of cheap microprocessors and memory elements means that it is a viable proposition to provide separate resources dedicated to each process. It is possible to provide for each process in the system a separate microprocessor, together with enough memory for the code element. If the designer specifies a new process, a new CPU/memory is slotted into the system.

Figures 3.1 and 3.2 illustrate, schematically, two commonly used configurations of multiprocessor hardware. In figure 3.1 the microprocessors use their own local memory to store program code. They communicate with one another via communications links that are set up to allow relatively long distances between the CPU/memory modules. There is a clear correspondence between the channels of the virtual machine and the physical links between the microprocessor modules.

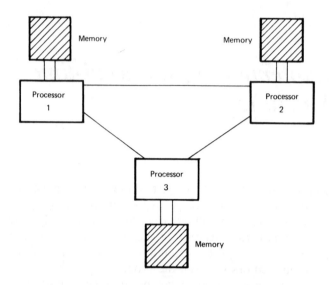

Figure 3.1 Distributed processor arrangement 1

Figure 3.2 shows processors connected via a common bus arrangement. The local storage for each CPU may contain all or some of the process code. If the local memory does not contain all of the program code for a process, then some will be held in shared memory. The shared memory is the logical place to hold the information in the system pools.

With either of the above configurations it is clear that we are in a position to provide a CPU/memory/code combination for each process. In order to create a process one need only load one of the memory modules with the relevant program code element. Clearly this simple and elegant approach should be utilised wherever feasible. It has, however, a number of drawbacks in certain circumstances.

(1) Cost

● Often economic constraints rule out the possibility of providing a unique CPU/memory module for each process. If insufficient resources are available, it becomes necessary to share resources between processes. None the less, in applications requiring a small, fixed number of processes, with modest reliability requirements, the simple multimicroprocessor realisation of the virtual machine would be the most desirable configuration.

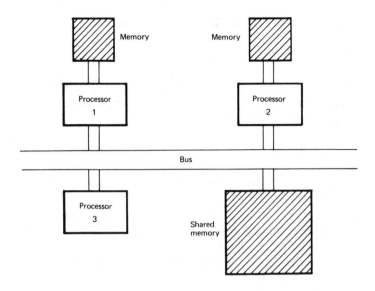

Figure 3.2 Distributed processor arrangement 2

(2) Lack of Flexibility

● There are more compelling reasons for introducing a more flexible relationship between processes and their hardware resources. A rigid allocation of process to CPU/memory implies that no new processes can be introduced into the system without altering the hardware configuration. In some applications this can prove a severe restriction. Some systems may require that the number of processes in the system vary with the workload on the system. A fixed CPU allocation would imply that the number of processes in the system is constant. This would severely impinge on possible expansion. The system could not be extended to include new activities without adding further hardware.

(3) Reliability

● Considerations of system reliability make it convenient to include redundant CPU and memory modules in the system. When a piece of hardware fails, the system can be reconfigured to use the redundant standby modules. This technique is difficult to employ if there is a rigid allocation of process to CPU/memory. With a distributed system it may be possible to transfer a process to another processor in the system, but this is not always possible if direct connection with external devices is involved. We shall discuss system reliability in some detail in chapter 5.

3.2   IMPLEMENTING PROCESSES — SHARED RESOURCES

3.2.1 Sharing the Processor

When discussing the ways in which a CPU (or CPUs fewer in number than all the processes) may be shared among the processes, it is necessary to consider three factors

(1) *how* the CPU is to be shared — in other words, what mechanisms are required to enable a processor executing the code element of one process to change its activity and execute the code element of another process;
(2) *when* the CPU is to be shared — that is, at what times, or as a result of what events, should the CPU change from executing one process to executing another;
(3) *which* process should the CPU direct its attention to, when sharing of the CPU is necessary.

Points (1) and (2) — *how* and *when* — we shall discuss in the following sections; point (3) — *which* process — we shall leave to chapter 4, where we discuss process scheduling.

3.2.1.1 Serial Execution

The simplest method of sharing a CPU is for the processes to be executed once through their code without interruption, one process after another.

This method causes the system to lose its responsiveness to environmental changes. It can only change the current process and thus its effect on the environment at the end of execution of the current process. The processes must of necessity be brief if the controlled system is to remain unaware of the fact that the processes are not running in parallel. If only one CPU is in use, the processes must not execute synchronising WAIT operations since, clearly, no other process can run to execute the corresponding SIGNAL operation.

Provided the application lends itself to short processes that carry out highly independent activities, then the simplicity of the serial approach has much to commend it. *How* is simple in this case: commence the next process at its starting point. Each process, when terminating, executes a piece of code that performs this function. And *when*? At the completion of the current process.

This does not mean however that such processes may not communicate with each other. Processes such as sample, filter, monitor and output may assume that the preceding process has left information that is required for the current process in a known place such as a pool. Such simple co-operative scheduling is quite suitable for many small real-time systems, thus avoiding a lot of the critical problem areas now discussed through serial execution with only limited pre-emption at the interrupt level.

3.2.1.2 Pseudoparallel Execution

The major drawback of the serial method occurs when processes take considerable time to execute, and the system therefore becomes very sluggish in its response to changes in the environment.

Ideally, in order to react to a change in the controlled system, it should be possible for a CPU to swap from one process to another at any time, giving the impression to the environment that the processes are being conducted in parallel. To make this possible we introduce the concepts of *volatile environment, process descriptor* and *dispatcher*.

● *Volatile environment* A process's volatile environment is that information that, if lost, would mean that the process could not continue from the point at which it last executed an instruction. It is the information that would be lost if another process used the CPU. The volatile environment includes such information as the contents of hardware registers, memory-management registers and the program counter. While the process is running on a CPU, the volatile environment is continually changing. If the process is denied the use of the CPU for a period, while the CPU is required by another process, then the first process's volatile environment must be preserved. If this is not done the process will be unable to continue from where it left off. If this *is* done and the information is restored to the registers, then the process will be unaware that it ever had anything but total use of the CPU. Note, however, that there is a significant overhead in stacking and unstacking the environment of a process every time a change is implemented, and this must be considered when designing process-swapping procedures.

● *Process descriptor* We must, therefore, provide a place to store a process's volatile environment while it is not using the CPU. At the same time, we could provide space for summary information about the process for system 'housekeeping' purposes. This storage element will take the form of a data structure that, in effect, models the process. We shall call this data structure a *process descriptor* (PD). So, as a further extension of the *process* concept we could state that the software element of a process consists of a process descriptor and the program code itself; see figure 3.3. The software elements that make up process A in this diagram consist of the left-hand process descriptor and code element. The significance of element S will be discussed in section 3.2.2.1.

● *Dispatcher*   The dispatcher is the mechanism that effects the *how* of process sharing. It can be implemented in hardware or software. When activated it stores, in the relevant process descriptor, the contents of the hardware registers that make up the volatile environment of the currently active process. It then replaces the contents of the registers with volatile environment information from another process's process descriptor.

● *Release of the CPU*   The *when* of process sharing is related to the conditions necessary for the current process to give up use of the

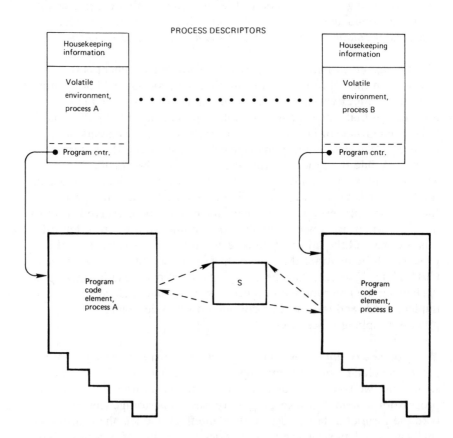

Figure 3.3 Processes sharing code

processor. A process may relinquish the use of the CPU voluntarily, or be forced to do so. A voluntary release of the CPU would occur when a process either terminates or executes an unsuccessful WAIT operation. A forced release of the CPU occurs when an interrupt occurs and an interrupt handling process is activated.

● *Interrupt handlers* The controlled system commands the attention of the software system by means of the hardware interrupt mechanism. Should an interrupt occur, the hardware saves a portion of the current volatile environment (including at least the program counter) in a fixed location and replaces it with the volatile environment of the process designed to handle the interrupt. When executing, the interrupt handling process is careful to ensure that it does not affect any of the unsaved portions of the interrupted process's volatile environment. When it has completed its action, the interrupt handler can execute a return-from-interrupt instruction, which restores to the registers the saved portions of the interrupted process's volatile environment. Clearly, the interrupt hardware acts as a simple dispatcher causing a forced, *restricted* process swapping.

● Note here that, as well as forcing the process to be swapped, the interrupt specifies exactly which process will subsequently be activated (the interrupt handler). The *when* and *which* aspects of process swapping are indivisible concepts when the swapping occurs as a result of an interrupt. Accordingly, we shall further our discussion of interrupts in section 4.1, when discussing scheduling.

On its completion, an interrupt handling process can swap the processor back to the interrupted process by executing a return-from-interrupt instruction. However, the occurrence of an interrupt normally implies a change in the status of the system's environment. This change may require the activation of a process other than the one that was interrupted. Thus, it is usual for the interrupt handling process to terminate by signalling the dispatcher, rather than executing a return-from-interrupt instruction. The dispatcher then finds which process should run next and effects the necessary swapping of complete volatile environments.

3.2.2 Sharing the Main Memory

If we assume that one CPU can be shared between more than one process, it remains necessary to provide main memory to hold the process code elements. The simplest way, and the one to be used if possible, is to provide in the system enough memory for each process to have its own unique area. Often this simple expedient cannot be employed. In most modern systems the cost of main memory far outweighs the cost of the CPU. For many systems the cost of main memory will force a reduction of main memory capacity. This implies that the available memory must be shared between the processes in the system. However, the falling cost of memory means that distributed memory becomes a possibility and the problem might go away. More likely, the requirements of the system will increase to match this advantage, and the problems of sharing memory will remain.

● There are two ways of effecting memory sharing — to share the code that resides in a section of memory, or to share the use of the section of memory itself. Let us consider the simpler method first.

3.2.2.1 Code Sharing

Real-time systems frequently contain a number of actions that form part of more than one process in the system. Conventionally, these activities are implemented as subroutines and a copy is built into the code element of any process that needs it. Now, if one of these subroutines were of any considerable size, a great saving in memory space could be achieved if the processes could share the code of the common routine, rather than each having a copy.

A program or subroutine consists of instructions plus data. Therefore, the shared routine will have local storage areas for its temporary working variables. In a shared CPU environment a process may be forced to give up the processor at any time during its execution. So, in figure 3.3 process A may be half way through executing routing S when it gives up the processor. Process B then takes over the processor and enters routine S. While S is executed, the temporary data in S will be manipulated according to B's requirements. If A then regains use of the processor, the temporary data used in S will have been changed by B's action. This fact is unknown to A and may cause it to malfunction.

There are two ways of avoiding this situation, as follows.

(a) Serially re-usable code   One method is to write the code in subroutine S in such a way that it makes no assumptions about the values in its local variables when it is entered. In other words, the initial values of the local data have no effect on the routine's action. Usually, the first action of the subroutine would be to set its local variables to a fixed, initial set of values. If a lock mechanism is applied at the beginning of the subroutine, and an unlock at the end, such that only one process may be executing its code at any one time, then processes can safely use the code, one after the other. The code is serially re-usable. The lock and unlock mechanisms can be implemented easily

using WAIT and SIGNAL operations. The use of these operations to ensure serial acces to code segments is discussed further in section 3.8.

(b) Re-entrant or pure code   If all the temporary data areas needed by S were to be part of the process currently using S, rather than part of S itself, then S would consist of executable code only. Therefore, it could be executed by more than one process at a time, provided that S did not modify its own instructions in any way. Code elements having this property are referred to as re-entrant or pure procedures.

● If a piece of re-entrant code is to act on different data areas, which are dependent on the process using it, it must access this data in an indirect manner. Typically, the re-entrant code module will access the data via a relocation pointer which is associated with each process. This relocation pointer containing the address of the beginning of the process data could be passed as a parameter when the subroutine is called.

● Each process will call the re-entrant subroutine by transferring control to the start of the routine. Some mechanisms will be needed to store the return address of the subroutine call. This is supplied conveniently by a stack mechanism. A stack can be regarded as a last-in-first-out queue of memory elements. The stack area must be part of the individual processes. In some implementations, the local data area is also included as part of the stack.

The amount of shared code that a process uses could be extended to include the whole of the process's code. In figure 3.4 there are a number of processes that execute the same code. They are, however, completely different processes because they use different data areas. Note that each process sees itself as consisting of its data together with

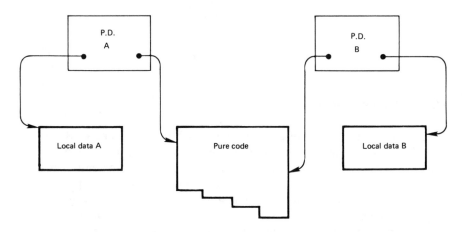

Figure 3.4 Different processes, same code element

its own code area. It is unaware, and unconcerned, that another process is actually using part of the same code for its action.

The device drivers in a conventional operating system are a good example of this situation. When building an operating system's facilities it is usual to include input/output processes to handle idiosyncracies of the different devices attached to the system. Figure 3.5 shows such a situation displayed as processes in the virtual machine. Now, to implement device-handler processes the systems programmer constructs the data structures and code modules shown in figure 3.6. The device descriptors contain device-specific information such as character set and speed. The device driver code uses the information in the device descriptors to tailor its actions. The device driver code, process descriptor, plus a device descriptor constitutes a process. To introduce a new process to handle another terminal, for example, the systems programmer need only create another device descriptor and process descriptor.

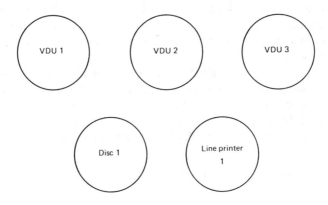

Figure 3.5 Input/output drivers

3.2.2.2 Memory Sharing

Even with extensive use of code sharing it will not always be possible simultaneously to accommodate all the process code in main memory. In this instance it will be necessary to hold code and data elements that are not currently being executed on a storage medium of higher capacity than the main storage. This medium, referred to as backing store, typically takes the form of magnetic discs and drums. Backing store is cheaper per unit of storage but slower to access than main storage. Code elements will be held on backing store and copied to main storage

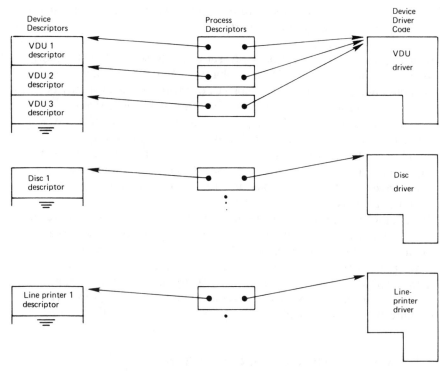

Figure 3.6 Input/output-driver data structures

when it becomes necessary to execute them. If a copy of a code element
is currently in main storage, it is *resident* and may be executed
immediately; if not, it is *non-resident* and must be copied to main
storage before it can be executed by the CPU.

● Most real-time systems divide main memory into two areas. The first
holds frequently executed code elements and the code elements of
highly time-critical processes. These code elements reside permanently
in memory. The second area is set aside as a free space to be shared
between the remaining code in the system. These remaining elements
consist of processes that are less time-critical in nature and code that is
less frequently executed. The relative size of the two areas will depend
upon the requirements and constraints of the particular system.

When to share The *when* of memory sharing occurs when an active
process wishes to execute a code segment that is not currently in
memory. It also occurs when a process wishes to access a data area that
is not currently resident in memory. This event is detected by

mechanisms in either the software or the hardware. The memory-sharing process, or processes, are then alerted.

How to share   A special process, or set of processes, is built to control the allocation of memory. Most mechanisms generally involve maintaining a list of all available pieces of memory. This list may be sorted in increasing or decreasing order of memory piece size or memory piece address. When a process requires space for its code element, a search is made through this list. If a suitably sized piece is found, it is allocated to that process. The required code element is then copied into this area from backing store. Once this code section is no longer required it may be copied to the backing store and a piece of memory made available for other processes.

● If a higher-priority process requests a large piece of memory store and finds it unavailable, a shuffler process may be called on to coalesce all the available free memory space. If this proves inadequate, then lower-priority processes may be called on to relinquish their current memory allocation, allowing the high-priority process room to run.

A fixed block size approach overcomes the fragmental problem at the expense of some overhead.

3.3   IMPLEMENTING SYNCHRONISATION

Many different synchronisation facilities or functions can be thought to be useful. They include DELAYME(time), ACTIVATE(other process), SUSPEND(other process) and DELAY(other process, time). DELAYME can be implemented as a WAIT on an event that will occur 'time' later. Facilities like ACTIVATE, SUSPEND and DELAY are dangerous. Their existence implies that the affected processes do not have total control of their synchronisation activities.

● In fact, all necessary synchronisation activities can be implemented using WAIT and SIGNAL. The detailed implementation of WAIT and SIGNAL depends on the system involved. At the lowest level they rely on a hardware lock-and-unlock mechanism to ensure that they are impervious to process swapping while they take action. At a high level they may be embedded in high-level language constructs.

3.3.1 Semaphores

Dijkstra (1968) has outlined a synchronisation concept against which other methods are measured. He introduced the idea of a *semaphore*, a simple data item that can only take non-negative integer values and can only be manipulated by three procedures: *initialise(semaphore, value)*, *wait(semaphore)* and *signal(semaphore)*. *Initialise* sets the value of the semaphore to *value*. *Signal* simply increments the value of the semaphore by one. *Wait* will decrease the value of the semaphore by one, but only if the result is non-negative.

Processes wishing to synchronise their activities execute *wait* and *signal* operations on shared semaphores. If a process executes a *wait* operation and the value of the semaphore is one or greater, then the process can decrement the semaphore and continue. If, however, the semaphore has the value zero at the time the process executes the *wait* operation, then decrementing the semaphore would result in a negative value. The process must therefore wait until such time as another process executes a *signal* operation in the semaphore, thus allowing the first process to decrement the semaphore and continue.

At any time, the value of the semaphore is equal to its initial value *plus* the number of *signal* operations that have been applied to it *minus* the total number of completed (that is, passed) *wait* operations. Now, because the value of a semaphore can never be negative, this implies that the number of completed *wait* operations on a semaphore must always be less than or equal to the initial value of the semaphore plus the number of *signal* operations that have occurred.

● Both *wait* and *signal* are indivisible operations; once begun, they must be completed. The processor cannot be swapped while they are being executed. This stipulation ensures that the vital incrementing and decrementing of the semaphore occurs without interruption. Examples of the implementation and use of semaphores are given in section 3.8.

● If we were to use semaphores as the synchronising agency in our real-time machine, then the significant event (see section 2.3) would be the incrementing of the semaphore. The semaphores themselves would reside in pools, monitored by the *wait* and *signal* operations.

● A *software trap* is a machine instruction that, when executed, causes an interrupt to be signalled to the interrupt mechanism. It is an interrupt generated by software. It is worth noting that, if *wait* and *signal* operations are implemented in such a way that they are entered as a result of a software trap, then they are in fact interrupt handling processes. The dispatcher will be activated on their completion.

3.4 IMPLEMENTING COMMUNICATION

In order to facilitate communication between processes, information available to one process must be made available to another process. This implies that an item of information stored in one area of the system's memory, accessible by one process, must be made accessible to other processes. This means that either the data is copied to another area of memory, or the same area of memory is available to all processes wishing to communicate.

In the discussion that follows, 'memory' will refer to both main storage and backing store. For the software designer the framework and principles remain the same; economics and performance requirements will govern his decision as to the location of data. Main memory can be accessed quickly, but more information can be placed on backing store. If large amounts of information are to be shared between processes then files on backing store would be most appropriate. If, however, real-time constraints make slow information access unacceptable, more expensive main storage will have to be used. The data itself must be unaffected by the location of memory storage. A data pool may be located on backing store or in main memory. Only the access procedures vary. The rapid advance in storage technology and the continual decrease in hardware costs make it vital to keep the data independent of the storage location. Unless the data structure is independent of the storage technology, it will not be possible for the designer to adapt the design to changing hardware economics.

3.4.1 The Channel

The purpose of the channel is to provide a pipe of information passing from one process to another. As well as providing a vehicle for communication, it provides an elastic link between processes within the system. For the processes to run truly asynchronously there must be some buffering of information; the larger the buffers, the greater the system flexibility.

The information to be passed from one process to another is best designed as a fixed format message. The format of message systems is discussed in subsection 7.3.4. It will usually contain identification information such as the name of the sending process. The message may contain the data itself, or it may be a pointer to the data. Commonly, either of two mechanisms is used to carry the message — the *queue* or the *hopper*.

3.4.1.1 The Queue

A widely used form of channel implementation is the first-in-first-out (FIFO) queue. Here, messages are placed on the tail of the queue by the sending process and removed from the head of the queue by the receiving process. Figure 3.7 illustrates this arrangement. Note that

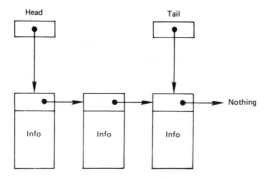

Figure 3.7 The queue

when a parcel of information is to be passed between processes, a
message must be built by writing information to a section of storage.
This storage is obtained from an available system freespace area. When
a receiving process finishes with the transmitted information, it will
return the storage element to the system freespace.

● A distributed processor arrangement complicates the situation only
slightly. In this case, the implementation of a channel requires the
provision of a communication circuit with its associated driving software.
The queue is in three pieces. One piece is in the sender's memory
awaiting transmission, another is in transit and the other is in the
receiver's memory.

The queue need not necessarily have a FIFO organisation. Messages
could be given priorities and placed in priority order within the queue.
Alternatively, certain sending processes could be given priority, and
their messages always placed at the front of the queue.

● When queues are operating there is always the possibility that they
will grow to the extent that the system freespace will become exhausted.
Steps can be taken to avoid this situation. For example, processes with
excessively long input queues could be given a high priority (see
chapter 4). However, in an overload situation, the available freespace
may still become dangerously low. There are two ways around this
situation. The system could refuse further work — that is, refuse
requests from its controlled system for action. For example, the system
controlling an airline booking system could refuse to process any new
transactions until an overload was reduced.

Many systems, however, are not in a position to ignore their
environment. A second solution to the overload problem is to allow the
system freespace to expand into the backing store (if present). Once
the freespace in main memory is exhausted, the queue would start using
a freespace area on fast backing store.

3.4.1.2 The Hopper

An alternative channel mechanism is a hopper or circular buffer. A fixed-sized buffer is set between the communicating processes. The storage is divided into a number of 'message'-sized elements. The buffer acts as a hopper; see figure 3.8. The transmitting process uses and moves the 'loading' pointer, while the receiving process uses and moves the 'unloading' pointer.

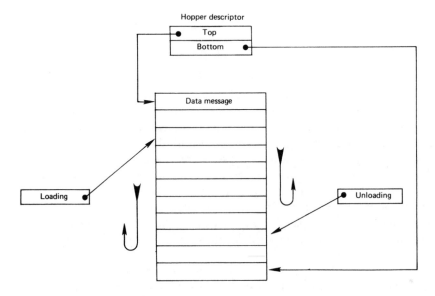

Figure 3.8 The hopper

The queue mechanism has the advantage that it can be extended for as long as there are package-sized elements of storage available in the system's freespace area. The hopper, on the other hand, is of fixed size, and this reduces its flexibility. However, it can be manipulated faster than the queue mechanism, as transfers to and from the system freespace area are not required. The decision as to which mechanism is used depends on system performance requirements.

The MASCOT activity–channel–pool (ACP) diagram does not distinguish between data-passing queues and synchronisation-control queues except by explicit use of names associated with the access procedures for IDAs and servers.

3.4.2 The Pool

● Pools usually take the form of system tables, shared data areas and shared files. In general, they consist of a piece of main memory or backing store which can be read from, or written to, by more than one process. They are used to store information that is relevant to more than one process in the system. The format of the data within the pools will depend on the particular application. They normally consist of data structures which model items in the controlled system or in the software system itself.

The data structures will take the form of tables, lists or individual storage elements held in main memory. In on-line commercial systems, for example, the pools will consist of on-line data files or a centralised database. These files will be read and written to by the processes controlling the on-line terminal activities and transaction processing. Often, for system security and recovery purposes, a regularly updated copy of this information will be held on backing store.

It is essential to control strictly the access to information in pools. If a large number of processes have direct access to a particular pool, a malfunction in one of the processes will cause corruption of pool information, and this will have ramifications throughout the system. Similarly, if any change is made to the format of pool information during the maintenance phase of the product's lifetime, the code for all the processes using the pool will have to be changed. These problems come about if processes using the pool are aware of layout details for the data structures in the pool. Usually, the processes do not need to know this detailed format information, as they are only interested in the data itself. If this is the case, we can introduce the concept of a pool 'policeman' or *monitor*. If a process wishes to access a piece of information in a pool, it does not go to the pool directly, but asks the pool's monitor to carry out the access. It will become evident that this concept of a monitor can be extended to channels and, in fact, to any item in the system.

3.5 MONITORS

While discussing channels and pools we have assumed that implementation of a data structure (queue, file, etc.) is sufficient to fulfil the communication requirements of our virtual machine. In fact, more is required.

● Processes should be unaware of the mechanisms driving the channel or pool. They should only need to present the channel or pool with information, or to request information from the channel or pool, and then expect that correct action will be taken. Furthermore, the processes should have no knowledge of the internal workings of the channel or pool. Unless this is the case, the processes will have to know too much about their environment for them to be regarded as free-standing programs.

● In the simplest case, we could provide the necessary facilities by creating a number of shared, re-entrant subroutines to be called by the processes. These access procedures would effect the necessary information transfers and, by suitable use of WAIT and SIGNAL operations, ensure that processes did not corrupt the channel or pool data structures. This type of data corruption is all too possible if asynchronous processes are allowed to manipulate common data.

We shall refer to this collection of controlling routines as a *monitor*. When a process wishes to read or write to a channel or pool, it asks the relevant monitor to do the reading or writing for it. Only the monitor is aware of the internal structure of the channel or pool.

Any changes — for example, from a queue mechanism to a hopper mechanism — need only be made known to the monitor. The user processes are unaware, and unconcerned. In this way, processes can be regarded as free-standing programs that utilise communication 'pipes' to interface with the outside world. We shall restrict our definition of a monitor to 'a collection of controlling routines'. Hoare (1974) has proposed a more formalised definition that includes the implementation in a high-level language of modules specifically declared as monitors.

3.5.1 Monitor Facilities

Monitors can be designed to provide increasing levels of service to a real-time system.

3.5.1.1 Basic Facilities

At its simplest, a monitor consists of a group of routines designed to implement the functions of its channel or pool. To do this, it must (a) provide the necessary data-transfer facilities, and (b) ensure adequate synchronisation of the user processes to avoid data corruption.

3.5.1.2 Watchdog Facilities

A monitor can be designed to act as a watchdog or policeman over the activities of its user process. The monitor can check the validity of the information passing through it. In a system test situation, the monitor could cause irregularities to be flagged. In an in-service environment, the monitor could instigate appropriate recovery action if invalid data were being generated by one of its user processes. We shall encounter further examples of monitor watchdog activities as our discussion progresses.

3.5.1.3 Testing/Debugging Facilities

● Monitors provide ideal agencies in a system-testing environment or 'test harness'. As they control the flow of information and act as the links between processes, they provide ideal points for inserting software test 'probes', and introducing test data.

Monitors can be built to include all of the above-mentioned facilities. When they are to be used in a time-stringent environment, all bar the basic facilities can be removed from the monitors by conditional compilation.

3.6 EXECUTIVE PROCESSES

Various 'special' processes have been mentioned: these include the interrupt-handling process, the process for swapping volatile environments and monitors. All these activities are needed to support the existence of the real-time virtual machine, and fall under the heading of *executive processes*. The executive may be regarded as that part of the real-time system which supports the existence, and controls the activity, of the processes in the system.

Processes that make use of the executive we will call *user processes*. The form and power of the services provided by the executive vary according to the size of the system being constructed. Typically they include: process swapping, interrupt handling, memory allocation, scheduling, interface monitoring, input/output device drivers and file-system control.

A user process, when it wants an executive service, calls on the executive to carry out the required actions. This call could be a simple subroutine call. However, it is desirable to isolate and protect the executive from the possible malfunctions of other processes in the system. The executive will normally be small and consist of highly reliable pieces of code. If the executive is corrupted in any way, it is difficult for the system to continue operation. However, if an individual user process becomes faulty, it may be possible for the executive to take some corrective action.

3.6.1 Protection

● In order that no rogue process can corrupt the executive, it is desirable to build a 'firewall' between the executive processes and other processes in the system. This protection is not always possible in a very simple microprocessor system. However, most modern minicomputer systems and the more powerful microprocessor systems include some form of memory-management hardware that does allow certain processes greater privileges than others, and does guarantee that processes cannot interfere with the memory allocated to other processes.

Each process is allocated a *protection domain*. A protection domain is the combination of the area of memory in which the process runs and the privileges — such as the ability to execute certain subsets of processor instructions — that the process possesses. Only the most privileged processes are given the power to transfer control of execution to another process's memory area. A simple protection set-up is a two-level 'kernel' and 'user' hierarchy. Processes in the kernel domain, or 'kernel space' would have access to all available machine instructions, while processes in user space would be restricted in the set of instructions they would execute.

Now, if memory-management and protection hardware is available to the system, the executive processes will be placed in a privileged area. This arrangement implies that a user process cannot obtain executive service by means of a simple subroutine call. The executive will be situated in a different protection domain, separate from the requesting process. A conventional solution to this problem is for the user process to execute a software trap instruction, after having placed suitable parameters in a location known and available to the executive processes.

The interrupt handling process will then recognise the trap as a call to the executive (system call) and signal to the relevant executive service process. Figure 3.9 shows this arrangement. Note that the executive is always entered via the interrupt service routine (or other closely guarded gateway). The executive is exited via the dispatcher.

● It is important that the software designer make full use of the protection mechanisms made available by the hardware. Some hardware systems provide more than two protection domains. If this is the case, then the designer would arrange to place the different processes and executive subroutines in suitable protection domains.

If no protection hardware is available, then a small amount of protection could be afforded by having the process call an executive monitor which checks the legality of the request, rather than calling the executive routines directly.

● The flexibility and low cost of Read Only Memories (ROMs) and Electrically Programmable Read Only Memories (EPROMS) allow us to

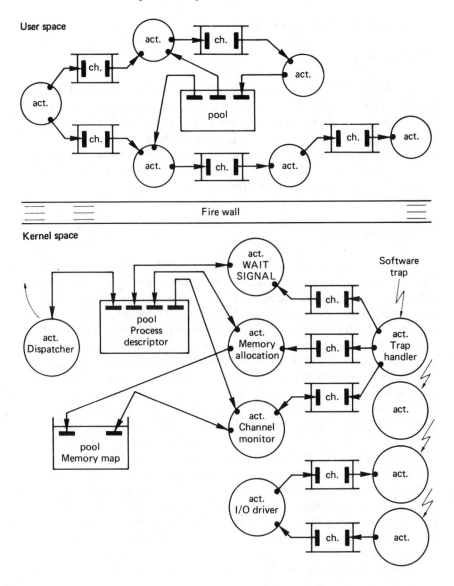

Figure 3.9 Some executive processes

fully protect the monitor code, since these memory devices cannot be accidentally overwritten. Such devices can be addressed within the normal address space (memory mapped) and constitute a guaranteed fire wall.

3.7   BUILDING THE SYSTEM

3.7.1 Bootstrap

Before we arrive at a fully operating real-time system we must build and test the software. In fact, at the outset, we must be capable of loading the process code elements into memory. The usual method is to employ a bootstrap technique. A small program consisting of a very few instructions is permanently stored in a non-erasable section of main storage. The purpose of this program is to load into memory a small process that is itself designed to load the system executive.

3.7.2 System Builder

Assuming that the executive has been successfully loaded we need to have yet another executive process. This process, the *system builder*, will be used to load the code elements of user processes and include their process descriptors in the process descriptor pool. A description of the system, including data on the activity/channel/pool interconnections, location of code elements and location of data elements, would be held on backing store in a system description file. The system builder uses this information to configure the system. Once the system is loaded, this process would terminate and the first user process commence.

● During the construction and testing phases of system development some of the processes may not be fully operational or even exist. Processes already built may not be fully tested and trustworthy. In this situation channel and pool monitors can provide an ideal test harness. Remember that each process is only aware of its environment through the auspices of the channels and pools to which it is attached.

● If only a single process has been developed, it is possible to test its operation by connecting its incoming channel to a file of test data, and its outgoing channels to test-result files. Provided that the test data conforms to that which the process expects to receive from its neighbours, the process will be unaware that this substitution of test files for real processes has taken place.

The system-description file will be designed to include information about completed processes, along with details as to which processes need to be replaced by test files. The system builder will tell the channel and pool monitors whether to use test files or process-generated data; see figure 3.10. In this way, from the very commencement of construction, the system can be loaded onto a comprehensive test harness.

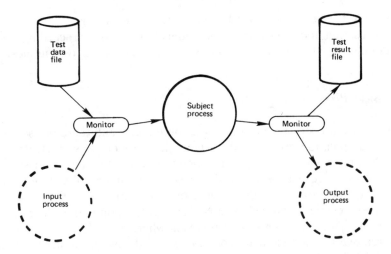

Figure 3.10 Monitor test harness

3.8 EXAMPLE

With the previous discussion in mind, it will be instructive to describe
the implementation of a very simple nucleus or 'kernel' of software that
will support the real-time machine. We shall make a number of
assumptions, as follows.

(1) The system will be implemented using a single CPU. If this is the
     case, then we can ensure that a process has temporary
     uninterrupted use of the processor by disabling the interrupt
     mechanism.
(2) There are no interrupting devices. We shall make this simplifying
     assumption until we discuss scheduling mechanisms in the next
     chapter.
(3) There is sufficient main storage in the system to accommodate the
     code elements of all the processes in the system. Accordingly, no
     memory allocation mechanism or backing store will be required.
(4) Semaphores will be implemented as the synchronisation primitives.
(5) The kernel resides in a protected area of store. This implies that
     the kernel can only be entered by means of an interrupt or
     software trap.
(6) Channels will be implemented as first-in-first-out (FIFO) queues of
     fixed-sized messages.

To provide the kernel we must facilitate processor sharing, synchronisation and interprocess communication. Before proceeding we will define some useful data structures and data-manipulation routines.

3.8.1 Basic Procedures

We will base the structure of the kernel on queues, and therefore some queue-manipulation routines will be helpful. Every queue will have a HEAD pointer and a TAIL pointer, pointing to the first and the last queue element, respectively. We shall also maintain a SIZE data item for each queue, containing the number of items currently in the queue. Each queue element will include a NEXT pointer, pointing to the next item in the queue. A pointer that points nowhere is NULL.

To remove the first element from a queue and leave it pointed to by a pointer ELEMENT we have

Remove ELEMENT from QUEUE
(1)   Make the value of ELEMENT equal the value of the HEAD pointer of QUEUE
(2)   Make the value of the HEAD of QUEUE equal to the value of NEXT in the item pointed to by HEAD of QUEUE
(3)   Decrement the SIZE of QUEUE.

To insert the element pointed to by ELEMENT into QUEUE we have

Insert ELEMENT into QUEUE
(1)   If the value of HEAD of QUEUE is NULL then make the value of HEAD of QUEUE equal to the value of ELEMENT. Otherwise make the value of NEXT in the item pointed to by TAIL of QUEUE equal to the value of ELEMENT.
(2)   Make the value of NEXT in the item pointed to by ELEMENT equal to NULL.
(3)   Make the value of TAIL of QUEUE equal to the value of ELEMENT
(4)   Make the value of ELEMENT equal to NULL
(5)   Increment the SIZE of QUEUE.

Figures 3.11 and 3.12 show the action of these two procedures. In figure 3.13 various kernel data structures are shown. Process descriptors contain the volatile environments of individual processes and a pointer field, NEXT, for use in creating queues of process descriptors. A semaphore consists of a value field, to hold the current value of the semaphore, and pointer fields that will be used to maintain queues of

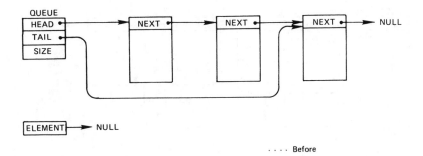

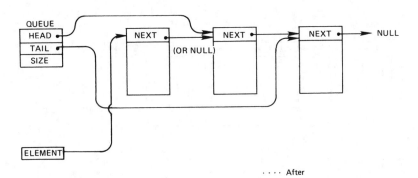

Figure 3.11 Remove ELEMENT from QUEUE

process descriptors. A simple queue item consists of the two pointers necessary for queue identification, together with the size of the queue. Figure 3.14 shows kernel queues. Each process descriptor will refer to an individual process. It will reside on one of the process descriptor queues, dependent on the status of its process. If the process is the running process, the descriptor will be the sole member of the *running* queue. If the process is waiting for use of the processor, the descriptor will be on the *runnable* queue. If the process is blocked, waiting on a semaphore, then the descriptor will be on the queue associated with the semaphore.

To complete our list of basic tools, we still need two procedures to affect process swapping

Save status of PROCESS
Store contents of all registers and other vital status information in the volatile environment area of the process descriptor pointed to by PROCESS.

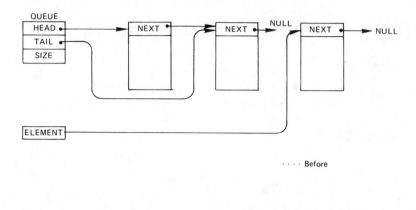

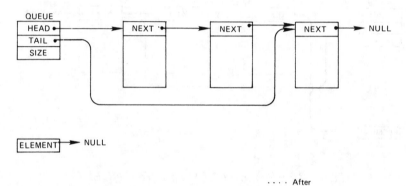

Figure 3.12 Insert ELEMENT into QUEUE

Restore status of PROCESS

Fill registers and status words with information obtained from the
volatile environment area of process descriptor pointed to by
PROCESS.

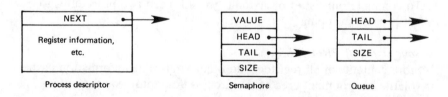

Figure 3.13 Executive (or kernel) data structures

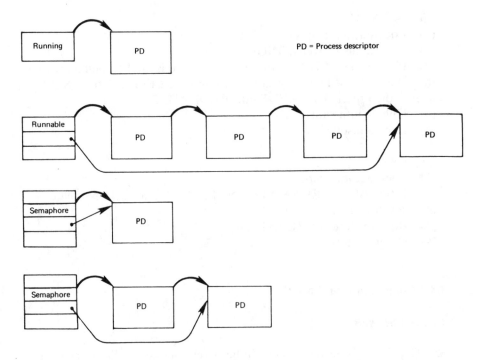

Figure 3.14 Process descriptor queues

3.8.2 Process Sharing and Synchronisation

Now, the running process remains the running process until such time as it is forced to stop by executing a WAIT operation. A SIGNAL operation may render runnable a process which is currently blocked. So assuming that WAIT and SIGNAL are trap handling processes, we define three processes that will implement processor sharing and synchronisation. WAIT on SEM and SIGNAL SEM will implement the two synchronisation primitives, and the dispatcher will effect the process swapping.

WAIT on SEM
(1) Lock out interrupts
(2) Save status of RUNNING
(3) If the value of the semaphore SEM is not equal to zero then reduce the value by one; otherwise, insert RUNNING into SEM queue
(4) Unlock interrupts
(5) Exit to dispatcher.

SIGNAL SEM
(1)   Lock out interrupts
(2)   Save status of RUNNING
(3)   If the value of HEAD of the SEM queue is NULL then increase the value of SEM by one; otherwise, remove ELEMENT from SEM queue, then insert ELEMENT into RUNNABLE
(4)   Unlock interrupts
(5)   Exit to dispatcher.

Dispatcher
(1)   Lock out interrupts
(2)   If the value of RUNNING is NULL then remove RUNNING from RUNNABLE
(3)   Restore status of RUNNING
(4)   Unlock interrupts.

3.8.3 Communication Facilities

3.8.3.1 Channels

●   The channels in the system will be based on queues. When needed, elements for the channels will be obtained from the system freespace queue. When no longer required, the elements will be returned to the freespace queue. To avoid corruption of the queue pointers, it will be necessary to protect the queues from simultaneous access by more than one process. For this reason we will provide two semaphores for each queue.

If a piece of code is bracketed by WAIT and SIGNAL on the same semaphore, and the semaphore is given an initial value of one, then only one process at a time may execute the bracketed code. If a semaphore is used in this way, it is called a mutual-exclusion semaphore. The first queue semaphore, then, will have an initial value of one, and be used to ensure that only one process is manipulating the queue at any one time. The second semaphore will have an initial value equal to the number of items in the queue, and be used to ensure that a process accessing items from the queue cannot do so if the queue is empty. The user processes will not have direct access to the queues and semaphores; they will only have the ability to call monitor procedures.

One fundamental queue in the system is the system freespace queue, FREESPACE. The semaphore *freespace-not-empty* is initially set to the number of items in the freespace queue, and the *freespace-mutual-exclusion-semaphore* set to one. The freespace monitor will provide the following access procedures:

Get item for QUEUE
(1) WAIT on queue-mutual-exclusion-semaphore
(2) WAIT on freespace-not-empty
(3) WAIT on freespace-mutual-exclusion-semaphore
(4) Remove ELEMENT from FREESPACE then insert ELEMENT into QUEUE
(5) SIGNAL freespace-mutual-exclusion-semaphore
(6) SIGNAL queue-mutual-exclusion-semaphore

Return ELEMENT
(1) WAIT on freespace-mutual-exclusion-semaphore
(2) Insert ELEMENT into FREESPACE
(3) SIGNAL freespace-mutual-exclusion-semaphore
(4) SIGNAL freespace-not-empty

3.8.3.2 Pools

● The detailed operation of the pool monitor-access procedures will depend on the structure of the pool data. We can, however, postulate a number of access rules: no process may write to a pool while other processes are reading it; no reader may start to read a pool if it is currently being written to by another process; more than one process may read the pool at one time.

In the following access procedures the purpose of the *mutex* (mutual exclusion) semaphore is to ensure that only one process may manipulate the integer *readcount* at any one time. Similarly, semaphore *w* allows only one process to write to the pool at any given time.

Initial values:
Integer readcount = 0
Semaphores mutex, $w = 1$.

Read pool
code A: WAIT on mutex
         readcount = readcount + 1
         if readcount equals 1 then WAIT on *w*
         SIGNAL mutex

            .
            .
         Do Reading
            .
            .

```
code B:   WAIT on w
          readcount = readcount − 1
          if readcount equals 0 then SIGNAL w
          SIGNAL mutex
```

Write pool
```
          WAIT on w
                       .
                       .
                       .
          Do Writing
                       .
                       .
                       .
          SIGNAL w
```

Assume now that a process wishes to read, and that the value of *mutex* is one. The process executes a WAIT operation on *mutex*, decrements the semaphore and passes on. It sets *readcount* to one and, accordingly, executes the WAIT on *w* operation. Note that while this process is in this section of code, no other reader may enter since *mutex* is currently equal to zero. The reader will only pass the WAIT on *w* operation when *w* has the value unity. Therefore if a writer is currently writing it will have decremented *w*, and so the reader cannot continue until the writer executes the SIGNAL *w* operation, at the completion of writing. The reader then passes into the reading code, having decremented *w* (ensuring no writing) and incremented *mutex*. More readers can now, one by one, enter code A. As *readcount* will now be greater than one, they will not WAIT on *w* and more than one process can be reading. Code B decrements the readcount and, when there are no more readers in the reading code, signals *w*, allowing a reader into the reading code, or a writer into the writing code, but not both. Notice that this arrangement could cause a writer to wait indefinitely while readers read.

Thus we complete the basic kernel of a real-time machine. We shall return to this discussion at the end of the next chapter.

3.9   SUMMARY

We have described the software that would be necessary to support the existence of processes, channels and pools. It is necessary to provide, possibly by sharing the resources, a CPU, memory and executable code for every process in the system. To control the access to channels and pools we must provide WAIT and SIGNAL operations and access-monitor routines. These facilities are centred in the executive or kernel. We have detailed the 'special' executive processes that make up the kernel of software necessary to support our virtual real-time machine. We must now provide a scheduling mechanism.

Concepts

Multiplexing; multiprogramming; volatile environment; swapping; process descriptor; serially re-usable; re-entrant; queue; hopper; monitor; executive; protection; memory management.

4 Scheduling

● The next facility to be discussed is the scheduling of process activity. The design of the virtual machine enables the software designer to separate considerations of process scheduling from those of process design. The processes think that they have sole use of their own processor and memory. In a one-process-per-processor setup, the processes can be thought of as running continuously, subject only to synchronisation requirements; in this case the scheduling problem does not arise. However, in a multiprocessing environment, the allocation of CPU/memory to the processes must be organised by agencies within the system. As a total concept, scheduling consists of deciding *when* the CPU/memory will be re-scheduled; *how* the CPU/memory will be re-scheduled; and *which* new process will be chosen. When and how to re-schedule have been discussed in the previous chapter. Here we will discuss how the system selects suitable candidate processes when a CPU/memory comes up for re-allocation — the *which*.

Priority

● Selecting a process to be run is a function of the relative importance of all eligible processes. Obviously, the process selected should be that which is most important or vital for the system's operation. The scheduling problem involves deciding which is the 'most important process'. It is convenient to think of process importance in terms of priority — a more important process having a higher priority than a less important one.

Priorities are not necessarily fixed. Conceptually, a process that samples a fluid flow rate every 5 minutes should gain in priority as the 5-minute period is approached. The more flexible the allocation of priorities in a system, the more flexible will be the system's response to changing environmental conditions.

● Note that the action of sampling is the critical action and can be separated from the subsequent processing of that sample by simple buffering. By operating a parallel sampler process, the critical timing can be removed. However, the processing must be carried out at some time before the next sample arrives, and so the problem remains.

64

Response

● Most commercial computer operating systems attempt to maximise the use of computing resources (disc drives, tape units, etc.). Accordingly, the priority of a certain process at a particular time may be strongly influenced by what resources it will use. Clearly, it is desirable to run a process that uses a tape unit at a time when the tape unit would otherwise be idle. However, once the system is expected to operate in real-time, the prime consideration must become that of adequate response to its environment. What is regarded as an adequate response will depend on the application. Real-time considerations must take precedence over the economic use of system resources. Our primary aim must be to design a solution to the scheduling problem that will ensure an adequate real-time response from the system.

Real-time Priority Levels

A process's priority is dependent on how important it is for the process to run immediately upon the occurrence of a particular event. This event may be something occurring in the controlled system, or simply the passing of a certain amount of time. The more stringent the deadline the process has to meet, the higher its priority.
● Three broad levels of priority can be identified.

(1) An interrupt level, which holds the service routine for those devices and situations that require instant or near-instant service;
(2) a synchronous, or clock level, on which repetitive processes such as scanning and sampling are run; these processes require accurate timing for their activation (but see subsections 7.3.3 and 10.2.1);
(3) the lowest or base level, which includes the processes that do not have to meet deadlines.

Pre-emptive and Non-pre-emptive Strategies

In order that the currently running processes reflect the relative process priorities in effect at a particular time, we shall specify a pre-emptive scheduling strategy. By this we mean that, if a process wishes to be activated, and it has a higher priority than the process currently running, then the current process will be stopped so that the high-priority process may proceed. For example, if a base level process is running, and a device interrupts, the relevant interrupt level service process does not wait for the base level process to finish, but will be executed immediately, before the base level process is resumed.

The alternative, a non-pre-emptive approach, would imply that the processes, be they interrupt, clock or base level, run to completion without interruption. Upon completion, each process would transfer control to the dispatching mechanism.

Note, however, that some re-scheduling by the real-time executive can happen when external events cause interrupts and when kernel support is requested through system calls. A simple system is illustrated in figure 4.1. The dispatcher runs the base level tasks serially, up to a clock 'tick' interrupt when the clock level tasks are run sequentially, and then returns to the base level after completion of all clock level tasks. Other interrupt level tasks (hardware or software) may occur, provided that the service routines are not time-critical and are short and infrequent enough to guarantee successful completion of all tasks at clock and base levels. Such a simple system implies a limited degree of pre-emption, but in a very controlled manner by selective enabling of the interrupt facility.

● Significant advantages are obtained when using this latter technique. Since the processes are not interruptable, poor synchronisation does not give rise to the problem of corruption of shared data. Shared subroutines can be implemented without producing re-entrant code or implementing lock and unlock mechanisms. However, as we have

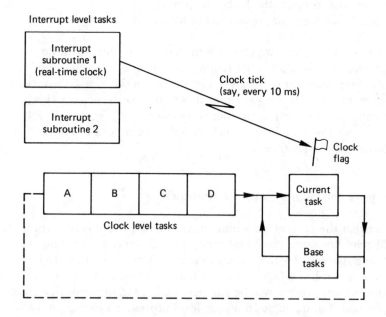

Figure 4.1 Simple system of serial scheduling

indicated in chapter 3, the main drawback with this approach is that while the current process is running the system is not responsive to changes in the environment. Therefore, system processes must be extremely brief if the real-time response system is not to be impaired. So, for the purpose of the following discussion we shall assume a pre-emptive strategy.

4.1 INTERRUPT LEVEL

It is at this level of process that the neat division between *when* to re-schedule and *which* to re-schedule becomes somewhat blurred. An interrupt forces a re-scheduling of the CPU to the corresponding interrupt-handling process. The system has no control over the timing of this re-scheduling. For this reason the amount of processing carried out at this level must be kept to a minimum. Normally, an interrupt level process will only do sufficient processing to avoid loss of data and status information, and will then channel the resulting information to a lower priority process for further servicing.

The interrupt forces a re-scheduling, and therefore the interrupt level processes must conduct a form of process swapping. As discussed in chapter 3, the hardware assists in the initial stages. The interrupt processes are designed to store whatever parts of the interrupted process's volatile environment they may need to use (normally a number of registers). They then carry out the necessary processing, replace the volatile environment and exit.

Even within the interrupt level, a priority structure will be necessary. The priority levels within the interrupt processes are defined by the relative time-critical nature of the interrupting devices. High-speed devices — for example, disc units — will need the ability to pre-empt the interrupt level processes associated with a slower device. The priority scheduling will normally be imposed by the hardware priority mechanism available on most modern processors. In general, these mechanisms work as follows.

The hardware includes a number of interrupt lines, each associated with an interrupt priority level. The CPU includes a register in which the current priority is stored (the processor priority). Associated with each interrupt line is a pair of memory locations (interrupt vector). The first of these locations holds the address of the start of the interrupt handling process for that interrupt line/priority level. When a device wishes to interrupt, it puts a signal on an interrupt line. If the processor priority is currently greater than the priority of the interrupted line, the interrupt is ignored. If not, then the current program counter is stored in the second location of the interrupt vector, the processor priority becomes that of the interrupting line and the value in the first location of the interrupt vector is placed in the program counter. When the interrupt handling process completes, it lowers the processor priority and replaces the program counter with the value previously stored in the second location of the interrupt vector. Note that interrupt handling processes may be interrupted by higher-priority interrupts.

The return from interrupt is normally to the interrupted process as implied by the previous comment, providing a stacking mechanism for several levels of interrupt activity. However, a return could also be forced via the dispatcher which may consequentially wish to re-schedule the processes after doing some essential housekeeping.

4.2   CLOCK LEVEL

4.2.1 The Real-time Clock

One of the interrupt-level processes is the real-time clock handler. A real-time clock is a hardware device which interrupts the processor at a regular rate. Virtually all real-time systems include such a device (see subsection 7.3.3). The reason for its inclusion is fourfold.

● First, not all activities carried out by a real-time system are a response to some external stimulus or interrupt. Very often, physical constraints (lack of available interrupt lines, for example) will prevent the device or mechanism that is being controlled from interrupting the processor. Therefore, in order to ascertain the need for servicing, it becomes necessary for the real-time system to inspect the status of the device at regular intervals. This technique, called polling, is used widely in communications systems to control distant terminals. The interval between servicing will, of course, be dependent on the performance characteristics of the device. Ideally, system control should be centred on the CPU. Interrupting devices command the attention of the CPU and are therefore exercising a degree of control. By regularly scanning the status of the devices, the CPU avoids the need for interrupt and retains full control of the system. It is necessary, then, for the system to be aware of the passing of real-time so that it may activate device-servicing routines at relevant times.

● Second, many devices controlled by the system will operate extremely slowly when compared with the speed of the CPU. This is especially true of electromechanical devices such as motors and relays. A process that causes a relay to close cannot assume that a relay has in fact closed immediately after execution of the instructions that initiate closure.

The process may well have to wait 20 to 50 ms before the relay is sure to be closed. It will, therefore, be necessary for the process to be able to wait a certain known amount of actual time before continuing.

● Third, it will often be necessary for the system to have a knowledge of real clock time in terms of a 24-hour day. In this way exact timing of certain events can be noted, stored and recalled for later report and statistics production.

Fourth, the real-time clock enables time-dependent scheduling — for example, periodic polling or sampling.

The real-time clock interrupting at regular intervals provides the system with a knowledge of, and thus the ability to measure, the passing of time. The rate at which a clock interrupts will depend upon the timing accuracy required by the system. It will usually be defined by the required rate of activation of the most often activated device-servicing routine. Typical values would be 20, 50 or 100 ms.

4.2.2 Clock Level Processes

Clock priority level processes are those which must run at strictly regular intervals. The real-time clock interrupt handling process, when activated, will normally update the time-of-day counter (some memory location) and transfer control to the dispatcher, having first left an indication that a real-time clock interrupt has just occurred. It is then up to the dispatching mechanism to select any clock level processes that must run at that clock 'tick'.

Some of the clock level processes will require accurate timing for their activation (the very reason they are at clock level). If the processes requiring the most accurate timing are always run first after a real-time clock interrupt, then they will be initiated at a regular rate. Those scheduled later will have some 'jitter' caused by the varying running times of the previously run processes. Here, priority is decided by the process's sensitivity to variations in timing.

It is possible, in certain circumstances, for processes running at clock level to take longer than the period between clock interrupts. Rather than let these momentary overloads disrupt the other processes that require high timing accuracy, it is possible to split the processes into two priority classes. The high-priority processes that are guaranteed to finish within the clock interrupt period are run first. Thereafter, the lower-priority clock level processes run the risk of being interrupted by the real-time clock on its next 'tick'.

The real-time clock will be designed to interrupt sufficiently often to initiate those clock level processes requiring the most frequent activation. Obviously, not all of the clock level processes will need to run at that rate; some will require activation every 5 clock 'ticks', some every 50 perhaps. A widely used method for scheduling these processes is to use a 'bit map' technique. This is explained in the following discussion and illustrated in figure 4.2.

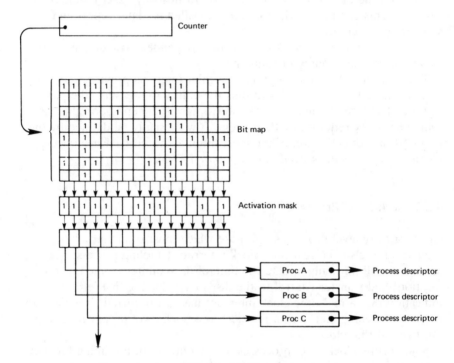

Figure 4.2 Bit map

Each clock tick is numbered, modulo N, where N is the number of ticks that will result in the eventual activation of all process. This tick number is used as an index to a timetable, each word of which has various bits set to indicate the different processes to be run at that tick. If a WAIT synchronising operation has been executed, a clock level process may not be runnable for some time. If this is the case, then the relevant bit in the activation mask will not be set. The tick number selects the word within the bit map. This word is logically 'anded' with the activation mask. The resultant word is then scanned from the most significant bit and the processes whose bits are set are executed in sequence. Note that the priorities of these processes are defined by the position of the process's column within the map.

● This is a good way of achieving a fairly fast control, indeed some of the bits may be used to activate parallel processes such as data acquisition or signal processing implemented in separate processors.

4.2.3 The Clock Queue

In the clock priority level we include device-scanning and polling processes that have stringent timing requirements. There is, however, another class of processes that use the real-time clock interrupt. These processes wish to 'delay' their activities for a fixed amount of time. The process cited earlier, which closed a relay, is such an example. We will set the priority of these processes within the base level group. Should it be vital that a process run immediately upon the expiry of its delay period, then we could allocate to it the highest-level base priority.
● A common method of implementing this delay capability is to introduce a 'clock queue' of process descriptors. When a process wishes to be delayed for a certain length of time, it calls upon an executive subroutine to remove its process descriptor from the runnable list and place it on the clock queue. The clock queue is a list of process descriptors of processes that have requested suspension. The process descriptor is placed in the list in a position relative to the time at which re-activation is required. When the real-time clock interrupts, the interrupt handling process updates the time-of-day counter. It then checks to see if this time corresponds to the time of the re-activation of the first process(es) in the clock list. If so, the process is made runnable by transferring the process descriptor to the queue of runnable processes.
● This repetitive checking of the clock list may be considered an unacceptable overhead for the real-time clock handler. After all, the interrupt handlers are meant to be short! To reduce this overhead, a special clock level process can be constructed. This process, designed to be activated every so many clock ticks, does the checking and process descriptor swapping. The period between successive activations of this process will define the minimum integral delay interval possible in the system. For example, if the process is activated every 20 ms, other processes may only delay themselves by 20, 40, 60 ms etc. Finer timing may be required for a few processes and this can be achieved by the use of programmable timers (see subsection 7.3.3).

4.2.4 Review

Before proceeding to discuss base level scheduling, we shall review the situation to date. Figure 4.3 summarises the different priority levels.
● Figure 4.4 shows a graph of process priority level against time. In this idealised diagram, it is assumed that each process has a unique priority and that the dispatcher takes zero time to do its job. The diagram represents the following sequence. Initially, a base level process is running, when a clock interrupt occurs. The clock interrupt handling

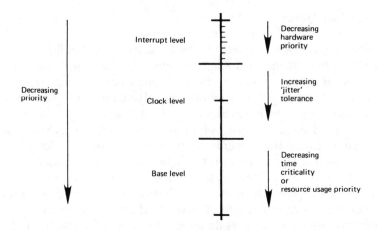

Figure 4.3 Priority levels

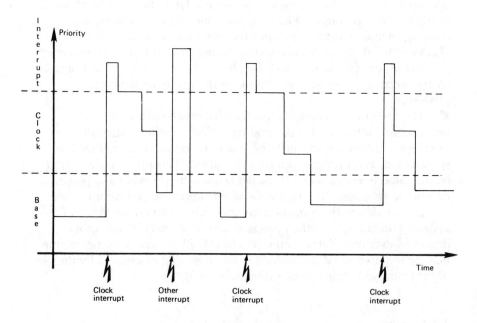

Figure 4.4 Priority vs *time*

process takes over and carries out any necessary processing before handing over to the highest-priority clock level process that is currently runnable. When this process finishes, a lower-priority clock level process takes over until it, in its turn, completes. The highest-priority base level process is then allocated the processor until it temporarily loses use of the processor to an interrupt handling process. In due course, the next clock interrupt occurs and the cycle is repeated.

4.3 BASE LEVEL

Once the processing requirements of clock level processes have been met, the remaining time in a clock period is available for use by the base level processes. Various scheduling methods can be applied at this level.

4.3.1 Time Slicing on a Round-robin Basis

This is relatively straightforward. At each clock period, one of the base level processes is selected to be run for the remainder of the period. This selection is done on a round-robin basis, a new process being selected each period. If the selected process, when activated, has no work to carry out, it returns control to the dispatcher immediately after it is activated. The dispatcher then chooses the next in line. Similarly, if the chosen process terminates before the end of the clock period, it returns control to the dispatcher.

Of course this method takes no account of the relative priorities of the base level processes. An implicit priority scheme can be introduced by giving higher-priority processes extra clock periods when their turn comes round on the round-robin. An alternative method is to set up a round-robin where higher-priority processes have more than one place on the round-robin, and are therefore selected more often. Re-scheduling the processes every clock period may prove too high an overhead, and so the dispatcher may re-schedule after every so many clock ticks.

In order to implement the round-robin method it is only necessary to provide the dispatcher with a circular list of runnable processes, and include within the dispatcher sufficient intelligence to maintain the round-robin.

● If we follow the basic philosophy that systems should always be as simple as possible, then the round-robin method provides the most applicable strategy. In many situations, a simple policy such as this will suffice. The designer should introduce more complex methods only when simple methods have been shown (by measurement of system performance) to be inadequate. Even if this is the case, simple methods should not necessarily be rejected. Considerable speed improvements in the processes themselves can often be obtained by the use of more efficient algorithms, simplifying processes by removal of unnecessary frills and constraints, and by judicious use of low-level code.

4.3.2 Pre-emptive Policies

Pre-emptive scheduling may be regarded as a variation on the round-robin technique. Here, the dispatcher chooses the highest-priority base level process to run. The process then continues, clock period after clock period, until such time as (1) it is forced to halt as a result of the execution of a WAIT operation, or (2) it runs out of work to do and voluntarily relinquishes the processor, or (3) a process of higher priority becomes eligible for selection. An advantage of this method is that the dispatcher is not directed to swap the processes as often as is necessary in the round-robin technique.

4.3.3. Priority Allocation among Base Level Processes

The priority assigned to a process may be fixed for the life of the system, or it may vary, dependent upon the conditions affecting the system at a particular time.

Fixed Priority

Process priority can be fixed and assigned at the time the process is created. Its priority would then be a function of the urgency of the job it must perform and often of the 'cost' or availability of the system resources that it uses.

● Unfortunately, it is very difficult for a designer accurately to forecast what will be a satisfactory mix of priorities for base level processes. This problem is aggravated by the dynamic and unpredictable nature of the system's environment. We can gain useful knowledge and experience by examining similar systems, but if this previous experience is not available then other methods must be used to gain information on system behaviour. This can be done either by analysing simulation models of the system, or by monitoring actual system behaviour under different priority mixes and environmental conditions. Chapter 11 will discuss this activity.

Variable Priority — The High-level Scheduler

The problem of forecasting can be avoided if process priorities are varied dynamically, dependent on the behaviour of the system when it is in operation. The *high-level scheduler* can be pressed into service to fulfil this function.

● This is an executive process that has the ability to alter process priority. It is activated at regular intervals and uses its knowledge of overall system status to re-allocate process priority. The calculation of new process priorities is an overhead on the system's workload, and so the algorithm that it uses should be as simple as possible. An example of a useful algorithm would be to give a higher priority than normal to a process whose input channel was growing excessively large. For commercial, batch-based operating systems, the algorithm chosen would be one that would tend to maximise the use of system resources or throughput of user jobs. For a real-time system, however, the algorithm must ensure that the time-critical processes are carried out. Therefore, when allocating a priority to one process, it must take into consideration process deadlines. More complex priority allocation algorithms will take into consideration the deadlines of *all* the processes in the system.

System Overload

● The scheduling algorithm for a real-time system must also ensure that the system adjusts itself to an overload situation in a correct manner. As an example, take a message switching system that receives and stores messages. Once a message is received in its entirety by the message switch, it is then re-transmitted down a selected path. Ideally, the message switch should never refuse incoming messages. Therefore, in an overload situation, the process reading in and storing messages must gain a high priority compared with the path selection and transmitting processes. This dynamic adjustment to overload is a necessity in all real-time systems and may, in cases of heavy overload, involve the system in temporary abandonment of some of its less vital activities. It is necessary for the designer to know what is the desired, acceptable or tolerable behaviour of the system under overload conditions. The formulation of suitable dynamic priority allocation algorithms is his most powerful tool in implementing these overload characteristics.

4.4 RESOURCE SHARING AND DEADLOCK

All processes in the system use system resources. At the least, these resources consist of a processor and storage for the code element. More usually, the resources would include disc files and peripheral devices. Whenever two or more processes compete for the use of a set of resources, a possibility of deadlock exists. Imagine that process A has the exclusive use of resource R and requests use of resource Q. Process B has the exclusive use of resource Q but requests use of R. Neither process can continue — they are deadlocked.

Commercial operating systems apply one of three strategies to solve the deadlock problem

(1)   prevent deadlock by ensuring that the conditions necessary for deadlock cannot occur;
(2)   detect deadlock when it occurs and instigate recovery action;
(3)   anticipate that deadlock may occur and try to avoid the situation that will cause it.

The simplest strategy is to demand that any process be allocated all of its resources at one time (normally when it starts). This approach avoids the possible deadlock, but it does not allow for the optimum use of system resources. Complex deadlock-avoidance algorithms have been designed and applied, in an attempt to allow more efficient sharing of resources between the competing processes. However, in a real-time system, the processing time required for the more sophisticated algorithms may prove unacceptable.

If we chose the simplest strategy, as described above, then the ideal process for allocating the resources is the high-level scheduler. The configuration and status of resources in the system would be described in system data structures. Each of these data structures (pools) would be protected by its monitor. The scheduler would carry out its resource allocation task via a dialogue with the resource monitors. In a real-time system, the resource-allocation responsibilities of the scheduler would focus on avoiding deadlock situations. Obviously, time limits permitting, it would be helpful if the scheduler could also cater for the optimum usage of system resources.

Figure 4.5 shows a possible layout for the processes involved in scheduling. The dispatcher would be a simple process primarily concerned with swapping the volatile environment of the process that is indicated in the process descriptor pool as the next to be run. The other three processes would use their particular knowledge of system status to manipulate the process descriptors so that they reflect the current priority requirements.

4.5   EXAMPLE

The scheduling strategy implied by the very simple kernel described in section 3.8 is simply: 'each process continues execution until it loses use

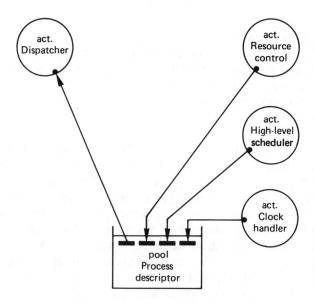

Figure 4.5 Scheduling processes

of the CPU by executing an unsuccessful WAIT operation.' For the sake of simplicity we did not include any interrupting devices in the system. Now, we will make the example more realistic by adding the following two assumptions.

(1) The system hardware includes a real-time clock.
(2) The CPU is provided with a priority vectored interrupt mechanism.

With these two facilities we can implement a more sophisticated scheduling arrangement. The scheduling of interrupt level processes is taken care of by the interrupt handling hardware. By using the real-time clock and its handling process, we can very easily produce a simple round-robin scheduling mechanism for the remaining processes. Consider the following processes.

Clock Interrupt Handler
(1) Save status of RUNNING
(2) Update time-of-day counter
(3) Set flag indicating clock interrupt
(4) Exit to dispatcher.

Dispatcher
(1)   Lock out interrupts
(2)   If clock interrupt flag set then insert RUNNING into
RUNNABLE and remove RUNNING from RUNNABLE
(3)   Restore status of RUNNING
(4)   Reset clock interrupt flag
(5)   Unlock interrupts

We now have a simple time-slicing round-robin. But the system still has
no concept of priority for non-interrupt-level processes. In order to
make scheduling more sensitive to process priority, we must extend our
simple process descriptor to indicate the process's priority. We do this
by introducing a new element into the processs descriptor data structure.
This element holds a value that reflects the priority of the process. We
must be able to assume that the process descriptors in the
RUNNABLE, and possibly the semaphore queues, are always in
priority order. To do this we must extend our 'insert into queue'
procedure so that it places the process descriptors at the correct location
in the queues.

4.6   SUMMARY

We have added a process-scheduling facility to our virtual machine.
Scheduling is based on process priority. We have identified three levels
of priority — interrupt, clock and base level. Because of the time-critical
nature of the system, we have emphasised a time-deadline policy, rather
than a policy that would optimise resource utilisation. The design of
scheduling strategies is totally divorced from the design of the scheduled
processes. The scheduling mechanisms used are standard models of
processes, channels and pools. The framework of our virtual real-time
machine is complete. A further problem remains, that of attempting to
ensure system reliability.

Concepts

Priority; clock; bit map; time slicing; round-robin; pre-emption; high-
level scheduler; deadlock; system resources.

5 Reliability

Real-time systems must be reliable. Ideally they will perform in a fault-free manner throughout their lifetime. In reality, this is rarely the case: systems *will* fail from time to time. Hardware systems fail when their components wear out, but software cannot 'wear out'. Why then does a software system fail?

Software Faults

● First of all, faults appear in software when particular circumstances occur which have not been catered for in the original design or, alternatively, when an error has been made at the coding stage and is not revealed during testing. As a result, the software does not perform in the correct manner. It can be stated with certainty that all software harbours a number of undetected design and implementation errors. It would therefore be unrealistic to assume that any piece of software is perfect, but one can demand that it perform to an acceptable level of reliability. What is deemed to be 'acceptable' will depend on the application concerned. Obviously the impact of a breakdown will have more serious implications for some systems than others.

System Availability

Reliability requirements are often expressed in terms of system availability: a system will be expected to perform with a certain maximum allowable time out of service during a particular time period. Also, no breakdown should take the system out of service for more than a specified time.

● Using a hardware engineering analogy, reliability requirements are expressed in terms of *mean time to repair* (MTTR) and *mean time between failure* (MTBF). Two factors, then, are important for system availability: (1) how rapidly the fault can be repaired; and (2) how often the system fails.

Consider the first point. Before the fault can be repaired, the cause must be isolated. Unless the software is well structured, and well documented, this can be a lengthy and tedious activity. Well-structured software increases system availability because it is easier to maintain. Further, if system availability is to be increased, the software must be designed to provide maintenance personnel with as much diagnostic information as possible in the event of failure.

The second point implies that system failures should be kept to a minimum in the first place. This chapter will concern itself with the methods of reducing the frequency of these failures.

5.1   TESTING

● Software faults can be attributed to residual design and coding errors or omissions. Reliability, then, is strongly influenced by the success of the testing phase of product development. Testing can only indicate the presence of errors, not their absence. To ensure maximum reliability, testing should expose the largest possible proportion of errors in the product. It is impossible to remove all the errors in a piece of software of any complexity. It should, however, be possible to gain a quantitative measure of the effectiveness of testing and, from this, to extrapolate a measure of future reliability.

● The occurrence of a software failure implies that a fault has been exposed by the execution of some untested pathway in the code. In the case of real-time software, further faults arise as a result of the occurrence of untested timing conditions. Ideally, testing should thoroughly exercise the software and thus expose all faults. Unfortunately this is impossible. Even if we leave aside the problem of timing errors, it remains impractical, for all but the simplest module, to test every pathway through the code. Take the simple module modelled by the flow graph shown in figure 5.1. There are approximately 250 thousand million unique pathways through this module. Even if we could test one path every millisecond it would take eight years to test the module exhaustively. Clearly it is impossible completely to test large programs, but there are a number of tools and techniques available to increase the effectiveness of the testing that *is* done.

Structured Walkthroughs

One of the most successful software engineering techniques is the structured walkthrough. Here, a small group of people associated with a particular module — the designer, the implementer, the tester — meet together to read through the module code, highlighting the errors and

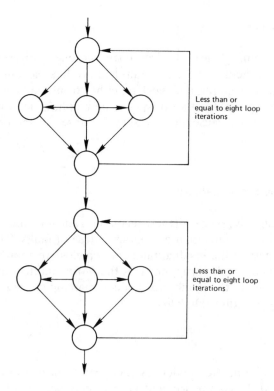

Less than or equal to eight loop iterations

Less than or equal to eight loop iterations

Figure 5.1 Program flow graph

any inconsistencies for later correction. This concentrated code scrutiny has proven to be a potent tool for uncovering errors. However, it can be time-consuming and hence expensive.

Profilers

● Once the code is submitted for testing, it is necessary to have some quantitative gauge of the thoroughness of the testing. We know it cannot be done completely. Even if it is not possible to test every pathway through the code, it should be possible to test every branch in the program. During a test run, profiling programs (see subsection 11.3.2) can be used to generate a source listing of the tested programs with an indication as to which branches have been executed and which not. This information gives the designer an indication of how thorough the test has been, and where further testing should be directed.

Test-data Generators

● A more comprehensive tool is a test-data generation system. This tool analyses the structure of the program and produces a control flow graph. Using this graph, and working either from the beginning or the end of the program, the tool traverses the graph, generating a set of input data that will cause all, or a specific subset, of the branches to be executed.

5.1.1 Testing and Reliability

● Unfortunately, even if all these techniques and tools are used it remains impossible to guarantee that a program is free of faults. The number and seriousness of the residual faults bear a close relationship to the future reliability of the program. It is therefore vital for the designer to have some idea of the number of faults remaining in the software in order to gauge future reliability.

Error Models

The history of a module under test can provide insight into its future reliability. At the commencement of testing, a large number of the more obvious errors will be uncovered.
● Later, the rate of fault exposure will decrease, as any remaining errors are necessarily more obscure. From the history of error detection it may be possible to create a mathematical model of the rate of occurrence of errors. Using this model it may further be possible to extrapolate the error rate into the future and thus to obtain a measure of future module reliability.

Error Seeding

Some practitioners attempt to gauge the success of testing by adding known errors to the module. The location and nature of these errors is unknown to the test team; however, they are assumed to have a similar distribution of location and nature as the 'real' errors in the software. After a period of testing, the percentage of 'seeded' errors that have been uncovered is calculated. The figure is assumed to be the same as the percentage of 'real' errors detected. From this information, the number of real errors remaining in the module can be calculated. Needless to say, the seeded errors are removed at the end of the exercise.

5.2   FAULT TOLERANCE

A more positive approach to reliability is to design the system in such a way that the system itself can recover from faults. If this is possible then the system will demand human intervention only when its automatic recovery mechanism cannot cope with the failure. By designing the system to automatically recover from error, we drastically increase the system availability.

● Systems that can continue operation in spite of faults are referred to as fault-tolerant systems. If a system is tolerant of faults, it implies that the system can detect the fault when it occurs, have sufficient information about the fault to correct its impact on the system as a whole and can then continue correct operation. Most software systems carry out the fault correction by means of 'rolling back'. Upon the detection of an error the system is returned to a state that existed prior to the fault, and then restarted. The system is restarted from a point called a *checkpoint*, where the system is known to have been operating correctly. We shall discuss this technique in more detail in subsection 5.4.1. Of course, if the fault is due to an error in the software, then the system will fail again if the same conditions are encountered.

Note, in passing, that a great deal of work has been carried out to ensure the reliability of hardware systems. The conventional approach is to use some form of protective redundancy scheme. Here the continued operation of the functions of a particular module is assured by the inclusion of one or more identical, but redundant, modules in the system. If an error is detected in the running module, a spare module is automatically switched into operation and replaces the faulty one.

A protective redundancy scheme can be very expensive and, since most modern computer hardware has a high mean time between failure, this technique would only be used in systems demanding a very high level of reliability. For the purpose of this discussion, we shall assume that any hardware fault protection mechanisms act autonomously and only inform the software of a malfunction if they are unable to correct the fault themselves.

5.3   FAULT DETECTION

Computer hardware is organised, to a greater or lesser extent, to recognise errors within the hardware system. Parity bits within words or bytes of storage, and majority logic circuits within processing hardware are designed to detect malfunctions. If the hardware is not equipped to handle the error itself, it will normally cause an interrupt to the software.

● Errors in the software itself are more difficult to detect; nevertheless their presence can be uncovered by placing checks at various levels in the software structure. Some arithmetic errors can be minimised or effectively eliminated by careful arrangement of the arithmetic — for example, the use of block floating point and limiting characteristics (see subsection 10.4.2). At this stage we shall simply assume that the presence of a fault is signalled to a 'recovery monitor' whose action on receipt of a signal will be discussed later. Specific provision for handling faults is made in some modern languages (see subsection 9.2.3). We will now describe the levels at which fault checks can be included in the software system.

5.3.1 Machine Instruction Level

The system hardware can be used to detect errors introduced by the execution of an individual instruction. Attempts to violate memory protection schemes, to execute privileged instructions or simply to divide by zero can all be detected by the hardware and signalled to the recovery monitor by means of an interrupt.

When part of a process's code element is loaded into the main storage, the first thing it can do is ensure that the loading operation has been carried out correctly. For this, a simple checksum technique will suffice. A checksum is a numerical value which is a function of the binary patterns comprising the code of a program. The simplest example would be the value produced by adding together all the words of the program as if they were integer binary numbers.

A checksum is positioned at a known location within the code element. Each time loading occurs, the process can calculate a checksum of the code element. This value is compared with the checksum embedded in the code. A discrepancy causes a fault to be signalled. Similar characteristics are used in serial communications systems, which is relevant to communication channels between different processors.

5.3.2 Code Module Level

Checks can be included in an attempt to guarantee the correct operation of code modules within the processes. One technique is the use of a *baton*. Here, each module of code passes a unique numerical value to the next module to be executed. This value is the baton. The receiving module checks the value. If it is incorrect, or not the value expected, it would imply that the normal progression from module to module has been upset. A fault would then be signalled.

Assertions

Fault checks can be inserted explicitly to form part of the code itself. This is most conveniently done by including an assertion facility in the program development system. The programmer can embed logical assertions in the code. These normally take the form of statements concerning the expected behaviour of the module at different points in its execution. Should an assertion prove false at run time, a fault is flagged and recovery action taken. The introduction of assertions automatically introduces additional, redundant code into the software.

Assertions take a number of different forms. Range checks ensure that the values of data variables lie within a specified range during execution. State checks verify that certain conditions hold among the program variables. Reasonableness checks analyse data input to or output from a module in an attempt to discover impossible or unlikely values. Figure 5.2 shows the assertion mechanisms available in a typical assertion system. The figure shows an ASSERT statement in the Program Evaluation and Test (PET) system produced by the Macdonell Douglas Corporation (Stuki, 1978).

ASSERT $(X(I) \neq X(J))$ FOR ALL (I, J) (1:8) WHERE $(I \neq J)$

This statement asserts the fact that:

For all values of I and J such that $1 \leq I, J \leq 8$ and $I \neq J$

then $X(I) \neq X(J)$

In other words, at the point in the program code where the assertion is made, all the first eight elements of array X will have unequal values. If this is not the case, the assertion will fail.

Figure 5.2 An assertion statement in the PET system

In a real-time software environment, assertion mechanisms are of most value during the construction and testing phase. The existence of assertion mechanisms, however, implies extra code, which can produce an unacceptable overhead in a running system. Therefore, the provision of assertion code can be made optional at the compilation stage. During the testing phase, the module could be compiled, including all the assertions in the program code. Later, the module could be recompiled including only a subset of the original assertions, the remainder being translated as program comments. Ideally, as many assertions as possible should be left in the code, since they are a powerful tool for detecting errors at the code module level.

5.3.3 Process Level

● Channel and pool monitors provide an ideal error-detection mechanism. Because they form the external interface between processes and provide processes with their interaction with the 'outside world', they can be used to watch for unexpected, and therefore possibly incorrect, process behaviour.

Any data being transferred out of the process can be checked and an error flagged if it appear suspicious. A monitor could be set up to initiate a time counter for each of the processes feeding its channel or pool. Should any of the processes not provide output within a certain time period, then an error condition can be flagged. Similarly, the fact that a channel begins to overfill could well indicate a fault in the receiving process. The monitor may not be able to pinpoint the exact cause of an error, but it will be able to indicate that certain processes are acting in a suspicious manner.

These fault checks will impose an overhead on the performance of the monitor. It would be desirable to make error-checking code an optional facility. This is commonly done in two ways. First, at compile time, successively detailed levels of error-checking code can be included in the monitor by conditional compilation facilities. Second, at run time, a pool of on/off switch data items could be set up. A monitor would regularly check the status of one or more of these switches and, dependent on this information, execute levels of error-checking code. A process associated with the system operator's console would change the value of the data switches when commanded by the operator.

5.3.4 Audit Level

Whole processes can be introduced into the system with the sole purpose of error detection. These 'audit' processes continually check system pools and hardware status for invalid status or conditions. They flag an error if their in-built view of 'correct' operation detects any discrepancies.

Watchdogs

A specialised type of auditor is the watchdog timer process. Figure 5.3 illustrates a watchdog set-up. The watchdog process, W, operating at clock level, regularly decrements the value of a set of data items in the pool. Each data item relates to one of the set of subject processes $S_1, \ldots, S_n$. The subject processes are designed to reset their data items at particular points in their execution cycle. Now, should a watchdog

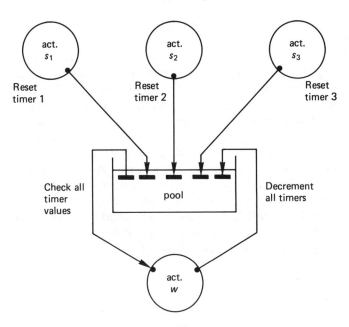

Figure 5.3 Watchdog timer

process, on decrementing all the data items, discover that one of the items has gone below a certain value (usually zero), it signals an error indicating the relevant subject process.

Redundant Information

● Most systems will include deliberate, or implied, redundant information. Audit processes can make use of this redundancy. The system state implied by one pool can be checked against the system state implied by the information contained in another pool. An audit process will flag an error it it finds two versions of system state information to be inconsistent.

Hardware Status

● A common source of error lies in the fact that the state of the controlled system is not accurately reflected by the data structures in the software. This is especially true in the case of electromechanical controlled systems. An auditing process can check the state of devices (relays, switches, connected remote terminals, etc.) in the controlled system and can compare it with the state indicated by the information held in the relevant system data pool.

● Should a discrepancy occur, an error could be flagged or, more simply, the pool state information updated. These auditing processes are particularly useful in systems where breakdowns and repairs are likely to result in parts of the controlled system being taken out of, or put into, service. Auditing processes can keep system state information up to date.

● Note that machine instruction, code module and process level checks detect errors at, or close to, the time they occur. Audit level checks detect errors by the side effects they cause in the system data structures. These checks are therefore slower detection mechanisms. None the less, there will usually be sufficient redundant information in the system data pools to justify the existence of low-priority audit processes that continually check the consistency of this data.

5.3.5 System Level

● In order to implement fault detection at the highest level, it is necessary to observe the system from an external viewpoint. This perspective is provided either by additional system hardware, or by a completely independent real-time system. The idea is to provide an observer totally detached from the observed system. For example, most mechanical systems include safety or fail-safe devices like governors, relief valves, etc. Electrical systems include voltage regulators and fuses. The activation of these devices would indicate a fault in either the controlled system or the controlling software. In either case, they can be used to trigger an alarm in the fault recovery system.

● Not only must the observer be totally independent of the system being observed, but also it must be possible to differentiate between a fault in the observed system and a fault in the observing system.

● Unexpected inactivity of a real-time system is often a symptom of faulty behaviour. For example, a common method of detecting failure in a teleprocessing centre is to include hardware to observe electrical activity on outgoing lines. Should all lines simultaneously become inactive for a number of seconds, a fault in the controlling software will be suspected.

● Not all real-time systems work in isolation. In fact an increasing number of systems are members of sets of systems distributed on a communications network. In these instances other systems in the network can provide an external monitor of a system's behaviour. Here a time-out mechanism is helpful. Each network member would be expected to communicate with its neighbours with a certain regularity. If a system does not respond to an enquiry from a majority of its immediate neighbours within a pre-determined period of time, a malfunction within it or its neighbours can be assumed.

In summary then, we can envisage a hierarchy of fault-detection mechanisms, all signalling the discovery of possible faults to a fault-recovery mechanism. Figure 5.4 summarises the situation.

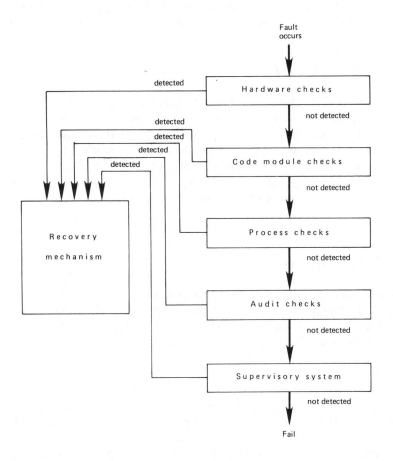

Figure 5.4 Fault detection

5.3.6 Fault-tolerant Programming

● It is vitally important that a real-time system does not halt, but it is also important that the effects of faults are minimised. A single missing event can cause a halt, but if operation is allowed to continue, assuming that only one event is missing (because of a temporary malfunction, perhaps caused by noise), the system can recover quickly. An important concept in improving reliability is defensive or fault-tolerant programming. The normal code is examined for likely causes of failure, perhaps because of temporary effects such as overflow, time-out, failed handshake and so on. By writing in procedures for handling such exceptions, local error recovery can be assured for all but the most persistent of faults, from which recovery must be organised along the lines suggested in the next section. This concept is discussed in more detail in subsection 9.2.3.

5.4   FAULT RECOVERY

Once the fault has been detected and signalled to the recovery monitor, it is up to that monitor to attempt to recover the system from the error. If correct operation cannot be continued, then the mechanism should, at the very least, ensure that the maximum error-diagnostic information is supplied to maintenance personnel before the system fails completely.

Initially we shall discuss a simple approach to system recovery, but we will also discuss some of the problems that this simple method tends to ignore.

5.4.1 Simple Approach

Early commercial data-processing systems often carried out lengthy calculations on hardware of questionable reliability. The following method was developed to avoid the necessity of repeating what could potentially run to hours of processing time.

Checkpoints

The programs were organised to create a series of checkpoints or footprints. These checkpoints were summaries of the current state of processing and were regularly placed on backing store. Whenever a fault was detected, the program needed only to be 'rolled back' to the last checkpoint before restarting. The checkpoints acted as a series of milestones. When each milestone was passed, the program was known to be acting correctly. This strategy can be readily applied to the real-time environment.

Figure 5.5 represents the flow of control in a hypothetical process code element. Many processes exhibit a circular control path, as shown in the diagram. However, even if the process is initiated at point A and terminated at point D, the following discussion will still apply.

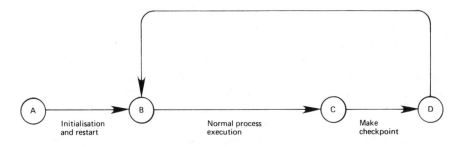

Figure 5.5 Process flow

When the process is first activated, it carries out initialisation activities. These may consist of checksum validation of correct loading of the code element, initialisation of variable values and, in the case of a process controlling a physical device, initialisation of the device (for example, positioning a disc arm). The data used to initialise variables, status words and device status information is not fixed, but read from a checkpoint data area. Ideally this data area is held in a highly protected area of memory or, better still, on backing store.

After the initialisation is completed, the process enters its main body of processing. On completion of one cycle of process execution, the current value of variables, status words, etc., are stored in the checkpoint data area. The process may then terminate or, more usually, return to point B for a second cycle.

Imagine, now, that an error has been discovered and the recovery monitor has been informed. The monitor will halt the process and cause it to be rolled back to its most recent checkpoint. To do this the monitor need simply restart the process at point A, having reloaded the code element of the errant process into main storage. The process will then continue from its checkpoint.

● The faulty process does not, of course, exist in isolation. All processes associated with the faulty process will notice, either directly or via auditing mechanisms within the channel/pool monitors, that the process is acting irregularly. Signals will then be sent to the recovery monitor. The irregularities will initially be caused by the faulty behaviour of the process but, for a period of time after the process is rolled back, irregularities will still be detected. This is because the process, by being rolled back, has had its normal sequence of operation changed and is therefore not behaving as the neighbouring processes expect. They will still signal errors. To avoid this unstable situation the reliability monitor will be designed to ignore error signals stimulated by recently rolled-back processes until such time as the subsystem surrounding the process has had time to settle down.

● If, after a pre-determined period of time, the process is still causing error signals, it can be assumed that the process producing signals is not the culprit. The problem will more likely lie in a nearby process. In this case, the whole neighbouring subsystem is rolled back. Again, the reliability monitor would ignore error signals from surrounding subsystems for a specified time period. If the error persists, then the whole system will be rolled back and restarted. Also, depending on the application area and on system performance requirements, it may be possible for the reliability monitor to abort faulty processes or subsystems and have the system continue operation at a reduced capability.

Should the error persist to the extent that the system could no longer remain operational, then alarms could be raised. These alarms could be messages to the operator's console, lights, sirens, bells, etc. Diagnostic information could be generated at this stage. This information would consist of execution summaries, snapshot dumps of parts of memory (see subsection 11.3.2.1), register contents and the status of hardware devices. The information would be dumped to backing store, high-speed hard-copy device or the operator's console.

This simplified approach to rollback makes a basic assumption. It implies that the faulty operation of the system was caused by a peculiar set of circumstances that will not readily recur once the system is rolled back. In many cases this is a valid assumption and, in the interests of keeping the system as simple as possible, it would be advisable to use this approach until it has been proven inadequate — for example, the auto-reclosing of circuit breakers after a lightning strike on the national grid. We have, however, brushed over a number of significant problems. It is well that we consider them.

5.4.2 More Complex Recovery Methods

Redundant Modules

● If the conditions that caused a piece of software to fail occur again, then naturally the software will continue to fail. The only way to attempt to cure the fault is to alter the software. As we mentioned before, it is usual for hardware reliability systems to include redundant modules. This technique can be used in software. Rather than roll back the current code element, a different code element is used. The replacement module will, of course, be designed to do the same job as the original module.

Obviously, the redundant code module will not be exactly the same as the currently running module. In the simplest case, the redundant code element could be an earlier version of the current module. Often, the correction of errors inadvertently introduces new errors and the use of a previous version of the software may clear the fault. A more satisfactory alternative would be to use a completely independent module. This module would have been produced to exactly the same design specification, but probably by a different programmer or team of programmers. As soon as the original code element has been corrected it is re-introduced into the system, replacing the backup module. The rationale behind this strategy is that the original module has been in service for a longer period and therefore undergone more 'in-service testing'. In this way the original module becomes more and more reliable as time goes by and the errors are corrected. It must be stressed at this stage that this, like any other technique that implies the production of redundant elements, is expensive.

Recovery Blocks

In our simple system a process has only one checkpoint. There is, of course, no reason why it could not be broken into a number of code elements, each with its own checkpoint (and redundant code element for that matter). This situation is shown in figure 5.6. Clearly the major drawback of this approach is the overhead of storing checkpoint information. Randell (1977) has suggested a formal solution to this problem. He uses a type of assertion mechanism in conjunction with a mechanism for storing checkpoint information. These mechanisms are invisible to the programmer.

A program is divided into *recovery blocks* headed by acceptance tests. The recovery blocks consist of a number of alternative code blocks, headed by a primary 'alternative'. Checkpoint information is stored prior to entering a recovery block. The primary 'alternative' is then entered and executed. Before the block is exited, the acceptance test (a boolean expression) is evaluated. If the test succeeds, the block is

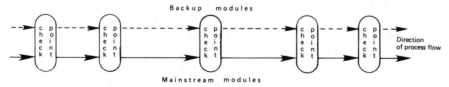

Figure 5.6 Multiple checkpoints

exited. If not, the situation is reset to the point where the block was entered and the second 'alternative' will be executed. Successive 'alternatives' are tried until the acceptance test is passed, or no further 'alternatives' are available, in which case the default error code is executed.

● The recovery block concept provides a convenient model for use in the design of the recovery structure of individual processes; however, real-time constraints may arbitrate against employing too complex a recovery structure. Storage of checkpoint information at the entrance to each block may impose too heavy an overhead. If this technique is to be used, it may be necessary to restrict the depth of recovery block nesting. .

Conversations

In both the simple approach and the recovery block approach, we return to a checkpoint by resetting the system to the state prevailing at the time the checkpoint was passed. This action is facilitated by a simple assignment of prior values to data variables.

● We have ignored the problem of irreversible processes. Consider a process that causes the reading of a card in a card reader. In order to roll back this process it is necessary to 'unread' a card. This is patently impossible. We have also ignored the problem of process interaction. What should be done if a process fails after receiving and destroying information from one process, and sending incorrect information to a third process? The failure and rollback of the central process implies the need for the neighbouring process also to be rolled back. Randall has suggested a design tool to be used in minimising these problems. He introduces a structure called a *conversation*, which provides a recovery structure common to a set of interacting processes.

Figure 5.7 represents a recovery block where the downward-pointing arrow indicates the overall progress of the process. The top edge of the square corresponds to the environment of the process on entry — the checkpoint information. The bottom edge represents the acceptable state of the process, as checked by an acceptance test, when it exits from the recovery block. The sides show that the recovery block is independent, from a recovery viewpoint, of any other activity operating in the system.

Now if we include part of the progress of another process in the same recovery block we have what is termed a *conversation*; see figure 5.8. We specify that all the processes must satisfy their respective acceptance tests before any may proceed beyond their test point. If any of the processes fail their test, all the processes must be rolled back to their individual checkpoints, where they entered the conversation.

The term 'conversation' is apt for this structure since, while in the

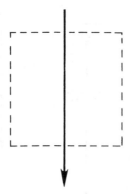

Figure 5.7 Recovery block

conversation recovery block, member processes may not communicate
or interact with processes outside the conversation. Conversations may
be nested, but may not intersect.

Figures 5.9 and 5.10 show conversations for the two examples of
irreversible processes described above. In order to implement the
conversation facility, it would be necessary to include calls to the
system's interprocess synchronisation mechanisms (WAIT and
SIGNAL).
● Recovery blocks and conversations are valuable design aids. An ideal
situation would be for the checkpoint creation and recovery mechanism
to be transparent to the designer and implemented as part of the
language compiler. However, even if these mechanisms are not
available, the structure they recommend is in itself a useful tool for the
designer when he is considering a recovery strategy for his system.

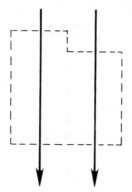

Figure 5.8 Conversation

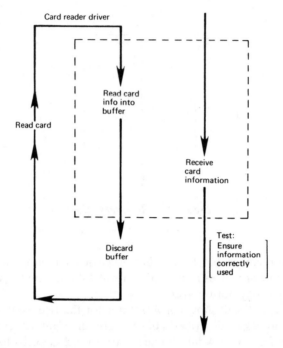

Figure 5.9 Card reader process and consumer process

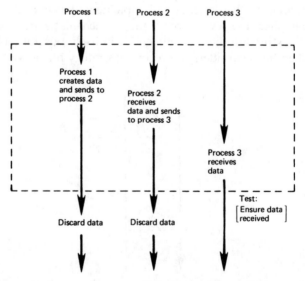

Figure 5.10 Three processes communicating a piece of data

5.5 RECOVERY LEVELS

● So far we have discussed a number of error-detection and recovery mechanisms which would be valuable should one of the system processes malfunction. For the recovery system to be complete, however, it must be able to recover from faults occurring within the recovery system itself. After all, there is no special reason why the recovery monitor, for example, should be exempt from failure. To overcome this problem, the virtual machine concept proves effective once again. We shall structure the recovery system in such a way that it provides successive layers of increasingly reliable environments. Each level will monitor the operation of the succeeding layer by means of a watchdog timer.

5.5.1 The Hardware Level

● We have already assumed that the hardware design includes error-detection and correction facilities. In order to highlight any faults in the hardware, we introduce a process that does nothing but exercise the hardware. It is used to execute the repertoire of CPU instructions, write bit patterns to memory, etc. If well-designed, the process should be short and exercise the hardware thoroughly. This process has as its watchdog the real-time clock interrupt. Should the process not reset its timer, the hardware bootstrap program will re-initialise the process. To allow for the possibility of a failure in the real-time clock, the independent system level watchdog can be used as a back-up stimulus to the exerciser.

The hardware exerciser provides a reliable environment where correct operation of the hardware can be assumed. The process acts as a watchdog to the code tester process.

5.5.2 The Instruction Code Level

● The code tester performs a dual function. By reading a process's code into its allocated space in memory it acts as a conventional process code loader. It also performs correctness tests on the code once it is loaded, such as checksum tests. This reliability level ensures that process code has been correctly loaded. The code tester process acts as a watchdog to the recovery monitor and the wait/signal process.

5.5.3 The Code Module Level

The recovery monitor lies at the focus of the reliability system and receives indications of malfunctions from both higher and lower reliability levels. It is the recovery monitor that implements process checkpointing and recovery block activities. By including the recovery monitor we ensure an orderly recovery from errors in code modules and thus assure a reliable environment at this level.

● In order that code sharing and recovery block conversations can be carried out, it is also necessary to guarantee a correctly operating wait/signal operation at this level. The wait/signal processes act as watchdog to the channel/pool monitors.

5.5.4 The Process Level

The channel and pool monitors attempt to ensure correct operation of system processes by monitoring their external behaviour. If necessary, the monitors can be designed to include a watchdog timer facility, or special watchdog processes can be set up for the purpose. At this level we provide an environment where the reliability of processes can be assured as far as is possible. Auditing processes can then be introduced to check the consistency and correctness of sets of processes within the system.

For a successful, functioning example of this form of reliability hierarchy the reader is referred to the ARPANET Pluribus Imp System, mentioned in chapter 6.

5.6   RECOVERY PRIORITY

5.6.1 Fixed Priority

● The previous discussion has made the tacit assumption that the recovery monitor will instigate recovery action the moment a fault is discovered. This implies that the monitor will be the highest-priority process in the system. It is vital the fault be prevented from propagating further and affecting other parts of the system. Faults have a habit of spreading very rapidly and it is very dangerous to ignore them. Giving the recovery monitor the highest priority is a sound practice.

5.6.2 Variable Priority

While bearing in mind the points made in the previous paragraph, the tactic of having a recovery monitor of very high priority is not necessarily ideal in all cases. While the CPU is engaged in executing recovery proceedings, it is unavailable for use in advancing normal system operation. When the system is in a time-critical situation it may well be better for a minor fault to go temporarily unheeded, and recovery postponed, while important processing is performed. Once the system workload slackens, recovery can be instigated.

Faults will normally be signalled to the recovery system via a software trap. The trap-handling process can be designed to note the fault, disable the offending process, update any relevant system status pools and perform a brief analysis as to the seriousness of the fault. At this point, this process could adjust the priority of the recovery monitor before exiting to the dispatcher. Recovery action would then take place at a time related to its importance.

● A better and more consistent approach is to centre the allocation of priority with the high-level scheduler. Recall from chapter 4 that part of the duties of the high-level scheduler is to dynamically adjust process priority so that the system may react correctly to an overload situation. Very often, the occurrence of a fault will result in system overload. A fault will reduce the system's performance capability while it is present, and increase the load by the necessary recovery activities. So, even if the system workload remains static during the fault, an overload may occur. Moreover, it is often the case that the system workload rises after a fault because of the buildup of a backlog of work to be done. This condition is particularly acute in systems which co-operate with others.

● The problems of allocating process priority during recovery and during overload situations are intertwined. It is sensible, then, to combine the operations in a high-level scheduler. If we do this, the software trap handler that handles fault traps would not alter the recovery monitor's priority, but rather transfer indication of the seriousness of the fault to the high-level scheduler.

5.7 EXAMPLE

For our example, we will use a very simple recovery scheme. Each process is assumed to use one checkpoint, in the manner described in subsection 5.4.1 and to have a control path as shown in figure 5.5. To instigate recovery it is necessary to restart the process at point A; see figure 5.5. To be able to do this we must have saved the volatile environment as it stands when the process is at point A. The logical place to store this information is in the process descriptor. So, yet again we extend the process descriptor to include the volatile environment of the process at its starting point. Another kernel queue will be necessary, the FAULTY queue.

Should a fault be detected, it will be indicated to the kernel via a trap. The trap handling process acts as follows

Fault Trap
(1)　Lock out interrupts
(2)　Insert RUNNING into FAULTY
(3)　Unlock interrupts
(4)　SIGNAL fault
(5)　Exit to dispatcher

The recovery monitor will WAIT on a semaphore *fault*. The recovery monitor acts as follows

Recovery Monitor
(1)　WAIT on fault
(2)　Transfer initial status to volatile environment in the process descriptor at the HEAD of the FAULTY queue
(3)　Remove ELEMENT from FAULTY then insert ELEMENT into RUNNABLE
(4)　Go back to (1).

5.8　SUMMARY

At this stage we should be in a position to create a system that is as correct and as reliable as possible. No complex system can be totally reliable. This is especially true of real-time software systems where, in the next minute, hour or month of operation, an untested or unexpected circumstance will occur, causing the system to fail. There are two main approaches to maximising system reliability: first, by using highly structured software and a thorough testing scheme, to minimise the residual errors in the software; second, to create fault-tolerant systems that can continue operation in the presence of errors. The first approach should be used in *every* system. The second is expensive, but it should be used as well whenever economically feasible.

● 　To summarise our discussion to date, it may be convenient to think of the processes in a real-time system as having positions in a hypothetical three-dimensional space. In one dimension we have the level of the process in the real-time virtual machine hierarchy, in another the process's priority and in the third the process's level in the reliability hierarchy.

Concepts

System availability; mean time between failure; mean time to repair; fault tolerance; protective redundancy; audit processes; watchdog timers; roll back; checkpoints; recovery blocks; conversations.

PART II: DESIGNING THE PROCESSES

6 Design Methodology

In chapters 2 to 5 we have introduced and discussed the form and construction of a real-time virtual machine. Although we have provided the designer with a useful tool, we have not provided him with a finished design. In his role as a designer, he must first be aware of the system for which he is to design the real-time software, and where appropriate, influence the system specification in order to help provide a system environment which is conducive to good software design and efficient reliable operation. Then he must design the layout of the processes, channels and pools, and specify the internal structure of the processes concerned.

In this chapter we shall take an abstract look at the entire design process, in order to discover some useful design techniques, drawing upon experience of past successes *and failures*. We first consider the system specification and the system designer's role in this, and then consider the software design process. A look at the important area of interfaces is then followed by an investigation of contrasting techniques used in the implementation of the internal structure of the real-time processes.

Design

● The fundamental aim of all designers is produce a 'good' design. This is rarely achieved without experience, and even then only if this experience has been gained in a 'good' environment! A good software design will result in a product which not only satisfies the requirement and performance specifications, but also is reliable and easy to maintain. Further than this, it must be produced on time at an acceptable cost. This usually means that it does not necessarily have the most efficient and elegant code or all the 'bells and whistles', but not surprisingly good software produced by experienced designers can often approach the 'ideal'.

The basis of good software design can be summarised in two basic concepts — correspondence and simplicity. Correspondence implies correctness, while simplicity contributes to reliability and maintainability.

6.1 SYSTEM DESIGN

Real-time systems embrace a wide variety of forms and it is beyond the scope of this discussion to attempt a study of the many types existing. Perhaps the commonest and most important class is that typified by the process control system, since most if not all of the problems occurring in this class are those collectively found in the other classes. While it is not necessary for the real-time programmer to be expert in control engineering, it is essential to know something of the nature of such systems in order to be confident of designing suitable software. This, then, is the starting point of system design.

6.1.1 Typical Process Control Systems

The simplest model of a control system is shown in figure 6.1, where we observe two fundamental blocks, namely the controlled process and the process controller. Note that these are linked directly in the forward path and by a feedback link passing information on the current status of the process back to the controller, which combines this information with the input or required status and processes the difference according to some control algorithm.

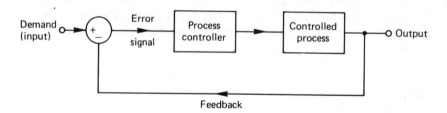

Figure 6.1 Simple model of a control system

In order to see more clearly the processes associated with the controller, which is of course going to be our real-time program running in a suitable processor, consider figure 6.2, which represents a simple linear, single controlled-variable system. The case illustrated is a rudder angle control for a small vessel. We will assume that the rudder actuator is, as in many high-power systems, a continuous (analog) mechanism, since this is very common, is likely to remain so, and highlights a number of problems.
● First of all, the output of the controller is a sampled data digital signal, which (a) requires updating at regular time intervals, and (b) will

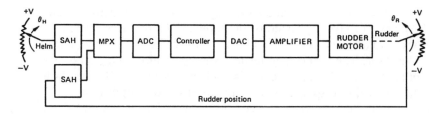

Figure 6.2 Simple linear rudder control system

be a fixed point number, usually shorter than that of the standard fixed point representation of the control processor. This will be communicated to an I/O handler in a server dedicated to the digital-to-analog converter (DAC). This element converts a fixed point number in its input register to an analog voltage output, scaled with respect to a reference voltage, whenever its input register is updated. The DAC element is omitted where a digital output transducer is employed (for example, in a stepper motor), but similar considerations still apply.

● The rudder position transducer produces an output voltage proportional to rudder angle which may be positive or negative about the neutral rudder position. This must first be sampled by a sample-and-hold amplifier (SAH), and then converted to digital representation by an analog-to-digital converter (ADC). The SAH is used to 'freeze' the varying input analog voltage while the conversion is carried out. The instant of sampling occurs when the SAH is switched from sample to hold. A recovery time is necessary after conversion is complete to enable the SAH to re-acquire the input analog signal. The ADC converts the held analog signal sample to digital form, a process known as quantisation, resulting in a sampled data digital representation of the analog input signal. Again, some problems arise: (a) the sampling and conversion process must be initiated at regular intervals which are commonly, but not necessarily, at the same rate as the updating of the DAC; (b) the conversion process is not instantaneous, and hence either a 'conversion complete' flag requires testing or a delay timer may be used to generate an interrupt indicating that the converted signal is available; (c) the data read from the conversion register of the ADC will have a shorter word length than that of the processor fixed point representation, and may also require justification and/or code conversion. The data so input will be processed by an input handler, as part of a server, to a pool where it will be accessed by the controller process. Note that the I/O handlers are commonly written in assembler to efficiently code the required bit processing (but see section 9.2).

● The input signal would normally be of a similar nature to that from the rudder angle sensor, but produced by a transducer mounted on the wheel whose angle is set and varied by the helmsman. This is seen in the diagram to be connected to the same ADC, but uses a separate SAH amplifier and is connected in turn to the ADC by an analog multiplexer. The latter operates in a similar fashion to a digital mutliplexer, this being a mechanism which selects one of several digital data sources, in response to a digital address, for output to a destination, perhaps via a shared line or bus. Note that after selection the multiplexer requires a finite settling time before conversion can commence and, after switching an SAH amplifer to sample an acquisition, delay must elapse before the signal is available to full accuracy. Clearly, the input handler must include these delays, which are fundamental to all such data acquisition systems; hence such a handler is a little more complex than appears at first sight. This is further discussed in subsection 10.2.1.

A final comment is that the input data pools are normally also accessed by an alarm monitor to indicate such conditions as excessive rudder angle and stuck at starboard limit. The functions carried out by the controller are discussed in subsection 10.2.2.

● Of course, most control systems are much more complex than the simple example given. A brief summary of the characteristics likely to be found in practice is useful, and further information may be found in Katz (1981).

Firstly, there are frequently several controlled variables, and some of these may be the objects of local closed-loop systems, each with its own controller. These are then the subject of a higher-level control system and the whole appears as a nested and interconnected set of systems, usually called a multivariable control system.

● Secondly, there may be non-linearities to contend with. This may simply be due to small deviations caused by approaching saturation, larger non-linearities caused by change of environment, such as aerodynamic force coefficients varying with altitude, or deliberately introduced effects, such as the bang-bang controller beloved of domestic central heating systems.

● Thirdly, there are time-varying systems in which certain characteristics of the controlled system are functions not only of several system variables but also of time. Typical of such systems are those found in aircraft and missiles where the mass, centres of gravity and pressure, and moments of inertia, all change as fuel is burnt. Further, inputs to many systems may themselves be time varying or time sequenced, such as the rate of climb and turn, altitude and course demands for a civil aircraft flight.

Finally, although many non-linear and/or time-varying systems operate satisfactorily with linear time-invariant controllers, a further desirable development is to employ an adaptive controller to give better

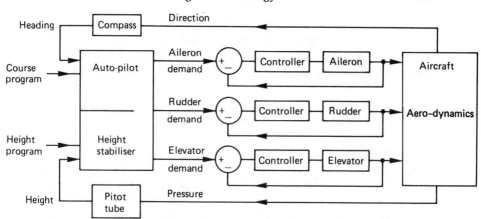

Figure 6.3 Simplified aircraft control system

performance. Figure 6.3 shows a simplified aircraft control system
illustrating many of these characteristics.

● Obviously such control complications have significant implications
for the real-time programmer, and some of these are discussed later in
this chapter and elsewhere, but it is useful to mention here some which
are not otherwise formally considered.

A multivariable system will have several feedback sensors, and it is
common to find that these are sampled at different rates. Further,
although they may be grouped together for control purposes, they may
be input in an inconvenient mix because of physical location or because
some are analog and some are digital. This has implications for the
digital control of multiplexers and interfaces, and of input channels.
These factors can result in software module coupling which is not
specifically related to the system block diagram. This is not generally
true for output channels.

● So far as non-linearity is concerned there are two considerations.
The first concerns the nature of the non-linearity, whether it can be
expressed as a mathematical function or as a look-up table, and the
second is whether the function is one of several variables or just a single
variable. These can be important considerations so far as processing
time and memory usage are concerned.

● Time-variable systems generally introduce complexity for the control
engineer, and for the programmer, in that control algorithms are more
complex. Again, complexity arises if the controller uses time-variable
functions which require computing.

● However, perhaps the most important issue is that of instability
caused either by non-linear and/or time-variable function software
implementation, resulting in limit cycles. The canonical form is not

necessarily the most satisfactory. This problem can also be caused by truncation and rounding, factors which also require consideration where fixed point operation is employed for speed, especially where short fixed point word lengths are employed.

6.1.2 System Specification and Modelling

The starting point of a real-time system is of course the requirements specification. This is 'simply' what the system is expected to do when complete. From this some basic system parameters are determined, often concerned with fundamental aspects, such as physical dimensions, mass, power requirements, etc., which are primarily the concern of electrical, mechanical, chemical, control and system engineers. From this, some fundamental limits of operation can be determined — for example, the natural frequency and bandwidth limits on, say, a supertanker steering control loop, which is clearly limited by the size of vessel! Control strategies and techniques are then determined for an initial design. At this point a block level scheme is available for the overall system. Using this and the requirements specification, an initial system specification is produced.
● From this a system model is produced, and the system is simulated to evaluate its performance relative to the requirements specification. Of course, in reality there are other considerations and problems in reaching this stage, not the least of which is how to obtain an accurate model, and the subsequent validation and verification of this model before reliable conclusions can be drawn from any simulation results obtained. Further discussion of simulation appears in subsections 8.2.3 and 11.1.2. Obviously, some iterations are required for this. The system may then require modification in order to improve its operation and performance which is another, outer level of iteration. Clearly, up to this point the software designer has had little or no involvement, but the above simplified discussion forms a useful backdrop to what follows.

6.1.3 Influence of the Real-time Programmer on System Choices

It is at the point reached above that the software designer should influence the computer system(s) on which the software is to run, and also determine the host/target configuration. There are many factors which affect the choice and configuration of hardware and system software, many of which have significant ramifications for both software design and operation. Perhaps the first consideration is the physical disposition of the system to be controlled. This is usually not something that is easily changed to better suit the computer systems, but changes are sometimes possible at this stage.

● Given that this is now fixed, the nature and disposition of all sensors, output transducers and instruments and warning devices must be considered to determine the requirements for local signal conditioning, multiplexing, sampling, digitising, processing and transmission. An important consideration at this point is the performance requirement in relation to any signal processing, such as digital filtering, to be carried out on sensor signals, since this may dictate a decision on whether this is to be implemented in software or perhaps in dedicated hardware with respect to the data and processing rates required. This is further discussed in section 10.2. In addition, an important requirement may be the provision of local control to ensure system integrity, so that a system may degrade gracefully rather than catastrophically in the event of failure.

From an analysis of such factors a picture emerges of some of the system requirements of both hardware and software. Decisions can also be taken with others in relation to the need for distributed processing and for provision of backup facilities. These conclusions, together with the major requirements for controllers and other functions, and the resulting capacity and performance needs of the computer system's hardware, provide an overall picture of the likely hardware requirements.

● From this information the software designer can consider what are the implications for the software systems. Important traditional considerations are of course the operating system, high-level language and assemblers. But to this list should be added a link editor, if not included in with the compiler as in a UNIX-type system, facilities for system construction involving linking of modules, and mapping the loadable code onto the hardware configuration. The latter is unlikely to be significant for a single processor system, but is important for distributed systems which are becoming more common with the increasing power and reducing cost of microprocessors. A further serious consideration is whether or not the software development is to be hosted, that is, to be developed on a different machine (the host) to that which will run the real-time object code (the target). If so, it is important to distinguish between the host development machine operating system and that in the target under which the real-time code is to be run.

● A relatively recent, but long overdue factor, is the environment in which the software is to be developed. The complex systems of today can fail, be unreliable or suffer late delivery to a customer simply because of the lack of an adequate support environment. These aspects are discussed in chapter 8.

● Closely related, but sadly still often not involving the software designer, is the choice and configuration of the hardware. This clearly involves processor power and type(s): main, subsidiary and backing store requirements, input/output channels, communications, command input, display and alarm monitors. If the hardware is determined by system and performance requirements only, then significant problems can arise later during software development, at a time when the hardware system design is already frozen. It is essential for those involved in software development to be involved at the discussion stage of system planning to minimise such problems. This is probably more important for real-time systems than for any other type.

● Some simple but relevant examples of the useful influence a software designer may have, arise in the choice of processors. Firstly, some 16/32-bit microprocessors have versions offering extended memory management, and selection of a cheaper processor without this option may turn out to be a significant disadvantage from a software point of view. Secondly, some systems make use of 8-bit processors for local processing or as input-output subsystems. If a processor from a different family is used, then cross compilers and/or assemblers are needed, adding complexity to the development process. Many 16/32-bit microprocessors have 8-bit equivalents which are cheaper and are fully code-compatible (but slower). Choosing a non-compatible processor set may be specified on the grounds of special facilities or performance, but this must be justified in an overall system context. Finally, and related to the last comment, is the availability of coprocessors and hardware accelerators. These should be considered in combination with standard processors as an alternative to special-purpose processors which may not have sufficient software support, especially that which permits easy integration with the rest of the software systems.

6.1.4 Correspondence

● The secret of the design of correct, maintainable software lies in the creation of a software structure which corresponds to the structure of the problem at hand. If the data structures, and the instructions and functions that operate on them, describe a model whose form reflects that of the application, any changes in the behaviour of the application can be readily incorporated in the software. Unless the activity/channel/pool (ACP) layout accurately reflects interaction of activities in the application, and the modular design of the activities themselves reflects their internal structure, an inelegant and inflexible design will result.

● Often, a great deal of analysis will be required to delineate the underlying structure of the application, and the true structure will often not be the one evident on first inspection. Although the resulting structure will frequently contain significant elements related to computer and external system hardware, and the latter is a useful starting point for some aspects of determining structure, careful systems analysis will usually reveal relationships where none were expected and some associations which will be purely coincidental. This activity, if carried out early enough, may well influence system choices as discussed above. Great care must be exercised at this early stage, for an error at the system design phase may well nullify any advantages gained by using well-structured program code or local optimisations of execution speed. Indeed, some parts of a design may even have to be scrapped. Perhaps the most important aspect of such analysis is the untangling of complex systems to permit restructuring along simpler lines, which ultimately provides for greater subsystem independence, reliability and fail-soft capability. This approach frequently helps to improve the designer's (and others'!) understanding of complex systems.

Software design, then, involves specification of the data structures and the functions that act upon them. Some design methods approach the problem from the direction of functions, while others focus the design on the data structures. We will first discuss the functional approach.

6.1.5 Top-down Functional Design

The usual approach to most large engineering problems is to effect a top-down modular decomposition of the problem. Top-down design involves breaking the problem down into smaller and smaller parts (or modules) to a point where each individual part is comprehensible and can be implemented. It is basically the 'divide and conquer' technique used in most problem-solving activities. We have in fact been applying this technique at the beginning of this chapter, by looking at the overall system to be implemented in order to obtain a satisfactory structure for the system, and hence determine the requirements and specification of the real-time software system that we are about to produce. We must now apply the technique to this software system. The virtual machine that we have designed facilitates this approach.

● The first step in a top-down, functional design for a real-time system is to divide the system into processes. Then, each process itself is broken down into subsections, and the function and interfaces between them are again closely defined. This must be done precisely, and to achieve this the interfaces between processes and the function of each process must be fully and clearly defined. It is a very common experience to find loose and/or incomplete specification of these, especially at the lower levels. It is fruitless to proceed further with the decomposition at any stage where there are ill-defined or incomplete processes or interfaces. A successful top-down design will result in a hierarchy of closely defined modules, each being small enough to be implemented as perhaps 20 to 60 lines of program code. This is about the maximum size that a program can be before it starts to become incomprehensible. It is worth noting that the result of this exercise has a significant benefit for both the members and management of a team of programmers, since each function and its interfaces is well-defined, and the styles, foibles and errors of individual members can be tolerated and controlled. Management of large software projects is a subject in its own right, but this approach is part of most successful projects.

Unfortunately, difficulties are often encountered, and the use of this technique does not automatically imply a clean design. These difficulties do not stem from the top-down technique itself, but from difficulties in decomposing the problem into modules. Some of these may arise because the software designer does not fully understand the system that he is asked to control, or the mathematics of the algorithms that he is asked to implement, and lack of experience can also contribute. One cannot, after all, be an expert in every aspect of such systems. Successful functional design is best learnt by experience, but all the same a number of guidelines can prove helpful.

● First, a top-down design must be iterative. We have already seen from the discussions presented earlier in this chapter that this is a normal and indeed essential part of good system design. In addition to software interfaces between modules, the programmer of real-time systems must himself establish interfaces with experts in other disciplines working on the same project of which the software is part. It is important to remember that, although the software is a vital, complex and sophisticated part of the project, it is upon the performance, reliability, cost, etc., of the entire system that the success or otherwise will be judged. The designer must be prepared, indeed willing, to retrace his steps up the design tree and redefine certain steps in the decomposition. This may involve system elements other than the software. He must do this if he finds that the structure of the lower-level modules does not correspond to the structure of the function in the problem area.

● Second, where practical, important design decisions should be put off as far down the design tree as possible. This remains true even though system designers may have a fair idea of how the problem is likely to be partitioned in the case of a distributed system, since the initial evaluation of this partitioning may turn out to be far from ideal.

Obviously, by the time a large system has been broken down into implementable modules most, if not all, of the design decisions will have been made. However, the earlier in the design a particular decision is made, the greater will be the influence of that decision on the final design. For instance, using our real-time virtual machine, it is possible to work a long way down the design path of each process before having to make any decisions as to the processor/memory configuration. If modules that require specific hardware characteristics are relegated to the lowest level of the design tree, the final design could be implemented on a variety of hardware configurations. If, on the other hand, a decision made at an early stage in the design compromised this versatility, a much less flexible product would result.

Although discussed in more detail later (subsection 11.1.2), a mention here of simulation is relevant to this discussion. The decision to use a particular solution to a problem, be it choice of algorithm or hardware, may be dependent on processing requirements and is often concerned with speed. However, at an early stage the software may be run slower than real-time, provided either that the external system does not contain time-dependent elements, whose time scale cannot be changed (and this is rare), or the external system can be simulated in slower than real-time. In this way, much of the software system can be tested for functionality and in addition a feel for processing requirements can be obtained. At this stage it is common to simplify structures and models, giving an early feel for how both system and software are going to perform.

6.1.5.1 MASCOT 3 Systems and Subsystems

● In subsection 2.2.3 we met the MASCOT 3 basic elements — *activity, IDA* and *server*. MASCOT 3, as distinct from earlier versions, also supports mechanisms for hierarchical decomposition of the problem. These are the elements known as *networks*, comprising elements *subsystem* and *system*, being part and all of an application respectively.

A *system* is a self-contained network constituting the complete description of the software of an application; it is the outermost level of the hierarchical structure. It has no explicit dependencies; all communication with external software and hardware objects is implied. This distinguishes it from a subsystem.

A *subsystem* usually has more than one independent scheduled thread of execution. Subsystems may possess *ports* and *windows*, and consequently can be interconnected by *paths* with the interconnections defined by *access interfaces*. It is clear from this that composite activities, IDAs and servers are examples of subsystems, and mixes of these can also be defined as a subsystem. An important feature of subsystems is that they may be nested to any depth, thus supporting the concept of top-down structured design. A graphical example of a subsystem is shown in figure 6.4. The outline of the graphical symbol is either bold or double to provide a distinctive form, and is usually a rectangle with rounded corners. The reader is referred to the official handbook of MASCOT (MASCOT 3, 1986) for a full and enlightening description of this valuable methodology.

It is often not clear which modular breakdown best corresponds to the structure of the problem. Different designers may well produce different breakdown schemes for the same problem. Constantine *et al.* (1974) have suggested that the relative quality of different breakdown schemes for one particular problem can be based on considerations of *cohesion* and *coupling*. While these concepts do not provide explicit guidelines for successful modularisation, they are valuable for the purposes of comparison of different designs. To some extent these concepts presume a non-distributed system and perhaps do not include considerations of the provision of fail-soft options. However, the concepts remain a valuable guide, and are now discussed.

6.1.6 Cohesion and Coupling

6.1.6.1 Cohesion

Cohesion describes how well or naturally a module holds together — its internal strength. Proceeding from a low level of cohesion, which implies poor internal structure, to a high level of cohesion, we have

(1) coincidental cohesion, where the components are in the module purely by coincidence, perhaps because, although unrelated, they were in a group of tasks given to a particular member of the software team, or were all to be written in assembler;

(2) logical cohesion, where the module performs a set of independent but logically related functions — for example, a set of sensor sampling routines or digital filters used in different processes;

(3) temporal cohesion, where the module performs a set of functions that are related in time — for example, system start-up routines, or data acquisition using common sampling times on sensors belonging to unrelated parts of the system;

(4) procedural cohesion, where the functions in the module correspond to the sequence of functions appearing in a section of a program — for example, sampling, filtering and process controller.

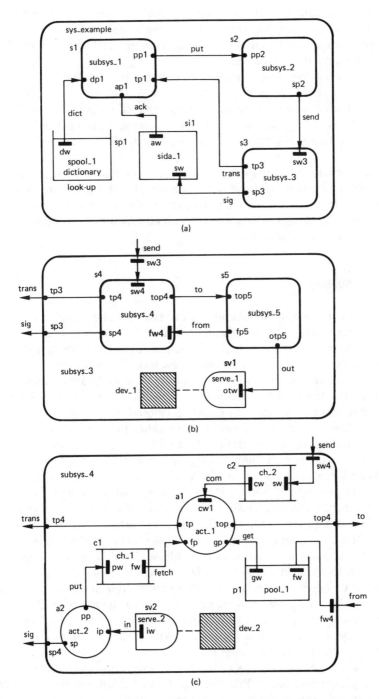

Figure 6.4 MASCOT 3 nested subsystems and hierarchical decomposition: (a) system example; (b) network decompostion; (c) lowest level of decomposition.

(5)   communicational cohesion, where functions operating on common
      data are grouped together — for example, calculation of
      proportional, integral and differential components for a controller
      from a common input pool;
(6)   functional cohesion, where every function in the module
      contributes to the performance of a single task — for example,
      examining, at each time slice, every selected variable for relevant
      error condition such as over-range, excessive increment or rate,
      and conditionally settling a warning flag or alarm indicator.

● Functional, sequential and communicational cohesion are most
desirable, whereas temporal, logical and coincidental cohesion are much
less desirable. Note that our design of the real-time virtual machine
encourages the design of processes with high functional, sequential and
communicational cohesion.

6.1.6.2 Coupling

● Coupling is a relative measure of the strength and complexity of
module interconnection. Ideally, there should be a minimum amount of
coupling between modules. It should be possible to remove a module
from the system and replace it with a new modified or alternative
module without affecting any other module or module interconnections.
If this is so, then both the cause of easier software project management
and the ideal of easy maintenance are furthered. By reducing
inter-module connections and defining modules that are, as far as
possible, free-standing, the designer stands a better chance of being able
to replace modules with minimum disruption at a later date.
  Whereas processes communicate via channels and pools, modules
internal to processes communicate with the rest of the module by
control mechanisms and data-transfer mechanisms. Take, as an example,
module B in figure 6.5. Module B's control interfaces are: called by A,
calls C and D. Its data interfaces are: parameters passed while being
called by A, parameters passed when calling C and D, and process-wide
data areas to which B has access. Ideally, we should be able to remove
B from the system and replace it with a modified or alternative module;
or, expressed another way, we should be able to change A or C or D,
or the form of the global data, without affecting B. If we hide from B
any information that it does not need to know, then we reduce B's
coupling to the rest of the system.
● Consider B's data interface. Module B will need to read from or
write to global data areas. Presumably, it uses the information to modify
its actions or those of the process. Normally, it will require only the

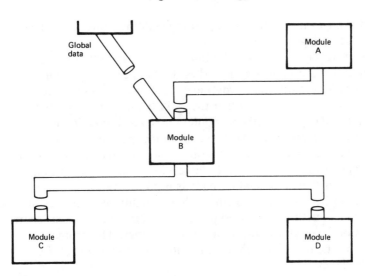

Figure 6.5 Module coupling

value of each item of information and will not be concerned how the information is stored. Provided that these values can be written or read, B will perform correctly. If B uses standard routines to read and write the information, it need have no knowledge of the layout of the global area. This means that the layout of the global area can be changed without affecting the action of B at all. If, however, B was aware of the global data layout, and used this knowledge, any change in the layout would imply the need for a change in B. This is frequently not a problem where data is stored as a file, since file access is normally under control of the operating system and users are advised not to attempt to bypass this built-in facility. However, smaller and faster data storage is commonly needed in real-time systems, especially those whose backing stores are relatively slow. The design of such stores (in the software sense) is often the province of the programmer. Knowledge of the access mechanism — for example, offsets and pointers in a rotating data set (see subsection 10.4.1) — can be used to advantage by a module, but this immediately gives rise to coupling not implied in the problem. While a designer may feel that he can handle this, it is not good practice since he may modify the data storage at a later date and forget or only hazily remember the implications for one or more modules. Worse still, he may have left the team or company. Those now responsible for upgrading or maintenance of the system will not thank him for his coding 'efficiency'. If the read/write interface had been properly defined,

. internal changes in storage organisation would not have any effect on modules accessing the store.

● Let us now consider the data interface with the other modules. If the total interaction between B and A, C, D operates by means of parameters passed during subroutine calls, B, A, C and D may be altered in any way, provided that they still transfer the expected parameter values to the other modules. It is worth mentioning that the updating of variables used by such subroutines can in certain circumstances get out of step if modifications are made to the control mechanisms which may have little discernible effect or be instantly disastrous. Further, if assembler code is used, an all too common total disaster is to lose control of a stack where conditional branches are used in conjunction with pushing and popping of registers, or from incorrect construction or modification of interrupt routines. The protection afforded by the use of a high-level language is mostly lost at the assembler level.

● Consider an example of undesirable coupling. Module A passes to module B an array of numbers from which B calculates the mean which is returned for use by A. The designer of A expects B to have available as a side effect the sum of these numbers and makes use of this fact informally. Subsequently, the designer of B modifies B to also calculate the standard deviation of the same set of numbers for additional use by module C, while correctly maintaining the mean for module A, but in doing so replaces the sum by its square. The designer of module A is unaware of this and module A now operates incorrectly as a consequence. The informal, undocumented connection between A and B created by A's designer having knowledge of the internal workings of B has not only resulted in unreliable software, but finding the source of such unreliability can be rather difficult, especially as the errors are data-dependent and therefore may be small or large.

When discussing the harmful effects of high coupling, Bergland (1978) quotes a telling example attributable to Alexander. He considers a system of 100 light bulbs, each of which is either on or off. The bulbs are connected such that, if a light is on, it has a 50 per cent chance of going off in the next second. If it is off, but connected to other bulbs, it has a 50 per cent chance of going on in the next second, provided that one of the bulbs to which it is connected is on. If none of the lights connected to it is on, the bulb remains off. Eventually, the system reaches an equilibrium where all the lights are off.

Now, if the lights are totally unconnected, the equilibrium state will be reached on average in the time it takes one light to go off. This is approximately one second. If we take the opposite case where every bulb is connected to every other bulb, the equilibrium would be reached in 10^{22} years! If, however, the lights were fully interconnected within independent sets of ten bulbs, equilibrium would be reached in approximately 17 minutes. In software terms, the last example would be equivalent to a set of highly cohesive modules with low inter-module coupling.

6.1.7 Data Abstraction and Data Structure Design

6.1.7.1 Information Hiding and Data Abstraction

● We have already mentioned in the previous section the advantages of minimising the coupling between modules and hence the complexity of the system. The policy is an ideal one to follow when designing a module. This means hiding as much information away from the module as possible consistent with proper functioning of that module. The same principle of 'need to know' is used in military and other secure information systems where each person has access to only as much information as is required to carry out the function.

● Information hiding at the process level is realised by the use of channel and pool monitors. A process does not 'see' the data structure in a channel or pool directly; it only sees an abstract model of the structure, as provided by the monitor's access routines. Well-known examples of this are: printing a file on either a serial or parallel interface printer, the latter feature being of no interest to the file handler or the output buffer, or even the user, but is handled at low level within the printer driver; and secondly, sampled data acquisition from an analog potentiometer via a digitiser or directly from a digital shaft encoder, where again it matters not what the nature of the source is, simply that data arrives via a channel into a pool. This principle of data abstraction is fundamental to most modern design methodologies. The topic of data abstraction is closely related to data typing which is discussed in subsection 9.1.4.

6.1.7.2 Data Structure Design

● Top-down functional decomposition does not automatically result in a program structure that exhibits close correspondence to the problem at hand. This is because it is often difficult to create a model of the problem by initially defining the activities to be performed. However, if we first model the system *items* as data structures it becomes a more straightforward task. The items in the system are easy to identify, and the best way to model them is usually apparent. It is for this reason that the data structure design method begins by defining these data structures (Jackson, 1975). The crux of the method is to make the structure of the environment dictate the structure of the data structures and, in turn, to make the structure of the data dictate the structure of the functions and processes in the system. In this way the functions will exhibit close correspondence to the problem environment.

● The correspondence between data structure and program structure can readily be seen at the program-code level. The basic program-structuring components are the sequence, iteration (loop) and selection (decision); see figure 6.6.

These structures have direct counterparts in basic data structures (figure 6.7).

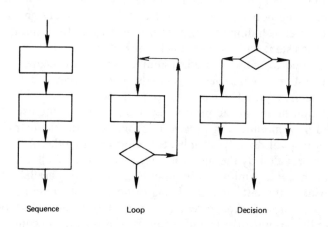

Sequence   Loop   Decision

Figure 6.6 Code structuring elements

The sequence

Data Structure A consists of: Item B;
                                     Item C;
                                     Item D.

Note that there is an important distinction between this structure and an array in that the length of the sequence is not declared.

The iteration

Data structure A consists of: Array (1 to index) of item B.

The selection

Data structure A consists of: if selector = 1st   Item B;
                                     if selector = 2nd Item C;
                                     if selector = 3rd Item D.

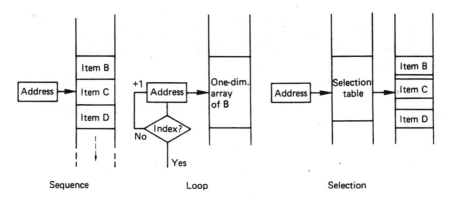

Figure 6.7 Data structuring elements

Just as the constructs can be nested, so the data structure constructs can be nested. Item B, for instance, may be a sequence, iteration or selection. In this way we can construct more complex and useful data structures — for example, a two-dimensional array, a record and a set. This correspondence between data structures and action structure is the key concept in the data structure design method.

To design the functional structure of a process, the designer proceeds as follows. First he models the input and output data with the basic structures mentioned above, using them directly or to create more complex structures as dictated by the problem. The designer should then be able to see elements in the output data structure that correspond to transformed elements in the input data structure. The purpose of the process is to effect these transformations. The program structure is a direct parallel of the structure of the data being manipulated. The designer does not need to invent the functional structure of the process: it is provided for him by the structure of the data. Sometimes the input and output data structures are totally incompatible. It will then be necessary to introduce intermediate data whose structure lies between that of the input and output structures. The process then performs two functions: it transforms the input data to the intermediate form, and then transforms this data to the requisite output form. For example, if the input data structure is a sequence of signal samples and the output data structure is a complex array of frequencies, the required processes are windowing of the input data structure (sequence) to produce a finite length structure (array or iteration), and Fourier transformation of this to produce the output data structure (complex array or iteration) (figure 6.8).

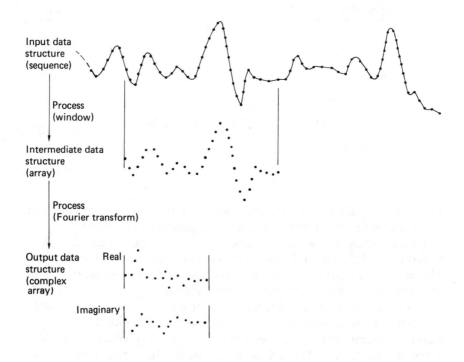

Figure 6.8 Data structures and processes

6.1.8 Real-time Software Design

6.1.8.1 Real-time Software Design Processes

Top-down functional design and data structure design approach the design problem from different angles. Each results in the design of data structures and functions, but one may be more applicable than the other in a particular set of circumstances. Other techniques such as bottom-up and modular design also have their adherents, however the authors' views are that for real-time software bottom-up design is usually inappropriate, and modular design is included within the preferred methods already mentioned. The decision as to which method is used is up to the designer's discretion. To date no universal design methodology has been accepted for real-time systems. We can, however, postulate a viable plan of attack, as follows.

● (1) Design and build a virtual machine that will support asynchronous co-operating processes. Earlier chapters have discussed this task in detail. Of course, previous experience of real-time systems may have already yielded a suitable virtual machine which can run on the selected host.

(2) Produce or obtain a requirements specification for the software part of the system, including all of the interfaces to the outside world.

(3) Identify all the items in the system and express them as data structures. This often highlights some incomplete specification details, and these must now be determined.

(4) Collect the data structures into pools and thus specify the processes that act on these pools.

(5) Specify any prerequisite synchronisation or information channels necessary for the processes to interact correctly, taking into account any inherent distributed processing requirements.

(6) Use a data structure design method to create the structure for each process.

(7) Express the data structures and process functions as high-level language programs.

(8) Iterate the above process where necessary to review and optimise the design.

(9) Map the software modules onto the hardware system(s).

● If one incorporates the above steps into a design framework and applies the framework to the production of software, the resultant code should correspond closely to the system under control.

6.1.8.2 Simplicity

The best panacea for complexity is simplicity. The simplest designs are usually the best designs. One has only to look at the world of nature to see that the simpler designs are often the most successful. Too often, designers implement a complex and ornate system in the mistaken belief that the more intricate or 'clever' it is, the more successful it will be. A useful rule is to get a basic system into operation quickly to verify the initial outline design. If 'hooks' are provided in the design the 'bells and whistles' can be added as and when they are necessary. It is much more important to get the essential core correct before adding enhancements which can so easily mask more essential tasks. Also, it may turn out that some enhancements incur a time penalty that makes them unacceptable.

● We have used a number of techniques to ensure that the structure of a real-time system is as simple as possible. Separating the different activities into discrete processes makes the overall structure of the system easy to grasp. By using highly modular, well-structured code we create processes that are clear and easy to comprehend.

6.1.8.3 Simplifying Real-time Systems

● When the system is tested in its real environment, timing problems may cause major difficulties. Each process may perform perfectly correctly in isolation, but faults will occur when the system as a whole reacts incorrectly to sequences of events. The cause of these faults can nearly always be narrowed down to problems with process scheduling and synchronisation.

If each process has its own hardware, and/or the system runs without interrupts to force unexpected process swapping, the whole question of scheduling and synchronisation is greatly simplified. These conditions imply that processes run to completion. If this is the case, the problem of synchronisation simplifies to that of ensuring that processes are only activated under certain circumstances. Scheduling simplifies to the job of avoiding deadlock over any shared resources.

● Of course, cost or system constraints may not permit such a simplification but the aim must always be to keep timing, scheduling and synchronisation solutions as simple as possible. Distributed systems help in some respects by off-loading processes onto local processors, but redundancy, reliability and fail-soft requirements will tend to obviate any advantages from the simplification point of view. In this case it is probably even more important to achieve as much simplicity as possible. One method of implementation is to avoid dedicating the processors of a multiprocessor system to a particular process, but to allow a processor to accept a process from a central list. This list is a priority-ordered queue of process descriptors requiring activation. Such a descriptor may consist of a number which identifies the process and also corresponds to the priority of the process in the system. When a processor takes a process from the top of the queue it will run the process to completion, and then access the queue again for the highest priority task. Of course, the maximum time for a process to run must be limited, although some processes may require a longer execution time but are interruptable. Accordingly, no process in the system may exceed the time that a high-priority process can be kept waiting. In order to prevent system deadlock, each resource is given a priority. No process may gain use of, and therefore lock out, a resource if it has already locked out another resource of equal or lower priority. Of course, such systems of process priority queues and resource allocation can put a considerable overhead on the software and consequently result in unacceptable response times. Such essential features may require either a dedicated processor or special hardware. The ARPANET Pluribus Imp (Ornstein *et al.*, 1975) is a useful if dated example which is easy to comprehend.

● As a general principle the designer should, at the outset, ask himself if it is really necessary to include the more complex aspects of real-time software in his system. Much of the discussion of the previous chapters centred around attempts to reduce the complexity of the additional system software whose inclusion is made necessary by constraints of hardware cost. The availability of sophisticated hardware elements at continually decreasing cost means that the cost–complexity–benefit relationships within real-time systems are constantly changing. One must continually ask the questions: Is it really necessary to multiplex a single processor? Is it necessary to have interrupts other than the real-time clock? Is it necessary to have a real-time clock at all? Should a single store be multiplexed? Should backing store be distributed? Is there a central system or can any processor behave as master? Are operating system functions distributed? The designer must address these and other questions with an eye to both simplicity and reliability.

6.2 THE PROCESS VIRTUAL MACHINE

In part I we developed a virtual machine with which it is possible to define a real-time system as a collection of co-operating processes. Assuming that a designer has progressed to the point where he has defined the function of and interfaces between the requisite processes, the next step is to design the internal structure of the processes themselves.

To design these processes it is necessary to specify the data structures and the machine instructions that make up their code element. Early in the history of computer applications it was found that the design of such programs, when they extend for more than one hundred or so instructions, becomes a difficult and error-prone task. This difficulty arises from the fact that machine instructions model the repertoire of actions and simple storage elements that are built into the design of the hardware. They do not reflect the actions and data structures that would naturally and clearly model a particular process activity.

● Notice, however, that the proliferation of more specialised VLSI microprocessors in the signal-processing area results in a hardware system which more closely reflects both the actions and the data structures required for this area of applications. This provides a basis on which the software processes and data structures can also be appropriately and more easily structured than for general-purpose microprocessors. This apparently encouraging note should be tempered by the realisation that, for the present, cross assemblers are the only mechanism by which software may be constructed for such machines (but see also subsection 8.1.2).

The traditional solution to this problem has been to create a suitable virtual machine, by superimposing a language translator onto the hardware. The language is designed to model the problem area. Hence the existence of COBOL in the commercial field, FORTRAN in the scientific field and PASCAL (Wilson and Addyman, 1982), and more recently Modula-2 (subsection 9.2.2) and Ada (subsection 9.2.3) and others, in the real-time systems programming area. These languages attempt to provide virtual machines suited to particular application areas. There is no reason why other virtual machines, more closely tailored to a particular project, cannot be built if the necessary support software is provided. This chapter will briefly describe the process level virtual machine provided by a high-level language and then will discuss two types of special-purpose machines.

6.2.1 The High-level Language Machine

As with the real-time virtual machine, the process virtual machine must reflect the underlying structure of the application. The software component of any application consists of a model comprising data structures and the action procedures that manipulate them. A useful virtual machine must therefore facilitate the definition and creation of data structures as well as allowing a highly structured representation of action algorithms. Most modern high-level languages incorporate these facilities.

The various high-level languages designed for real-time application share similar structure. They allow the designer to

(1)   define data structures, both in terms of the primitive data storage elements (bits, bytes and words), and in terms of more complex

data structures defined previously in the program (see subsections 6.1.7 and 9.1.4);

(2)   declare that instances of pre-defined data structures exist and that access to and knowledge of these data structures are restricted to different parts of the program (subsection 9.1.1);

(3)   define a hierarchy of modules, consisting of data and action sequences, which forms a logical whole;

(4)   describe the action sequences within modules in terms of structured loop, conditional and sequential blocks.

Currently, there exist a great number of real-time, high-level languages; however, attempts are being made to encourage use of a standard for real-time applications. Meanwhile Pascal, with its excellent control structures and strong data typing, has filled the gap. Two major contenders for a standard are Ada, developed by the US Department of Defense (DoD) and suitable for large, distributed systems, and Modula-2, developed by Wirth, suitable for smaller single processor applications. Chapter 9 examines the real-time features of these languages and develops an appreciation of their relative merits.

6.2.1.1 High-level Languages vs Assembler Languages

Real-time software systems have traditionally been written in assembler level program code. The main argument in favour of this approach has been the time-critical nature of most real-time applications. Programs written by experienced assembler programmers are generally more 'efficient' in speed and memory space requirements than those programs produced by compiler translation.

Efficiency

The criticism most often levelled against high-level languages is that the code produced by the compiler is relatively inefficient. When considering small amounts of program code (say 100 to 200 lines) this will usually be the case. A compiler cannot be as astute as a human programmer and often cannot find minor, local optimisations in particular programs. As the program increases in length, however, it becomes more and more difficult for the human programmer to maintain a grasp of the overall structure of the program. As the program grows more complex, so the programmer's ability to optimise lessens. The compiler, on the other hand, is unconcerned with program length and its optimisation activities operate with equal efficiency no matter how long the program. For a certain length of program, a programmer may produce twice as efficient code as a compiler. Nevertheless, for programs of moderate length, a modern compiler cannot hope to produce code as efficient as that of a programmer writing in assembler code.

● However, it must be said that in certain cases the best of both worlds can be achieved by selectively using assembler coding, confined within a module or subprogram body, as discussed in subsections 10.4.2.4 and 9.1.6, or by using specialised processors, as in subsection 10.4.3, restricted to essential critical areas only. The latter represent only a small proportion of the total code for the system. Some mention should be made of the necessity of making a compromise between portability and performance, achieved by using quirks of a particular processor.

Life-cycle Costs

When compared over the entire life cycle of the product, the high-level language has considerable advantages over assembler language implementation. Applications can be coded far more rapidly in a high-level language. The code produced is clearer to read and therefore better documented, and is easier to debug, maintain and extend. Further, by producing well-structured high-level language code, where important decision and control points are highlighted, it is possible to implement a reasonably thorough testing scheme. The high-level language compiler and run-time system is able to do sufficient checking to avoid many of the pitfalls of assembler level programming. For example, it is not possible to inadvertently transfer control outside the bounds of a subprogram, something all too possible in assembler level programming. Moreover, automatic array bounds checking can be implemented and automatic variable-type checking conducted. The programmer is, in many ways, protected from himself.

During the software maintenance phase, a product coded in a high-level language is, without doubt, more economical than one coded in assembler code. The properties of good self-documentation, clear modularity and explicit structuring, inherent in a well-disciplined high-level language program, are vital to speedy and economical maintenance. Overall, these considerations have led designers in a strong swing toward the use of higher-level languages in real-time software.

● Support for low-level input/output in Modula-2 and Ada removes much of the conflict by permitting most of the code to be written in the high-level langauge with its powerful support environment (IPSEs, see subsection 8.3.2), including at least integral documentation of low-level code.

6.2.2 The Interpreting Machine

As useful as a general-purpose high-level language may be, it is possible to create virtual machines even more closely tailored to the problem at hand — and create them with relative ease. The first example that we will discuss is the interpretive code machine.

6.2.2.1 Interpreters

A compiler translates the sequence of actions specified by a high-level-language program into an equivalent machine code program. When the program thus generated is run, the processing hardware reads an instruction, interprets the instruction to mean that it must carry out a certain action, and then executes that action. A piece of *software* that acts in this way, reading, interpreting and executing a sequence of coded instructions, is called an interpreter.

● A software designer may discover that the behaviour required of a particular part of the application at hand breaks down into a number of specific, small, closely defined actions, carried out in differently ordered sequences throughout the application. For example, in a certain industrial application, the activities 'move left', 'move right', 'move forward', 'move back', 'grasp' and 'release' may occur in differing order throughout the application. Now, if he were to program a virtual machine that executed programs couched in terms of the above six instructions, then the designer's job would be greatly simplified.

● It is unlikely, however, that there would be available a high-level language that included as part of its instruction repertoire the specific actions required by a particular application. It is also very unlikely that it would be economically viable to create a special-purpose compiler for only one application. It may, however, be possible to implement an interpreter. This is further discussed in subsections 8.1.2 and 10.3.1.

6.2.2.2 Implementing an Interpreter

Let us assume that a particular application breaks down into a small set of actions, say A, B and C, repeated in different sequences throughout the application. In order to create a virtual machine which will execute a program of these actions, the designer proceeds as follows.

Each action in the set of actions will be given a unique instruction code. Also, each action will have associated with it a program, written in a suitable language, which carries out the functions necessary to implement the action. The interpreter is designed to read an instruction code, decide which program corresponds to that instruction code and then transfer control of execution to the beginning of that program. Upon their completion, each of the action programs will transfer control back to the interpreter. The interpreter then reads the next instruction code in the program of instruction codes and the cycle is repeated.

Figure 6.9 shows the data structures that could be used by a simple interpreter. The code to be interpreted consists of a sequence of 8-bit storage elements. The left-hand four bits of each element will be interpreted as an action. The right-hand four bits will be interpreted as a parameter to be used when carrying out the action.

Both sets of bits are interpreted as numbers and used as indexes for data tables. The *action code address table* contains the value of the start location of the program code that implements each possible action. In this case there are sixteen possible actions. The *actual parameter table* contains a set of parameters. Each action is given an instruction code which corresponds to its location in the action code address table. When each action is executed, the interpreter makes the parameter indicated by the right-hand four bits of the code available to the action program. The instruction pointer indicates which code is to be interpreted next. On each cycle of the interpreter it is incremented to point to the next code in sequence. Non-sequential jumps within the interpreted code can be implemented by allowing action programs to manipulate the instruction pointer. The conditions under which such jumps occur may be defined by flags internal to the machine or from the outside world. The latter may also be used as part of the instruction counter to point to alternative code, depending on external conditions.

6.2.2.3 Advantages of Interpreters

Flexibility

Once a designer builds the software necessary to create the data tables, and builds the interpreter itself, he is in a position to create a virtual machine tailored to part of the sytem he is designing. In fact, he is now in a position to create many different virtual machines. For each new machine all he need do is create a new set of tables and action programs. The same interpreter can be used in each of the machines.

Space Saving

● A great advantage of the interpretive technique is the space saving that it engenders. If there were, for example, sixteen different possible actions, then they could be implemented as conventional subroutines

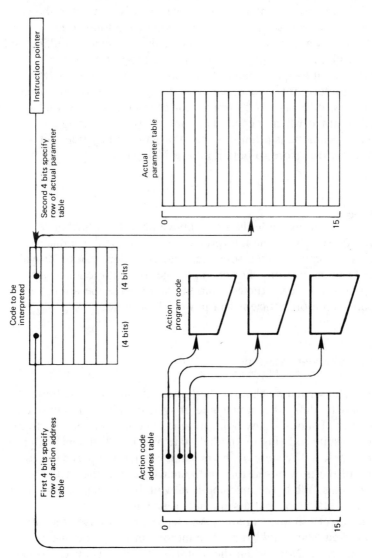

Figure 6.9 Interpreter data structures

and called from a main program. This method implies the use of at least one or two computer words per call. However, by using an interpreter, each of the actions can be represented by four bits — a significant saving in space. Of course, the price paid for this saving is the time overhead in running the interpreter. However, it is very often the case in real-time systems that only a small portion of the total code is time-critical, and a large amount is rarely activated (error-handling and diagnostic code, for example). So, for a large proportion of the application the time–space tradeoff may well come down heavily in favour of an interpretive technique. This is particularly true if portions of the process code have to be stored, for economic reasons, on backing store and returned when needed. The time overhead in using an interpretive technique is often less than that imposed by frequent accesses to backing store to obtain non-resident code.

Macros

● The robot arm example discussed above provides a further interesting possibility. If the interpreter code is defined as a macro with appropriate parameters, then some generalised actions can be provided as higher-level instructions. For example, 'get part', 'orientate part', 'deliver part' can be constructed from the more basic operations to provide an even more efficient and powerful machine.

6.2.3 The Finite State Machine

Another useful virtual machine is the finite state machine. A finite state machine may be defined as a machine or system which exists in one of a finite number of states at any point in time. The machine moves from being in one state to being in another state as a result of some external event or stimulus. The state of the machine at any one particular time is a function of the previous history of the machine, together with the current stimulus. While the machine is moving from being in one state to another, it may carry out a sequence of actions.

Consider a very simple example. An electric motor has two control buttons marked 'start' and 'stop'. The motor can be in one of two states — on or off. Now, when the motor is off, two events can occur. The start button is pressed, or the stop button is pressed. If the stop button is pressed, the state of the motor remains the same — off. If the start button is pressed, the motor changes its state to on. If the current state of the motor is on, then pressing the stop button will result in a change of state to off; pressing the start button will not cause a change of state. Note that the future state of the motor is a function of its current state, together with any events that occur.

● The 'state' nature of a machine is often represented graphically within a *state transition diagram*; see figure 6.10. In this diagram the states of the machine are represented as boxes with curved sides. For the machine to move from being in one state to being in another, some event must occur, signified here by a flag symbol. When passing from one state to another any actions carried out are represented by rectangular boxes; these will appear in later diagrams. This form of representation of a finite state machine is that recommended by the CCITT (1976), an international standards organisation, in their Specification and Design Language.

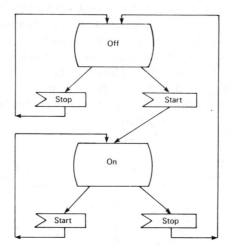

Figure 6.10 Simple state transition diagram

The electric motor is, of course, an extremely simple example. It is, however, possible to model many complex real-time applications as finite state machines. Consider the states of an individual call in a computer-controlled telephone exchange. The call passes from being in an idle state to awaiting dialled digits, ringing, talking, then terminating the call. A process that is sampling an input stream of characters and looking for certain patterns of data is another example. Such a process may be, for example, a syntax analyser for a compiler or text-translating process, or it may be the input process in a message switching or TELEX centre.

Consider the TELEX example. Let us assume that an input process is reading in messages. These messages consist of a string of characters. In actual systems the message would begin with the pattern ZCZC and end with the pattern NNNN. We could model the action of the input process as a finite state machine. An event in this case is the receipt of a character. This is shown in figure 6.11. Here we have made the simplifying assumption that the message starts with ZC and ends with NN.

The process remains in the idle state until such time as a Z character is received. Once Z is received the state changes to that of waiting for a C. Should any character other than a C be received, the state returns to idle — remember that ZC is the start of message sequence. Should, however, a C be received at this point, the state of the machine becomes that of receiving and storing a message.

Should the process receive an N while in this state, then it may mean that the N is the first of the pair of Ns that signify the end message. Accordingly, the process changes state to that of awaiting the end of message. Should the next character again be an N, then the process designed to handle complete messages will be signalled, and the input process will return to a wait state. Should any other character be received, then it implies that the first N was simply part of the message text, so it is stored together with the current character and the process state becomes that of receiving a message.

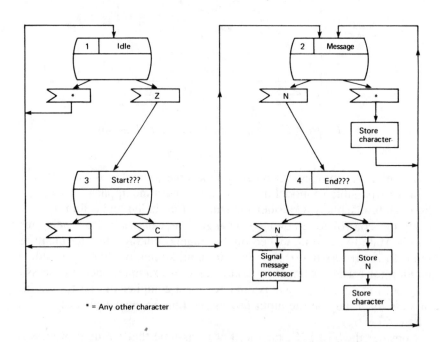

Figure 6.11 State transition diagram for message analyser

6.2.3.1 Implementing a State Machine

If we assume that a finite state virtual machine would prove helpful, how can we create it in software? We shall investigate the implementation of a finite state machine in some detail in order to highlight the ease with which a powerful virtual machine can be created.

A Simple Approach

A first attempt would be to set up the data structures shown in figure 6.12. The data structure is a simple mapping in tabular form of the information implicit in the state transition diagram. The *state table* has a row for each state in the machine. The row holds the number of the state, together with two integers which correspond to row numbers in the *action table.* These row numbers point to beginning and end rows of a section of the action table. Each section of the action table contains information about a particular state. Each row in the action table corresponds to an event which can occur; the action to be taken as a result of that event; and the state that the machine would enter on completion of the action. Figure 6.12 contains values corresponding to the state transition diagram in figure 6.11. The arrows in figure 6.12 show the situation if the machine were in state 1. The *current state* indexes the state table. The *begin* and *end* fields of row 1 of the state table indicate the section of the action table that represents state 1.

Once these tables are created the next step must be to construct a program which simulates the action of a state machine by acting on the information in the data structures shown in figure 6.12. The algorithm is quite straightforward

(1) *Get next event*
(2) Search down that part of the *action table* that corresponds to the current state, looking for the row corresponding to the event just received
(3) Carry out the action specified in the *action* column
(4) Set the current state register to the value in the *next state* column
(5) Go back to step 1.

The behaviour of the function *get next event* will depend on the system implementation. Its purpose is to provide the finite state machine with events in the order that they occur. If the finite state machine is implemented as a process in our real-time machine, then *get next event* will be a function which reads, from a channel, data representing events.

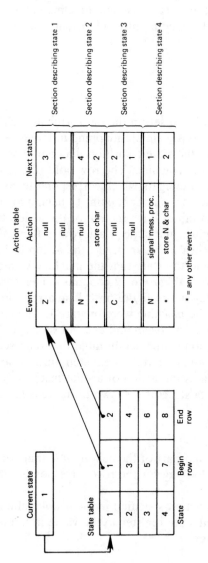

Figure 6.12 Finite state virtual machine — data structures

A More Useful Model

● The previous simple implementation implies that there is only one possible *next state* that can result from the occurrence of a particular event. This conforms to the formal mathematical definition of a finite state machine. However, when attempting to model real systems as state machines, it is frequently necessary to have more than one possible next state after the occurrence of an event. This is because the actions that result from the occurrence of an event may result in more than one outcome, which in turn may result in more than one set of actions and next states. Figure 6.13 shows an extremely simplified case of an on-line system that allocates a working buffer to each user. If, on receipt of a 'log on' request it can allocate the buffer, then the user is logged on. Note that the outcome of the decision box is a function of the action 'allocate buffer'.

To accommodate this situation we must refine the software model of a finite state machine. Because there is now possibly more than one next state for each current state–event combination, the state table must be extended to include an *auxiliary table*. The auxiliary table contains the additional action/next state information for those current state–event

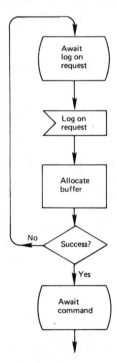

Figure 6.13 User log on scheme

combinations which have more than one outcome. The state table must include a new column to store a flag which indicates whether the auxiliary table is to be used. In the following discussion, refer to figure 6.14. The auxiliary table would normally be an extension of the state table; it is shown separately for clarity. Consider the following points.

(1) Every action procedure acts as a function, returning an integer value to the state machine's main procedure. This integer value corresponds to the outcome of the action and is a member of the contiguous set of positive integers, including zero. If an action has only one possible outcome, it will return to zero, if two outcomes zero or one; if three outcomes zero, one or two; and so on.

(2) If the flag for a particular row is one, then the next-state field is interpreted as the next state. If the flag is zero, then the next state is interpreted as a pointer to the first row of a section of the auxiliary table.

(3) The auxiliary table is divided into sections consisting of a variable number of rows. Each row corresponds to the set of possible actions and next states that could eventuate when a particular action is carried out while the machine is in a particular state.

(4) The rows in the auxiliary table also include a flag bit, implying that actions in the auxiliary table could also lead to further actions and different next states.

The algorithm for the state machine program is now

(1) *Get next event*
(2) Search down that part of the action table which corresponds to the current state, looking for the event corresponding to the one just received
(3) Carry out the action specified in the action column of the current row
(4) If the flag bit *is* set, then set the current state register to the value in the next state column and go back to (1)
(5) Otherwise, add the value returned from this action function to the value in the next state field and use the result as an index to a row in the auxiliary table. Go back to (3), using this row index as the current row.

The event scanner   We have already mentioned that the *get next event* procedure will read events from an input channel. In the example shown in figure 6.12, an event is the receipt of a character, so the *get next event* procedure will read a stream of characters from the channel. But, of course, these characters or events must have been generated by some

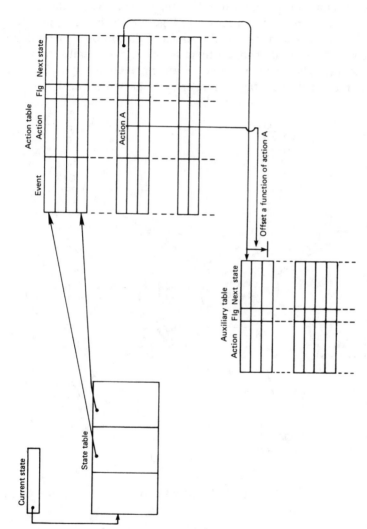

Figure 6.14 Finite state machine — extended data structures

process at the other end of the channel. We shall call this process that generates events the *event scanner*.

Events are detected by scanning the system and comparing the present status with that found by the previous scan and reporting any differences as events. It is important that the events are passed to the finite state machine in the order in which they occur. Accordingly, careful event queueing will be necessary. Figure 6.15 shows a possible scenario. The event scanner reads the status of the various system pools. If it detects any events, it channels them to the relevant finite state machine process. The channel would be implemented as a queue in this case, while the event could be an integer value passed down the channel.

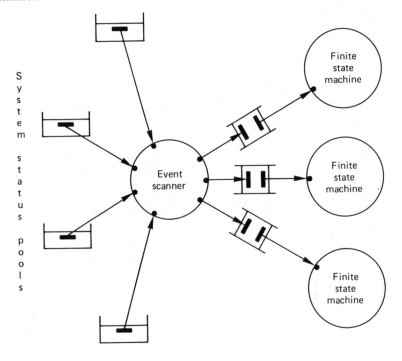

Figure 6.15 Event processor

● *Parallel machines in one process*   Note in figure 6.15 that one event scanner is serving a number of finite state machine processes. It is possible to coalesce these state machine processes into one process which stimulates the action of a number of finite state machines running in parallel. To create such a process it is only necessary to extend the basic data structures and to provide action/auxiliary tables for each of the machines in the process.

Rather than having a current state word, a *current state table* is provided. Each row in this table holds the current state of one of the machines in the process, together with a pointer to the machine's state table. The current state table is shown in figure 6.16. One extra integer is required to indicate which machine is in action at the current moment.

The message from the event scanner will also need extending to include an indication of the particular finite state machine to which the event refers. This could simply be an integer corresponding to the machine's row number in the current state table.

● For very small applications involving sequencing and timing of hardware, the finite state machine, implemented with electrically programmable read only memories (EPROMS), is a popular alternative to discrete logic, because the ease and speed of design and the rapid reprogramming without hardware changes make this very attractive.

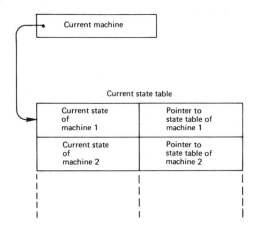

Figure 6.16 Current state table

6.3   SUMMARY

In order to make the design of real-time processes a manageable task, and to minimise the complexity of their implementation, it is necessary to employ a virtual machine abstraction. High-level language compilers provide useful general-purpose virtual machines. Moreover, it is possible, at relatively little cost, to provide software to support special-purpose virtual machines that are tailored to the requirements of a specific set of processes.

The implementation of the two special-purpose virtual machines described in this chapter are examples of the general technique of writing *table-driven* software. The idea is to produce a small, general-purpose program which will define its actions by looking up instructions in data tables. A major advantage of this technique is that the performance of a particular system can be altered simply by altering the contents of the tables.

● It is often the case that for more complex real-time applications no single particular process virtual machine type is suitable. It is eminently possible to consider including modules of any type under the overall control of one, provided that the problem can be sensibly partitioned. This may be particularly true for distributed systems, especially those with differing processor types.

Concepts

High-level languages; interpreters; finite state machines; state transition diagrams; table-driven code.

7 Interfaces

Embedded real-time systems are concerned with measuring and controlling the world outside the computer and of communicating with other systems or parts of a system in the case of distributed processing. Knowledge of the techniques of interfacing and the associated software implications and complications is a vital part of the work of the real-time programmer. It is an essential but messy end of the software design job, involving bits, part words, and packing and unpacking of both data and control. Absolute addresses are also necessarily involved, often with different read and write formats at the same address and having implied parameter FIFOs associated with particular functions. Isolating this level of detail in I/O modules is an important part of the designer's task.

The following discussions are brief and indicative of the general principles involved in various aspects of interfacing without recourse to specific interface chip designs. It should be noted that the discussion involves (elementary) hardware concepts with which the reader may not be familiar, and should be read in terms of what design decisions need to be made considering the features provided by interface devices, rather than a treatise on how to program specific devices in detail. Although reference to any particular manufacturer's product is omitted to avoid dating, some similarities are inevitable.

7.1 THE SOFTWARE INTERFACE

In general-purpose applications of computer software the latter has relatively few but important interfaces. These are commonly restricted to keyboard, screen, mouse and printer. The human computer interface (HCI) is considered to be vitally important and covers such considerations as operating system, high-level language, keyboard layout including function keys, and screen functions including the use of windows, nested menus, help facilities and graphics. Such facilities are now so important that the whole areas of HCI and the support environment for program development and testing have received considerable attention in recent years. HCI is beyond the scope of this

145

text, but support environments are covered later in chapter 8 (section 8.3). In this chapter we take a detailed look at some of the interfaces that commonly occur in real-time systems and which are less frequently the concern of those involved in general applications programming. As real-time systems are involved with monitoring and controlling external devices and systems, there are many aspects of interfacing that normally are of no concern to the average programmer. The real-time software will have to communicate with serial and parallel hardware interface chips, and this involves details of handlers for such devices. These are normally dealt with by the operating system writer or perhaps the person who writes the input/output routines for tailoring an operating system to a particular machine. Some knowledge of the requirements of the devices being monitored or driven is needed before such I/O code can be produced, and this leads to the generation of low-level processes which then interface to the high-level code of the main body of the software. The low cost of graphics hardware, and the improved communication that visual presentation of information provides, means that most modern real-time systems will include some form of graphics display even at the low-cost end of the market, and although still having some problems with recognition, speech input and output are being increasingly used. Consequently, real-time systems will have to communicate with speech recognisers and speech synthesisers.

Distributed systems offer many advantages and bring with them a few problems as well. Interfacing to external processes and processors is becoming a common requirement. Often this is achieved through standard networking systems involving communications protocols conforming to the ISO standard (International Standards Organization 7 layer communications protocol model) (Tanenbaum, 1981; Marsden, 1985).

7.2 LOW-LEVEL PROCESSES

● It is highly desirable that all real-time software is written in a high-level language. There are, of course, many reasons for this, not the least of which is the compactness of the source code resulting from the relative power of the high-level instructions provided by such languages. This *can* make the code easier to read and understand if it is well written. Perhaps the biggest advantage is that the facilities provided for program development and testing are far greater for high-level languages than for assemblers. However, until recently the facilities for dealing with the specific requirements of input and output were omitted from many high-level languages, on the assumption that the majority of programmers do not need them as input and output facilities are provided via the operating system. This leaves the real-time programmer in some difficulty, since he cannot normally get away with such a simplistic approach. There are now two alternative solutions to this problem.

● The first, and probably at the time of writing still the commonest, is to employ a high-level language where possible and to use an assembler for the rest. This approach seems to be satisfactory except for two problems. It is fairly common to find that a suitable assembler is not available — by this is meant a relocatable assembler that runs under the same operating system as the compiler — and the compiler includes a linker for assembler code. Also there is the problem of having to learn both high-level and low-level languages whose constructs and features tend to be rather different. A further problem arises with respect to target systems employing a different processor from the host development system. Cross assemblers are readily available, but cross compilers of production quality are rare and expensive.

● The second solution is much more attractive. There are two relatively new high-level languages which are specifically designed for real-time (and other) applications. These are Modular-2 and Ada. Both include facilities for low-level processes. The first is suitable for small to medium sized systems, both host and target, and the latter for medium to large systems. Both have adequate support for program development and testing, and hence it is desirable to employ one of these languages for real-time work. The former is rapidly gaining the popularity it deserves, and the latter is the language specified for the majority of new military applications and hence should rapidly become rather popular, but will only run on a sufficiently large host. In the non-military sphere the choice of language is often dictated by previous experience, the cost of mounting and supporting a new language, and the size of available host.

● It must not be assumed that low-level processes are necessarily confined to input/output functions. Occasionally severe timing constraints will dictate an improvement in coding efficiency. Typical situations where speed can be improved are those involving nested loops, where replacing the inner loop only by more efficient code can have a dramatic effect on overall execution times. This can sometimes be carried out by simplification of processes, but where this is not practical the traditional approach is to replace small code segments by assembler code. The reason this is effective is due to the use of short fixed point arithmetic (2 bytes instead of 4), short loop counters (1 byte), and compound control orders, etc. Note, however, that the use of the special quirks to be found in every machine is to be avoided, since others wishing to modify the segment may not know of such *tricks*. In the new languages mentioned above many of the 'fast' features available via assemblers, such as those just mentioned, are available from within the language, rendering the use of assemblers largely unnecessary and thus greatly simplifying the task of the programmer.

7.3   THE PROGRAMMER'S VIEW OF HARDWARE INTERFACES

The majority of interfaces on most modern computers are support chips from a microprocessor chip family. This is a cheap and very effective means of providing what used to be a fairly complex piece of logic design. Such devices can, for the most part, be categorised under three headings: serial I/O, parallel I/O and counter/timer. Many devices from different microprocessor families have somewhat similar characteristics. Consequently a general view of these will suffice, and will give an indication of these characteristics and the implications for the low-level module writer.

7.3.1 Serial Interfaces

●   Perhaps the most common serial interface is the RS232, commonly used to connect terminals to machines. However, many modern serial interface chips handle several different protocols. This makes such devices much more versatile, but as a consequence the user must carry out more initialisation before the chip can be used for a particular purpose. To do this the programmer must understand not only the protocols and why a particular protocol is being used, but also how the registers are set up for the protocol desired. A simple example is the initialisation of control registers to achieve the desired number of stop bits and character length for a character transfer, together with the parity convention, baud rate and whether synchronous or asynchronous transmission is required. For block transfers, information such as frame length, and address and control fields must be initialised. There are further complications. Block transfers are usually associated with error detection, both of format violation and data error. The latter is achieved by a frame check sequence (FCS) or cyclic redundancy check (CRC), this being relatively trivial in hardware but very slow in software. This in turn gives rise to the question of the actions to be taken when various errors are detected, both from the reporting point of view and error recovery by, say, frame retransmission, with all that this implies in real-time systems. Last but not least is the complication of having two or possibly more such programmable serial interfaces in a single device. From a software point of view the latter complication is trivial, since the fact that they are associated in the hardware is an example of coincidental cohesion. It is likely that the device is memory mapped into the I/O space as separate but adjacent sets of locations, and any association can be disguised by assigning suitable but different names to the two channels. Fortunately, code modules for such devices can often be lifted from other applications but must be checked with care before use. Unfortunately, use is sometimes tailored to a specific application and/or the latest devices are specified, requiring a new module to be written.

● Asynchronous character transmission may be characterised by the general format of figure 7.1a. A programming model for a typical character serial interface is then illustrated in figure 7.1b. The first observation concerns the addressing of the device registers. Just two register addresses are provided which have different meanings depending on whether they are read or written to. This is a common feature of most interface chips of almost every type, not just serial devices. In this case, one address is used for data input and the same address is used for data output, which also provides for simple unambiguous software use. The other has the function of a command register when written to. This register has a collection of bits having such functions as transmit enable (TxEN), request to send (RTS), data terminal ready (DTR), software reset (SR) and error reset (ER). This list is not exhaustive or device-specific, but serves to illustrate the nature of the command bits. As, in general, some combination of bits in command words are valid and others are not, the supporting code must correctly assemble the command words and inhibit illegal combinations.

This observation implies a general requirement for inserting particular bits in a word without disturbing other existing bit patterns, and will be returned to later. When the command register address is read, the information returned is the status byte, as shown in figure 7.1b. This contains bits indicating such conditions as framing error (FE), receiver ready (RxRDY), overrun error (OE), transmitter empty (TxEMPTY), parity error (PE) and synchronous detect (SYNDET). Again the list is not exhaustive or device-specific, but shows the variety of conditions that the interface handler will have to deal with. The particular model illustrated may have more than one mode of operation and this may be set by writing to the mode register (not previously mentioned) as the byte sent immediately after either a hard or soft reset. Other devices have an additional address for mode bits and other flags. The sequence implied by soft reset, mode byte, command byte is also a common general approach to sending instructions followed by parameters in many types of peripheral chips, and will also be returned to later. The mode register contains a code for character length (5 to 7 bits), a code for baud rate/synchronous operation, a code for the number of stop bits, enable and odd/even parity bits, a 1 or 2 sync. character bit and an

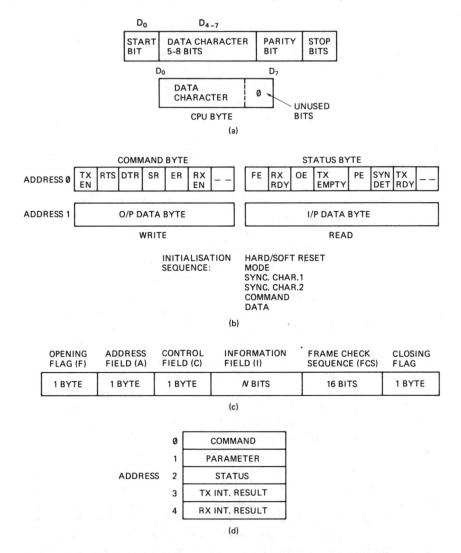

Figure 7.1 (a) Asynchronous character transmission. (b) Typical programming model for asynchronous character transmission. (c) Frame transmission — typical frame format. (d) Typical programming model for frame transmission

internal/external sync. detect bit, all packed up into one or more bytes.

Synchronous operation is not included, as the above brings out most of the important issues for low-level software design for simple character interfaces. This discussion has highlighted the complexity of something as simple as character serial interfaces.

● For many applications the simple type of interface suffices; however, communications have necessarily been developed for more sophisticated systems involving higher-level protocols for sending information between a number of destinations in a network. This has given rise to interface chips capable of software configuration for different protocols. In particular, the ISO standard High-Level Data Link Control (HDLC), the IBM Synchronous Data Link Control (SDLC), and CCITT X.25 protocols may all be programmed onto such chips. This type of serial data transmission is organised around frames, as illustrated in figure 7.1c. These frames have data fields which are bit-oriented and are therefore code-independent, so that, for example, either text or binary code segments may be sent via the same communications channel. Supervisory frames may be used for control purposes, and non-sequenced frames for secondary station control or initialisation, in addition to data sent via information frames. For real-time systems in which distributed processing is used such protocols are useful for CPU–CPU, terminal–CPU, and CPU–terminal applications, where terminal includes sensor/transducer/display cluster interfaces. Information may be sent via direct memory access (DMA) or non-DMA data transfers, and be interrupt or non-interrupt driven. Interface chips have a generous register structure in line with the modern practice of large memory mapped I/O space. Typically, such devices will have a programming model as in figure 7.1d. As the number of commands is large for such a chip, an example only of the use of the command and parameter registers is given:

Command byte:	Transmit frame
Parameter byte:	l.s. byte of frame length
Parameter byte:	m.s. byte of frame length
Parameter byte:	Address field of transmit frame (A)
Parameter byte:	Control field of transmit frame (C)

Here we return to the principle of sending a sequence of bytes to a single address, as mentioned earlier. The status register contains bits such as command buffer full (CBF), command parameter buffer full (CPBF), receiver interrupt (RxINT) and transmitter interrupt result available (TxIRA). Some of these bits are used for command control purposes and the remainder are interrupt flags. The normal sequence of operation is a *command phase* in which commands (with parameters) are sent to the interface, followed by an *execution phase*. The latter may be independent of the CPU (for example, DMA) or require intervention by the CPU. Completion of this phase is followed by a *result phase*, the successful completion of an operation or an error condition. This is indicated either by an *immediate result* (such as clear to send, carrier detect or a user condition) via the result register for quick response, or an interrupt for a reason specified in one of the interrupt result registers. The latter contain bits such as address match, CRC error and DMA overrrun for a receive interrupt result register, and bits such as frame transmit complete, abort complete and clear to send error for a transmit interrupt result register. Clearly, it is important that the interface software module be capable of dealing with all possible conditions and of reporting errors requiring action for fail-soft recovery to other appropriate modules of the system.

The reader is referred to other volumes in this series for a full discussion of communications systems (Cole and Gee—see page i).

7.3.2 Parallel Interfaces

● These provide a faster data transfer rate than serial interfaces, and can be arranged to provide for functions of any appropriate width from a semi-nibble upwards by a combination of hardware and software configuration. Such interfaces are generally restricted to short physical path lengths for economic reasons, but are very useful for connecting such devices as analog-to-digital converters (ADC), digital-to-analog converters (DAC), BCD switches and numeric displays. A typical device will contain 2-byte-wide data registers. These may be set to have an input, output or bi-directional function at the byte level by mode control bits in a control register. As an alternative, they may be programmed to be input or output registers by means of a second pair of registers known as data direction registers, also 8-bits wide. A complication arises from the versatility of the latter, which allows individual bits to be input or output. This caters for the packing of bits required for various functions to make efficient use of the interface. The result is somewhat like the collection of flags in a CPU status register, except that they may be input or output. Clearly, the complication for the software designer lies in the packing and unpacking of the required collections of bits, bearing in mind that bit manipulation can be a slow process in some languages. It is in this sort of situation that the software designer should influence the hardware design in order to foresee and avoid difficulties later. This is indicated in figure 7.2. Further features of some parallel chips are the provision of additional bits which can be used in various ways. As output they can be programmed to be high or low and hence be used as a flag, or as a clock for an external data latch. As an input they may be used to generate an interrupt or be an acknowledge signal. The interrupt flag can be set to trigger on positive or negative edges. A further register is for control, and may include bits to

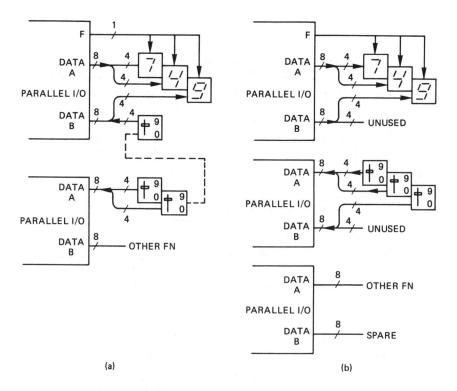

(a)

(b)

*Figure 7.2 Parallel interface techniques: (a) not recommended;
(b) preferred*

enable/disable/reset the interrupt flags and set positive/negative edge
response, etc. (figure 7.3a).

● A programming model of this type of device is shown in figure 7.3b,
it is not intended to be a particular chip, but exhibits features to be
found in many variants. The data registers are programmed on a bit
basis in any combination of input or output, or on a byte basis to
tri-state (see Glossary) mode for bi-directional use. The data direction
registers are used to define input or output function for each bit.
Tri-state operation is selected by control register mode bits. The control
registers also contain fields to define the mode of the additional control
input/output bits. These may be programmed as outputs to be set or
reset for control or flag purposes, or to produce a single pulse (see
Glossary) of width equal to the clock period for, say, latching external
data. The control registers represent a particular example of the
bit-packing problem referred to earlier; writing to, say, one control

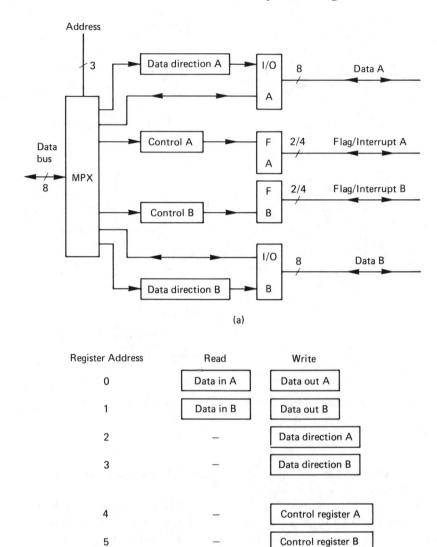

*Figure 7.3. (a) Parallel interface organisation. (b) Programming model
for parallel interface*

output to set it must in no circumstances interfere with a previous
initialisation of another bit such as a positive edge-triggered (see
Glossary) interrupt input. The interface software module must lock out
any possibility of interaction between non-associated functions, even

though the built-in hardware coupling cannot be avoided. This can, of course, be achieved by accessing each function as though hardware coupling was absent and maintaining mutual exclusion by assembling the resultant control or data word by suitable masking, shifting and or-ing.

Other parallel interface devices include ADC, DAC, motor controllers (see Glossary), etc., which are directly connected to processor buses and memory mapped, have similar characteristics from the software point of view, but clearly have rather different functions.

7.3.3 Counter/Timer Interfaces

● Not surprisingly, many real-time functions are associated with counting events or sequences, and with measurement of time intervals. With both of these functions come the further requirements of synthesis and measurement. Provision of a real-time clock (from whatever source) permits software generation of ticks, events and sequences, and consequently of implementing time measurement systems. However, the growing use of digital techniques in external systems, and the speed that these are required to operate, can place increasingly severe loading on processors for these functions. A popular solution for time-critical applications is to provide local counter/timer and control functions using either dedicated hardware or local processor-based hardware under the control of the real-time system and its software. There is an increasing tendency to make external systems more flexible by adding programmable features where previously these were hardwired. Fortunately, along with this development comes a range of support chips for counter/timer applications. Again, the low cost of silicon chip technology and the availability of memory mapped I/O register space have provided sophisticated programmable facilities. As with the serial I/O chips, some careful initialisation is necessary before particular user functions can be reliably realised. Figure 7.4 shows a typical multichannel counter/timer chip programming model. Three 16-bit down counters are provided. These may be easily separated as they are associated with unique addresses. Each may be loaded or read as required. The control register provides a wide range of facilities. An address field selects a particular counter/timer channel. A second field controls the read/load conditions: For loading, the options are load l.s. byte only, load m.s. byte only, or l.s. byte then m.s. byte (two byte load). The read operation is to latch a counter into a buffer while it is counting; this may then be read to monitor the current count. A further bit may be used to dictate binary or BCD operation. A final field sets the counter mode. Typical modes are, for an initial count of N:

Interrupt on terminal count (count = 0), that is, after N clocks.

Single pulse length of length N clock periods, triggered by external gate input.

Rate generator (divide by N). Produces a pulse every time the count reaches zero, or generates a square wave of period N clocks.

Triggered strobe. Generates an output pulse N clock periods after either N is loaded (software strobe) or a hardware trigger is received.

Register address	Function
0	Timer 1 low byte
1	Timer 1 high byte
2	Timer 2 low byte
3	Timer 2 high byte
4	Timer 3 low byte
5	Timer 3 high byte
6	Timer control register
7	Interrupt flag register
8	Interrupt control register

Figure 7.4 Counter/timer programming model

The address field effectively isolates the control between channels, but again the control words must be carefully assembled to avoid unwanted effects. Some microprocessor chips include timer/counter channels on chip, but the features are similar. The timers appear as registers; their functions are part of the instruction set.

● The many real-time applications of such devices include motor controllers, real-time clocks, time and sequence measurement and generation. All these can lead to substantial benefits for the software designer by relieving processors of these tasks and effectively decoupling and simplifying the processes.

7.3.4 ANSI/IEEE Std 488–1978/GPIB Interface

This, the IEEE Standard Digital Interface for Programmable Instrumentation, developed from the Hewlett–Packard General-Purpose Interface Bus (GPIB), one of the more common and sophisticated world standard interfaces, is for measuring instruments and related applications. It is a byte-wide external bus system, and is quite popular as many manufacturers world wide make provision for connection of instruments and subsystems by this method. It differs by an order of magnitude in complexity, power and programmability from the simple parallel interfaces discussed above. An outline of its features from a software point of view is useful in that it raises issues relevant to other such complex interfaces existing now and those that will exist in the future. Loughry (1983) provides a detailed insight into hardware, system, and low-level and medium-level software standards and their application for this useful interface system. A system model of the interface is shown in figure 7.5 from which the main features can be seen. Four types of system may be connected to the external bus. Input devices or subsystems are talk only (sources) — for example, digitisers or digital output sensors. Output devices or systems are listen only (destinations) — for example, digital indicators or stepper (pulsed) devices. The third category are I/O devices, talker/listeners — for example, collections of sensors, motors or indicators. The final category is controllers of which, if there is more than one, then only one can be

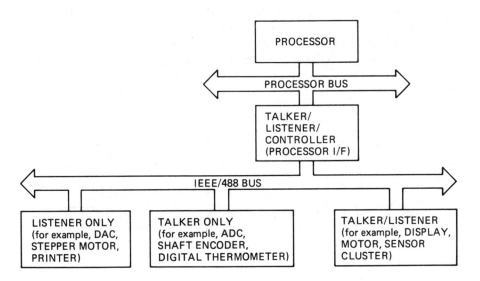

Figure 7.5 IEEE/488 bus system

active at a particular time. Devices in this category are connected to central or local processor buses, and are usually memory mapped.

● The typical register model of figure 7.6 illustrates the level of complexity for talker/listeners. The model exhibits the by now familiar features of differing read/write functions for a particular register address, and of data, command and status registers. Additional features are further mode registers for polling, addressing and auxiliary purposes,

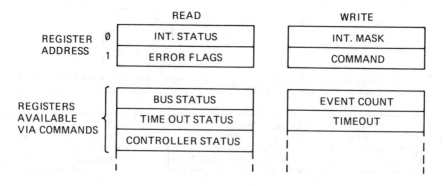

	READ	WRITE
Ø	ADDRESS	ADDRESS
1	DATA IN	DATA OUT
2	COMMAND	END OF SEQUENCE
REGISTER ADDRESS 3	ADDRESS STATUS	ADDRESS MODE
4	SERIAL POLL STATUS	MODE (SERIAL POLL)
5	INTERRUPT STATUS	INTERRUPT ENABLE
6		AUX. MODE

Figure 7.6 Talker/listener programming model

and registers for sequences, interrupts and device addresses. The model for a controller (figure 7.7) has mask registers for both interrupts and errors, and status registers for interrupts, the bus, the controller itself, and the status (current count) of an event counter. A timeout counter is also featured. These give an indication of the flexibility designed into

	READ	WRITE
REGISTER ADDRESS Ø	INT. STATUS	INT. MASK
1	ERROR FLAGS	COMMAND
REGISTERS AVAILABLE VIA COMMANDS	BUS STATUS	EVENT COUNT
	TIME OUT STATUS	TIMEOUT
	CONTROLLER STATUS	

Figure 7.7 Controller programming model

this interface system. The following presentation of aspects of the standard for the software to be followed by implementers of the system has some interesting features that are useful in general, not just for this bus.

Communication with devices using this bus is via *messages*. These are of four types: program message, measurement message, status message and display message. A message has the general structure indicated by figure 7.8a for all types. The measurement message is a useful starting point and has the structure of figure 7.8b.

Headers are one of the three types indicated in figure 7.8c. These are an alpha string, a formatted alpha string, or a string of any printing

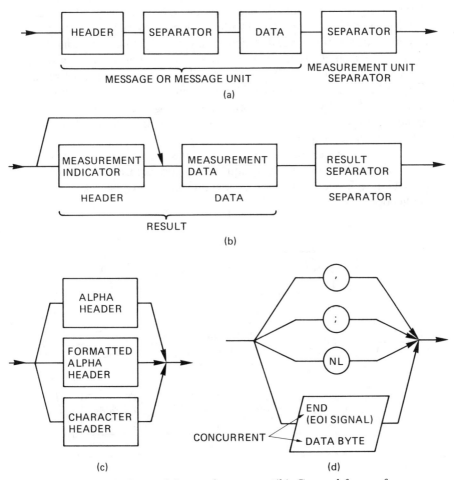

Figure 7.8 (a) General form of message. (b) General form of measurement message. (c) Headers. (d) Separators

ASCII characters with the exception of the reserved characters required for parsing. All headers must start with an alpha character.

Separators are indicated in figure 7.8d. Here there are levels of separator and preferred separators at each level. The lowest level is to delimit message elements or data fields. The semi-colon has higher precedence than the comma, as in normal grammar. The middle level is new-line (NL), or CR LF, and is used to separate a sequence of message units. The highest-level separator (END) denotes the completion of a sequence of measurements or instructions. A talker, having sent END, may not output further bytes without first receiving a specific device-dependent command to do so.

Data is of three types: numeric data, block data or string data, as shown in figure 7.9. Numeric data may be signed or unsigned, integer, or have fixed or floating point formats. Block data may have many formats, but has the general structure illustrated. It has a preamble of # followed by a single alpha character denoting the particular data format. The data, always necessarily sent in bytes, may be sequences of binary, text, single or double precision floating point, octal or hexadecimal numbers. Check type may be none, sum or CRC, and length of the sequence may be determined by length bytes or the use of END. String data is delimited by quotes.

Program messages have a similar form and features as data messages, but usually have multiple data sequences. They are distinguished by particular addresses and codes used within the messages in a particular application.

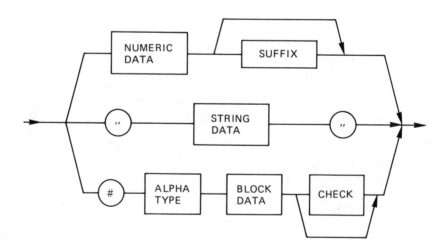

Figure 7.9 Data

Status messages are much simpler in principle and are characterised via parallel poll or serial poll mechanisms which have related characteristics to polled and vectored interrupts in a processor, but related to activities in the interface. Status may be read at any time but a device may request service for a particular reason subsequently identified by reading appropriate status registers in that device. Specifically, in serial poll mode if enabled, a request service message (RQS) may be sent concurrently with a status byte (STB).

Display messages are specifically for device input or output where intervention by a human being is required. Either program and measurement message types may be used, and character and string data are probably the most appropriate.

Full definition of systems for programming, data transfer, status and display functions within this bus standard is contained in ANSI/IEEE Std 728–1982. This is included in Loughry (1983).

● Although this discussion concerns a specific system, it does give a very clear indication of some of the features desirable in a distributed processing system. The message mechanism is a popular way of communicating between processors and also between processes. It highlights the variety of message types required and hints at the need for a hierarchy of message priorities. It clearly provides for many different data structures from single bytes to complex instructions and sets of information. It also indicates a requirement for an ordered approach to communication between subsystems of widely differing characteristics. These abound in real-time systems. Such a systematic approach does much to ease the complexity involved in implementing communications in complex systems and helps to decouple the subsystem characteristics from the communication mechanisms. This improves simplicity, and must help with subsequent reliability. It is essential to provide a clean simple software interface between low-level handlers and the high-level specification part of such I/O modules, a point returned to in subsection 9.1.6.

7.4 THE GRAPHICS INTERFACE

A revolution has been taking place in the availability and use of colour graphics in almost every sphere of the application of computers. This has come about partly because of the revolution in desk top and home computers. The expectation of most users now includes some form of graphics facility. It has been known for some time that pictorial presentation is a highly efficient way of communication for human beings. The world wide success of television tells its own story. Where does this fit then into real-time systems? The more obvious places are the block diagrams, flow charts and structure charts associated with specification, system design and documentation. But these are appropriate for the general-purpose computers on which system developments are hosted, and have been available for some time. Such systems were moderately costly but inclusion of a graphics terminal does not represent a large fraction of the total cost. Many real-time systems are relatively small and inexpensive and/or have remote subsystems of this nature.

● Three simultaneous developments have made the low-cost colour graphics terminal a reality, and will continue to do so with even more effect. These are: the higher storage capacity of memory chips at the same or even lower cost than their lower capacity predecessors; the ready availability of medium-resolution colour video monitors; and the increasing number, variety and power of raster scan graphic display controllers.

● Many control systems feature indicators, meters, chart recorders, mimic diagrams and control panels, all providing information for human monitoring. The cost of this provision is high. Further, a text screen for man–system interaction is often required as well. A colour graphics screen *could* provide some or all of these facilities on a switched function basis. The hardware cost at the time of writing was of the order of $1100 or £750 and expected to fall, a clear indication of financial viability. Consider a monitor panel with a conventional thermometer, a voltmeter, a numeric display and a set of lamps indicating the states of switches and valves, as in figure 7.10. Such a panel can be generated as a graphics image and fed with data derived from sensors, and presented in a familiar manner. Teletext type of presentation is also available but

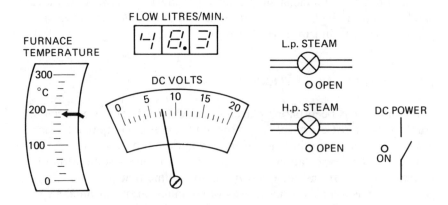

Figure 7.10 Monitor panel

provides relatively poor screen resolution. Derived displays are clearly possible, such as volume delivered calculated from mass flow rate. Text windows and window managers are an essential feature of most modern software support systems. Graphics windows play a similar role in graphics displays for real-time and other contexts. Keyboard control can select and format the parameters displayed, and alarms can automatically overlay existing screens. Many future real-time systems will employ graphics displays, and the applications to which they are put will increase in both number and complexity.

● A useful but not definitive view of such systems is a programming model of a typical graphics display controller, as in figure 7.11. A very large number of features is provided via just two memory mapped registers. The first, when written to, is the command register and this is supported by a command stack. The latter allows the supporting processor to send several commands without having to wait for the first to be completed. This helps in freeing the processor for other tasks. Clearly, the stack is of limited length since it is in hardware, and stack overflow must be avoided. The register in read mode is a status register which provides, among several flags, stack full which is used to stop the processor from sending any more commands. The second register is a data register by means of which parameters associated with these commands are sent. This is also a hardware stack with similar advantages and problems of the command stack. When read, this is a data register from which data in picture element (pixel) form may be read from the screen for a graphics dump on a suitable dot matrix printer if required. Similarly, pictures in pixel form may be loaded to the screen, although this is mainly in connection with display processing of pictures captured, for example, from a video camera via a separate frame buffer. This type of block move is usually carried out under DMA control. Graphics pictures are created by successively drawing objects, with each object being made up of a sequence of basic elements such as lines, circles and graphics characters.

● This is best understood by means of a hardware diagram (figure 7.12). A graphics display controller (GDC) chip has several functional blocks. A counter system working from a clock generates the basic synchronising pulses initialised in terms of pixels/line, lines/frame and

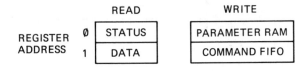

Figure 7.11 Display controller programming model

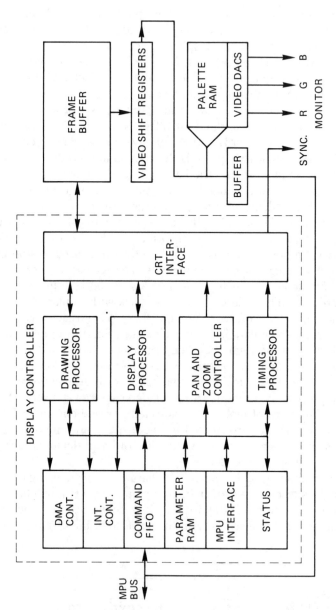

Figure 7.12 Raster scan colour graphics system

picture frame refresh rate, all of which are under software control (with some limits, of course). A second block supplies timing signals to the memory from which the screen is refreshed (frame buffer). A third block is concerned with command, parameter and data control. The fourth block is a drawing processor which, using digital differential analyser (DDA) techniques draws lines, circles, ellipses, rectangles, etc. Additional logic is provided for cursor control, light-pen and DMA control. The GDC is seen to be the interface between the processor bus and the frame buffer. The latter is read continuously to refresh the video monitor, with dual access for writing to this memory. Text may be written to the screen in two ways. First as graphics characters, usually as a pattern 8×8 pixels (8 bytes) which may also be used to construct other useful shapes such as parts of meters, valves and thermometer scales (or space invaders!). The second way is to use part of the frame buffer or a separate memory to store coded characters (and associated attributes) which are then interpreted by a character ROM or RAM, the latter providing a 'soft' character set. Additional features are zoomed *write* of graphics characters, and pan and zoom *read* onto the screen. An important feature of such systems is the ability to access a frame store larger than the physical screen. This allows for large mimic diagrams over which the screen can be panned up/down and left/right, and/or several simultaneous diagrams. The latter are selected by a simple change of display start address, changing to a new picture in one refresh period. Extra hardware is required to provide additional facilities and so a typical system would include other memory mapped registers for this. Perhaps the best example of this is a palette store. The frame buffer stores logical pixel colours of, say, 4 to 8 bits. These are read and used to look up the actual colour, commonly of more bits — for example, 24 bits (8 bits for each of the red, green and blue signals). The user may change this small high-speed memory at any time, without changing the frame buffer contents but simply the colours on the screen. Several different palettes may be available simultaneously, selected by a single parameter.

● It can be seen from this brief discussion that considerable power is available in these graphic processor systems, and only an outline is provided here. Developments in such processors are likely to be rapid. Fortunately, there is a standard for such systems to enable software writers to communicate relatively easily with such systems. This is the Graphic Kernel System (GKS), described in Hopgood *et al.* (1983). The detail of how to draw a line, circle or, say, character K at 52 degrees in italics of size 5, and so on, is hidden from the programmer who simply calls the appropriate routine with parameters as required. On top of this, he builds a superstructure of higher-level graphics objects such as a set of axes, voltmeters, chart recorders and mimic diagram elements, with parameters such as axis labels, voltage and pen position. These objects are assembled to form a graphics file for each picture with parameters for that picture. Once the picture is written to the screen only changes such as pen position, voltmeter reading, etc., are required to update the pictures, including those drawn in the display buffer but not actually displayed.

● The real-time software designer should ensure that the code module for the display has a simple interface. This should be driven by a channel through which is sent the graphics file to draw the required pictures, and subsequently the parameters for updating those pictures. In this way the complexity implied by the discussion above is hidden.

Currently, the interpretation of the graphics file has to be done by a general-purpose processor associated with the graphics processor. Future systems will have chip sets when these functions are better integrated.

7.5   VOICE INPUT/OUTPUT

Much work has been done on speech recognition and synthesis in recent years. Many systems of speech synthesis are available and are to be found even on small home and business computers. In real-time work it is arguable that voice output from a software or hardware assisted synthesiser could prove useful in many ways. For instance, in the cockpit of a commercial aircraft there are visual display devices such as artificial horizon, course indicator, engine monitors and so on. In addition, there are alarm annunciators. The captain and crew have a lot to monitor and, of course, most of the time all is well. When action is required it often involves more than one member of the flight crew. In an emergency the crew have to cope with many tasks simultaneously. A voice system giving warning of impending problems, information on unusual conditions, and of course alarms, has the advantages of being independent of head position, or of requiring notice to be taken of, say, a dial whose indication is out of normal position. Similarly, giving a command by means of voice is also useful, freeing the hands for other tasks.

7.5.1 Voice Synthesis

● The synthesis of the human voice is quite a complex task and, because of the data rate, is normally supported by special hardware speech processors to provide adequate speech quality. The processor is supported by one or more memories containing the coded speech parameters required to produce particular phonemes or phrases. These are selected in user-programmable sequences to produce words and sentences. To improve speech intelligibility, it is desirable to include context parameters such as the loudness and pitch of each phrase. It is the latter which cause problems when reproduction of the printed word is required, for example, but they are satisfactory for the production of a pre-programmed set of commands or sentences. It is clear from this discussion that a set suitable for a particular application could be pre-programmed and the speech output initiated by a simple coded command via a channel. Alternatively, sentences could be constructed according to a set of rules to produce acceptable modulation. Of course this is more flexible, but inevitably more difficult to achieve. It is inadvisable for the real-time programmer to be involved with any detail below this level, and preferably not even at this level. Hence the interface should be kept very simple, but the result can be rather effective.

7.5.2 Voice Recognition

● This area has some notorious difficulties. Word recognisers are quite good for a limited vocabulary and a limited range of speakers unless the system is complex and expensive, although this is liable to change. There are also, in a control environment, some hazards in getting it wrong! However, it would be unwise to dismiss such systems since developments in this day and age tend to be rapid. Perhaps the biggest problem is recognition where context is important, and this calls for a lot more computer power. In view of the difficulties, such systems are usually self-contained and can provide a relatively simple interface for input of perceived speech and output of commands such as store new word, enable speech interrupt, select mode or vocabulary. The job of the real-time software writer has to be limited to interfacing the speech recognition system to a channel and writing a module to respond to speech input as appropriate to the system being designed.

7.6 EXTERNAL PROCESSES

● These can be categorised in two ways. First consider a 'simple' system comprising a controller and a controlled process. Here the controlled process is an external process. It may be a process in which there is no programmable action, it simply responds to commands and can be monitored. The interface situation can be generalised in a useful diagram such as figure 7.13. The interface here is seen to be between the physical external process and the controller dividing the functions on

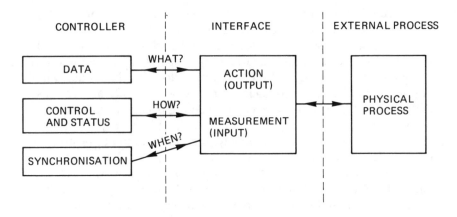

Figure 7.13 Input/output model

a basis of what? when? and how? Input and output are perceived to be measurement and action. The external process and its interface may be regarded in some senses as a peripheral, although this tends to direct one's thought processes towards conventional computer peripherals, which is rather restricting. This is the traditional computer-controlled system with or without feedback, monitoring, alarms and so on. It is likely that in the modern equivalent of this the external process contains a microprocessor or two. The popular dot matrix printer falls into this category. It has a flexible set of operational modes and functions but is not programmable in the accepted sense. The second category covers systems where external processes are more complex and involve a processor which may have a power equal to or greater than that of the controller. In this case, perhaps the controller has the function of a system supervisor or performance optimiser. Clearly, there is the possibility of a network of such external processes. The question then arises of whether such a system should be viewed as having a central processor at all, or be considered as a network of communicating partners. This is particularly true of systems in which redundancy is achieved through duplicate processors. A further consideration is the possibility of human access to the external process and whether this is restricted to that process or can by some mechanism have access to the controller/supervisor.

● These discussions lead us more and more to regard the normal situation as one of communicating processors rather than the traditional star system with a central computer communicating with peripherals. The modern small computer is in any case such a system in its own right. Usually comprising a general-purpose CPU with maths coprocessor, peripheral processor, a graphics processor and a disc controller, it will communicate with a printer which includes a processor, and possibly have a communications processor and a GPIB controller. This is not yet generally seen as a distributed system.

7.7 EXTERNAL PROCESSORS AND DISTRIBUTED PROCESSING

● Industrial processes usually require real-time operation and are sometimes distributed over considerable distances, and this often forces a decision to use local processing. There are several reasons for this. Firstly, one of reliability. If processing is centralised, then a failure of the central system implies failure of local systems. Next there is the problem of communication data rates. In closed loop systems, delay in transmission is translated into extra phase shift around the loop, and this does not improve stability. Thirdly, there may be sufficient local processing need to justify the cost of a local processor. Finally, simplicity: partitioning a problem into processes relating to geographical location may be coincidental cohesion, but is sometimes desirable.

What then are the considerations for real-time systems constructed as a distributed network?

● The hardware may include processors of different types. If possible the software designer should, at the outset, minimise this by recommending use of one manufacturer's processors, whether these are computers in their own right or members of a microprocessor set. The reason for this is code compatibility, especially for the situation where the software is to be developed using a host development system (see subsection 8.3.1). Many microprocessor families have 8, 16 and 32 bit processors which are code-compatible but clearly execute at different speeds. This makes development a simpler task and certainly assists with profiling the software onto the distributed system. Of course, this is not always possible, particularly where a special processor is chosen for performance or other reason as, for example, for digital filtering. However, the special code can be constrained to be within a module and hence maintain simplicity.

● The communication systems (channels) connecting processors must have adequate bandwidth and the protocols must allow for various types of data to be communicated. For reliability they should also be arranged to provide redundant connectivity to permit nodes to be bypassed using an alternative route in the event of failure or heavy traffic.

● Operating system functions can be distributed to advantage (see subsection 8.1.1). In particular a common kernel, resident in each processor, simplifies the system, makes it more reliable and reduces transfers of operating-system components between processors. Similarly, files and library routines can be kept in more than one place, as can copies of compilers, assemblers and utilities, although these requirements will be dependent on the system, and in particular on the availability of storage, especially the size and presence or absence of discs at a particular node.

● Perhaps the most significant aspect of distributed real-time systems is the influence of the distributed hardware on the software design and performance. It is of paramount importance that those responsible for writing the software are involved at the earliest stage of the system specification and proposal. A mention was made earlier of the need to delay major design decisions as late as possible and this is never more true than for the choice of hardware, including communications, and the ramifications for all aspects of software design and performance.

7.8   SUMMARY

In this chapter we have looked at interfaces, which is often a neglected area of real-time systems, especially those in which the computer system(s) are embedded. Important issues are seen to be communications, the complexity of modern hardware interfaces and the subsystems to be interfaced, and the consequential need for the real-time programmer both to understand these and to ensure that the inevitable low-level code specific to many interfaces is confined to the modules handling them. The consequences for software development of device-specific code in terms of the availability of suitable and compatible tools are mentioned in relation to host/target systems. The growing importance of both graphics and voice input/output are highlighted and discussed with respect to the advantages of improved HCI and the software interfaces available to the designer.

Concepts

Software interface; hardware interface; communications protocols; serial and parallel interfaces; counter/timers; low-level processes; messages; raster scan graphics; graphics kernel system; external processes; distributed processors.

8 *Design and Development Tools*

● Real-time systems are, and probably will be for some time to come, developed in environments which are not conducive to the efficient and reliable production of the software element. Perhaps the biggest thrust of the 1980s has been the recognition of the importance of software design and development tools under the banner of software engineering. It is absolutely vital that designers are provided with the necessary tools and are capable of using them to the full. It is important for the designer to be aware of the features of such tools required specifically for real-time systems. This chapter considers the conventional tools in the light of the specific needs of such systems.

● It is important to distinguish between a host system on which the software is to be developed, and the target system on which the resulting object code is to be run. Sometimes these are one and the same system but, as we shall see, the development facilities available on target machines are not necessarily adequate for the job, resulting in the use of different machines for the two tasks. This in itself can also give rise to incompatibility problems related to the code being generated by one system being required to run on another, because of discrepancies in hardware and operating systems, often caused by incompatible versions.

● As a consequence, the operating system of the host may be quite different from that of the target system. Indeed, for very small target systems (for example, a washing machine) there will be no disc filing system and probably very little random access store. The software will reside in read only memory and run under a simple real-time executive. This will have been developed for the specific application or possibly reshaped from an earlier model. By contrast, the host development system will require a full-blooded operating system capable of running all of the software tools needed for the construction and testing of the end product.

8.1 CENTRALISED AND DISTRIBUTED SYSTEMS

Some systems are built around a single central system connected to the outside world with which it reacts. Although this will continue to some extent, it must be recognised that many such systems already have more than one processor. This arises from the ease with which a microprocessor can be introduced into a system to reduce both product cost and development time, and the advantages and flexibility of the consequent programmability. Often the microprocessor will be many times more powerful than is necessary, but the economics of the over-kill justify its inclusion. For example, consider a typical desk-top PC system, apparently based on one particular microprocessor chip. The system will probably include a floppy disc and Winchester hard disc controller implemented with a second processor; a third processor will handle the screen graphics, and a fourth will handle communications. Outside, the printer will have one or more processors to provide all of the smart features such as soft character set, bi-directional printing and proportional spacing. Here we see distributed processing in the hardware sense. The (single) user will expect several of his tasks to operate concurrently, such as screen functions, printing, keyboard interaction and perhaps an I/O task. It is clear that if such small machines can use multiprocessor systems, both local and distributed, then this is likely to be the case for real-time systems on a larger scale. This development has significant implications for the system software traditionally provided.

8.1.1 Operating Systems, Memory Management and File Handling

Various aspects of operating systems have already been introduced as they relate to the target system and its run-time needs. In particular, activities such as input/output, file and command handling were discussed in subsection 2.4.2; resource sharing, synchronisation, monitors, executive processes and system building were discussed in chapter 3 and scheduling in chapter 4. Here we concentrate on the development of the real-time software, and on some run-time aspects for distributed systems.

● Operating systems in the traditional sense will continue to be required for development work such as compilation, linking and loading, for conventional storage and file management, and for I/O functions. Additionally for real-time systems with distributed processing, a kernel is required for each processor to provide a local run-time environment, and which avoids unnecessary transfers of operating system code along transmission channels. The principal requirement of such a kernel is to provide synchronisation facilities. In particular, mutual exclusion must be provided so that a process must be sure that no other process may intervene during a critical set of actions — for example, when an instance of a shared process is saving its status. Secondly, a signalling system must be provided to allow processes to communicate at the control level — for example, buffer full when writing. Such a kernel should be simple, robust and not impose too many restrictions on the designer. It should also provide adequate performance without introducing high run-time overheads. Operating systems are often proprietary to a particular manufacturer's computer ranges, and therefore choice of hardware dictates choice of operating system which is not ideal. High-level languages are usually chosen independently of computer system, but operating systems less so because of the hardware involvement. However, decoupling aspects of operating systems from the hardware is an increasing trend and this and its multiprogramming features make UNIX a popular choice, but see chapter 12.

● Memory management is a feature of many operating systems. Distributed systems necessarily have local memory, and this is managed by the local kernel or monitor. What is required may be minimal in the sense that dynamic allocation may not be necessary. Indeed, some local systems may have the operating system kernel and user code modules implemented in read only memory (ROM) which affords complete protection against over-writing under fault conditions. However, to speed up development, user code may initially be run from RAM until fully tested (even though erasable ROMs (EPROMS) are available), as down-loading code from a host is usually quicker than erasing and blowing ROMs. The kernel must also support file access, even though file store may not be available locally. This should be transparent to the user, except for access times. It is useful, but not essential, that a local system have the capability of terminal access to other parts of the system and under fault conditions be capable of stand-alone operation, albeit with reduced performance in some areas.

● It is clearly possible that only user code resides in a dedicated local system. This feature is possible via code generated and down-loaded from a host, particularly where a language such as Ada is employed. However, it must be stressed that a common basic kernel is a highly desirable feature which will provide tested and reliable synchronisation and communication, even if some sacrifice of speed is made relative to application-specific alternatives. The latter should only be considered if all else fails, and this usually is the consequence of poor design at an earlier stage.

8.1.2 Compilers, Assemblers and Interpreters

We have seen in subsection 6.2.1 that the high-level language machine is one of several possible ways of implementing the real-time virtual machine. To do this we will require a compiler for the selected high-level language, and indeed if one of the other implementation methods is chosen, the code for this will need to be written in a high-level language.

● In a distributed system, compilers will reside in backing store in a host or file server. Copies may be run on other machines in the system, where appropriate, to support parallel development. For most real-time software development, it is essential to provide either a language which supports user-defined data typing and low-level facilities (see section 9.2), or a compatible relocatable assembler whose objects can be linked with compiled code. Specifically, any part of the system having special-purpose processors, to support signal processing or graphics for example, must have assembler support producing code that can also be linked. Structured design can sometimes produce top-level whose code comprises calls to lower-level modules. This type of code can be run under an interpreter since the time for interpretation is relatively short compared with the execution time of code modules. This is particularly true for array operations such as those found in signal processing. If the modules are fully tested, then compilation is unnecessary as the top level(s) will execute directly. This approach, although not always suitable, does make for fast development. Clearly, the type of interpreter provided for BASIC or FORTH language computers is unlikely to be of use in a real-time application (one should mention, in passing, that although compiled BASIC or FORTH may offer sufficient performance for some applications, the lack of real-time features may severely limit its usefulness).

8.2 ADDITIONAL FACILITIES

8.2.1 Libraries

● We have seen earlier that certain entities in our software systems — for example, the channels and pools of section 3.4 — are common to most applications. It would make sense then to have prototypes of such entities available from a library for inclusion into the system structure, without having to redesign these for each instance with the attendant potential for errors. Other examples of such generic entities might be basic procedures such as the queue operators of subsection 3.8.1, the real-time clock of subsection 4.2.1 and the watchdog timer of subsection 5.3.4.

Libraries contain frequently used self-contained code modules, and as such are useful features of most efficient software systems. Some compilers generate minimal applications code, relying heavily on run-time libraries for execution of different types of statements. Users will also generate procedures, functions and macros which if commonly required may also be consigned to a library function; these might include data acquisition, digital filtering and controllers of generic types, for example.

● Two basic problems arise in real-time work. If the code is not available on the local store, calls to library routines from file store or other processors result in delayed execution. Hence, copies of all required library routines must be available locally unless non-time critical processes are involved. Secondly, parallel operation in a single processor or in distributed processors with shared store may require calls to a particular library module from different processes. This can result in several processes having simultaneous access to a common run-time routine. Unless mutual exclusion is arranged, which itself may cause problems, corruption of variables and data is highly likely. The solution is to implement the routine as a pure procedure or generic program unit in parametric form. Instances are then created involving compile time parameters for each process. Support for such features is provided in modern real-time languages.

8.2.2 Debugging Aids

'Debugging aids' is a description of a loose collection of tools to aid the commissioning of software and systems. We have seen in section 5.1 the various ways in which the system may be tested and exercised to make sure that it operates correctly. In chapter 11 a rather different view is taken of the system operation, that of performance monitoring. It is clear that a significant overlap between these views exists. If testing indicates that the software operates correctly as designed, we may initially feel that this is satisfactory. However, we must then take the wider view of the performance requirements to determine whether further modification is necessary.

● Traditionally, these aids have been provided as a set of debugging tools at various levels. The lowest level, the hardware level, employs specialised equipment such as logic analysers or in-circuit emulators. Its main use is for time-critical hardware debugging and interaction with machine code program execution and debugging. This level is important to engineers and may have interaction with software faults at the lowest level. This is supported at the lowest level by monitors providing information at the register and memory location level, perhaps best implemented as a software front panel. Modification of registers and memory locations is necessary, along with insertion of breakpoints in the code.

Above this is the high-level language statement level. Here the user may monitor and interact with program variables.

● The next level is the operating system level, where a similar software front panel can be used to display data structures such as a RUNNABLE list or task control information. Task synchronisation and communication information may also be displayed, preferably symbolically. The use of windows to permit simultaneous display of concurrent activities is a useful feature.

At the application level, the user is only able to modify selected system parameters, such as constants in controllers.

● A better view of debugging is the provision of a complete environment, rather than a set of tools, to provide a logical approach to interactive debugging at various levels in the system, with logging of activity to provide a history of user interaction. Complex distributed systems usually require significant debugging in the early stages of implementation. Interactive system building involves loading and initialising modules and data structures, and activating tasks in various processors. During development, different versions of modules may be tested, often with simulated external system components to avoid damage and/or waste of time and materials. A kernel debugging system should reside in each processor, with overall control from a centralised source. Such a debugging system should have a powerful but simple command language, allowing extension to provide hooks into every level of software. In this way, tools specific to the system can be created and used as required, alongside the more general tools previously described.

8.2.3 Simulation Languages

Simulation is an important technique for system development (subsection 4.3.3), testing (section 5.1) and evaluation (section 11.1). Simulation can be used in many ways for real-time systems development. Firstly, in order to control a system it is essential to have a model of that system. This is obtained by using one of several system identification techniques from which a model is developed. The model is then verified and validated. This may now be studied with confidence and used to evaluate control strategies. The real-time software system can be interfaced to the model and tested before connection to the real world. This principle can be applied to parts of the external system as well as the whole. Indeed our modular software approach may also be applied to simulation.

● Given a model description, comprising probably both analytical and empirical elements, how do we create a software simulation of the model? The answer is to use one of the many simulation languages designed for just this purpose. These may be of two basic types. For simulation of continuous dynamic systems there are the continuous system simulation languages (CSSLs), such as CSSL IV and ACSL. For discrete event systems there are languages such as SIMSCRIPT (event scheduling) and SIMULA (process interaction). Of course, some systems have a combination of continuous and discrete event elements. If these can be separated into discrete and continuous modules, then the appropriate language can be selected. However, more complex approaches such as the COSMOS language allow combined continuous discrete models. In the modelling and evaluation phase it is essential to have fast interaction, and when complete the model must be able to communicate simply and reliably with the real-time software that we have been designing. The implication of this is that the code be linkable and runnable under the same operating system as the real-time software. A further feature of using simulation instead of the real external system is the ability to change the time scale. For example, a super-tanker navigation system will necessarily operate at very low speeds, with a course change taking many minutes to execute. A simulated tanker can be operated at, say, 10 or 100 times real-time to speed up testing and evaluation. A word of caution. If human interaction is involved, whether in control loops or simply monitoring operations, then no time scaling is feasible unless human modelling is permitted!

8.3 DEVELOPMENT ENVIRONMENTS

As we have seen, a wide range of software tools is required for the efficient production of reliable real-time software. In the past, such software has been developed using only basic and essential tools such as editors, compilers, operating systems and command languages. The tools required have tended to be isolated entities linked only by a common file system. As the amount of code required has increased with system complexity, the need for adequate support for software development has also increased. It is essential that an adequate development environment is provided on a suitable host.

8.3.1 Host Development Systems

● It is sometimes necessary to carry out development on the system which will run the resulting object code. This has the advantage of a common operating system, and down-loading of code to other processors in the system is fast and straightforward. However, target systems may well not be large enough to support software development properly. This is particularly true of distributed target systems, where computing power, main store and file store are divided between processors, resulting in no one processor having adequate resource. The processors of the system may of necessity be of different types, some of which may be unsuitable for software development because of their special-purpose nature. Even if one processor is large enough, suitable software tools may not be available on that processor.

A further complication may lie with inadequate provision of peripherals such as terminals and printing facilities, and of file store to support a team of system designers. Perhaps the most common example of the need for a separate host is where Ada is the language selected for software development. Ada requires a large amount of store in which to run the compiler, and this is further compounded by the need for parallel development of modules by a team. It is unlikely that the target system will include a processor capable of supporting an ADA compiler. Subsets of Ada should not be entertained since, as we shall see, many of the facilities provided in the full implementation are distinctly advantageous for real-time systems. Subsets inevitably lose some of these and can also give rise to compatibility problems.

● Of course, a host does not necessarily have to be a single large processor. Several processors connected by a network, or a network of work stations supported by a file server, can be just as effective, perhaps even more so. The principal requirement is for a common database.

8.3.2 The Support Environment

We have seen in chapter 6 that the design process has many phases. If these are developed and progressed in an ordered way by means of an integrated software support system, then the resulting application will acquire fewer errors on the way, be much more controllable in a team situation, and will more quickly come to a successful conclusion.

● The starting point of any project is the requirements specification and the end point runnable correct code — the delivered system. In between there are several levels of representation of increasing complexity and precision. Between levels transformations are required, usually involving added knowledge. The first requirement for support is a database management system, through which the entire system may be developed, modified, configured and monitored. Access to the design database is required for several purposes and at many levels. Source code is only one form in which information is represented and stored. The availability of bit-mapped graphic systems makes possible representation of information at various levels in terms of block and structure diagrams, graphs and trees. For example, both the ACP

(Activity, Channel, Pool) diagrams illustrated earlier and data structures can be screened. Such graphical representations require suitable editors for creation and modification via menus and mice, and also for creating the data structures necessary for the storage of such information in forms which are accessible by other structures and not just convenient for display purposes.

● An essential part of any program development system is, of course, an editor in the textual sense. Many existing editors have limited facilities and are difficult and frustrating to use. This is especially true of some of the smaller microprocessor-based systems. A temporary solution is to use a word processor which produces a text source code file compatible with the operating system under which the compiler is run. Word processors are powerful text editors and are easy to use. They have some facilities which are not relevant to code input and editing, but these can be ignored. All such editors allow input which violates the syntax of the programming language, leaving errors to be detected during the compiler syntax analysis phase. More recent developments include language-oriented editors and structure editors. The former restrict the choice of input to that which confirms to the correct syntax of the chosen language. The latter are more general and provide considerable help in developing the structures required of the code, in addition to restricting the possible input to syntactically correct forms. A simple Pascal fragment illustrates this:

```
    Program filter (input, output, parameter);
begin
{Statement}
 repeat {Statement} until {Condition};
end
```

---

begin if case repeat while for with call ◊   (◊ = cursor)

● This would appear in a text window. The text in the brackets { } is the name of a syntactic class and represents a hole for the user to fill in later, thus allowing him to create the structure without initially worrying about some of the details. The editor may also allow display of condensed forms, again supporting the structural view of the code. The menu restricts the user's options when expanding the syntactic class of the hole pointed to by the cursor. Nested windows and window managers are useful features for examining and modifying code and structure. Such techniques support good programming style and inherently lead to more reliable software production at source.

● At an early stage of development, application of formal methods can save much subsequent wasted time and effort. Formal verification can be used to show that a program satisfies a formal specification. Formal methods lead to correct programs and consequent reliability. It is desirable to speed up development to make use of existing code modules developed for other parts of the system or from earlier systems. The concept of re-usable code is a good one but difficult to achieve in practice. Great care must be taken when doing so. It is a temptation to assume a correct piece of code will operate correctly in its new environment.

● Complex software systems require considerable management to keep control of their development. A *history manager* may be used to maintain source versions and histories. Frequently, a working module is 'improved' to produce a non-working version, resulting in a desire to return to an earlier version. A *change manager* records changes made anywhere in the system and provides a means of planning and tracking the consequences for other modules. A *monitor manager* notifies users when particular modules are changed. Finally, a *configuration manager* is used to build programs from specified module versions. It will also record source versions used in a particular program version or release.

● MASCOT, a Modular Approach to Software Construction Operation and Test can be described as an early example of a support environment for real-time (parallel processing) systems. It provides a formal methodology for expressing software structures which are represented diagrammatically (ACP diagrams), independently of computer configuration and programming language, as previously illustrated in section 2.2 and subsection 6.1.5.1. It supports all aspects of the software life cycle, including design, implementation, test, documentation and maintenance. It can be implemented on a bare machine to provide the kernel executive which is compact and efficient, and can be implemented on top of an existing operating system or be fully integrated. The current version (MASCOT 3) has overcome the shortcomings of earlier versions, in that it copes with large systems and multiprocessor targets. It allows both decomposition of structure and grouping of structures into subsystems, and has an improved communication model.

Some of these techniques are still in the development phase. They are grouped under the general heading of integrated project support environments, IPSEs (McDermid, 1985).

● Just as it is clear that no one programming language is suitable for every application area, then it is likely that no one support environment will emerge as being appropriate for all applications. The designer must elect to choose the support environment in relation to several aspects of his anticipated application. Cost and size of the development will dictate the affordability of such a system if one is not already available. He must also consider — Is the application stand-alone or embedded? Is the target system likely to include distributed processors and/or special-purpose processors? Is the application data or processing intensive? Is the application time critical? and so on.

8.4 SUMMARY

In this chapter we have looked at some of the tools and facilities needed to implement our designs and how to manage the complexity. Host development and target systems are introduced in relation to the differing needs of the two types of system in many applications. Some specific advantages and problems of distributed systems as they relate to real-time systems have also been discussed. The part that simulation plays in modelling, developing and testing of real-time systems cannot be under-estimated. The time and cost savings resulting from the use of simulation can be immense, and the consequences of attempting to use faulty or unreliable software to control the real world can be disastrous. Simulation languages provide the best method of quickly achieving successful simulation, and are to be preferred to standard high-level languages.

Concepts

Distributed systems; generic libraries; operating system kernels; software front panel; simulation; support environments.

9   High-level Languages

In section 6.2 we saw that the high-level language machine was an important way of implementing a process virtual machine. Here we look specifically at high-level languages in some detail to ascertain their suitability for our purpose. Many such languages are used for real-time applications. Often, for a particular organisation, the choice is determined by past investment in support for particular languages. Until the early 1980s, most available languages exhibited a considerable lack of facilities to support this important application area. This chapter first examines the requirements for real-time systems, and then considers three rather different real-time languages.

9.1   REAL-TIME FEATURES

9.1.1 Modules and Separate Compilation

Essential to all large software projects is program structure. Means for implementing such structure are features of several real-time languages, but each tends to use a different set of names for describing these features. Such structure has two dimensions. The first is spatial and concerns the decomposition of a process into entities of a manageable size, the structures which link these and the relationships to the problem to be solved. The second is temporal and concerns decomposition of a complex problem into a number of smaller parallel or quasi-parallel processes running at the same time.

9.1.1.1 Spatial Decomposition

This has at its lowest level the subprogram (that is, a function or procedure). These have three important aspects:

● (1)   A specification of the subprogram interfaces.
   (2)   The description in detail of the action(s) to be carried out.
   (3)   How that action may be called.

182

A subprogram contains two essential parts: a definition or specification part, and an implementation part or body. The specification part gives the name of the subprogram, what effect it will have and the parameters it requires. The implementation part has the detailed code for the action required when the subprogram is called. The two parts may be separate or associated and may be compiled separately. How the subprogram is called is a function of the language in which it is implemented. A subprogram may be large enough to be regarded as a separate module, but is usually small and consequently easy to understand.

● The next level is the module, which includes one or more subprograms. The overall structure is similar to the subprogram. However, the specification part must include the specifications of each subprogram. Thus we have the concept of separating the use of a facility from its provision which allows the program to exhibit what is desired without being cluttered by implementation detail. A module does not necessarily have an implementation part. The specifications of the subprograms provide all the information required to call them. A module may then be called in another part of the program; indeed, modules may be nested, thus providing upper levels of structure and hence a means for both writing and understanding complex software.

● Often a particular program unit is required in several places in a program. Sometimes such a unit has already been written for a previous version or project. Re-use of such units is obviously desirable for efficiency. Such a program unit could be written directly, involving the actual parameters used for the required purpose. When such a piece of code is required elsewhere it must be modified for that purpose before use. Alternatively, the program unit may be written with separate specification and execution parts. The specification part is a more general style and the execution part may be tailored for a specific application. The most general and useful approach is to write the program unit entirely in parametric form. This form is not directly executable, but requires substitution at compile time of the actual parameters of the instance. Many such instances may be created of the same general form, providing similar but not necessarily identical actions. Such *generic* forms are created and stored as library units. Some examples of useful generic units might be

General computation:	input/output handler; stack manipulator; queue handler.
Real-time systems:	MASCOT pool; IIR digital filter; PID controller; timer; data acquisition.

● Separate compilation is desirable for a number of reasons. The most obvious is the consequence of a single minor change in a subprogram requiring re-compilation of the entire program. When a large system is involved, individual modules can be compiled and tested prior to incorporation in the system. During development, modules will undergo a number of revisions and have optional versions or require replacement. Separate compilation permits re-compilation of only the affected parts of the system. At any time a system may be configured from defined versions of its parts to produce a current variant which can then be mapped onto the hardware. Clearly, sometimes modifications are only internal to a module and do not affect its interface. Often this is not the case, and then the compiler needs to know which other modules are affected.

● This leads us to consider the *scope of visibility*. A variable local to a subprogram or module should be invisible outside of that program unit. This is important where different members of a team use the same name for different variables without the need to inform each other. Unique names are, of course, essential outside of this scope, and the compiler must carry out module interface consistency checking. A language therefore needs rules for determining the visibility of declarations. Recompilation must be carried out in a carefully defined order. Specifically, if a parent unit is changed, all subunits must be recompiled. If a library unit is changed, then every unit referencing this must be recompiled, and if a program unit specification is changed its implementation part must also be recompiled.

9.1.1.2 Temporal Decomposition

Embedded computer systems — that is those in which the computer hardware and software are embedded inside a larger system involving other components — are usually required to have many activities occurring simultaneously. Several sequential strands of program activity may be identified which can run in parallel. Such strands may be called concurrent processes or tasks, and may run on a single processor by time sharing these activities or be distributed among several processors which actually execute in parallel, or even some combination of these. This is a simplistic view, however, since most processes do not run in isolation and therefore need to communicate with one another. This leads us naturally to the topic of concurrency.

9.1.2 Concurrency

● Concurrency concerns the problem of providing reliable synchronisation and communication between parallel processes. The problem exhibits some subtle features which, if not implemented satisfactorily, can lead to disaster. Two important features are needed to allow parallel operation to occur, and these are necessarily independent of any parallel hardware provision. The first is the use of shared variables and resources. In principle, this appears to be simple. In practice, two processes, which, for example, expect to see the same value of a shared variable at a particular time or under defined circumstances, cannot always be guaranteed to do so unless special provision is made, since timing and circumstances are usually data-dependent. Secondly, co-operating processes need to communicate with each other using signals. After completing a particular action, a process may wish to communicate a result to another process. The receiving process may either not be ready to receive this result or may already have passed the point where the result was needed unless synchronisation has been arranged by some signalling method. Features are clearly desirable in any language selected for concurrent programming to allow such provision to be made in a well-structured and easily comprehensible way. Different languages have various features to support implementation of such synchronisation.

9.1.2.1 *Mutual Exclusion*

● Concurrent processes normally need to communicate with one another. Fortunately, it is usually possible to arrange that such communication is based on loose coupling, and consequently each process spends most of its time not involved in mutual activities. It is possible then to consider the structure of a process in terms of critical and non-critical parts. Before entering a critical section, a process must execute instructions to establish the right to enter the critical section and exclude all other processes. On leaving that section it must execute further instructions to indicate to other processes that it is relinquishing its right to exclude them. Note that the pre-protocols and post-protocols must also be considered critical, since failure to complete these protocols exclusively will lead to severe problems.

A simple, well-known example is the 'return from interrupt' instruction at the end of an interrupt service routine for a system with a single level of interrupt. The problem is that the two instructions 'interrupt enable' and 'return from interrupt' should be executed without interruption to avoid a possible loss of control of the stack. This is usually avoided by the hardware delaying the execution of 'interrupt enable' by one instruction.

● Returning to the general discussion of mutual exclusion, the non-critical parts of processes can be run in parallel by interleaving. If a process terminates unexpectedly because of incorrect code or external device failure, then this should not cause the system to fail. It is likely that the critical sections are exercised often and consequently will be tested in practice, resulting in few if any errors. The non-critical code of a particular process can, if precautions are taken, be organised to promote recovery from error conditions.

● 'Correctness' is a feature that assumes greater importance in concurrent programming and especially in real-time systems. There are two aspects of this which are important. The first is that the real-time software must never halt. Whatever situation arises, the program must continue to execute to allow some processes to continue normally and others to be temporarily suspended pending detection, isolation and correction of the problem(s). The second concerns that response to action requests. This splits into two further areas. One is to ensure that if an action is supposed to happen, then eventually it will. The other is to ensure that all processes get a fair share of the action in relation to their needs and response times. It is vital to ensure that the situation known as deadlock does not occur. There are many descriptions of this phenomenon. Not all such situations are concerned with time or indeed computing. Deadlock does occasionally arise with small specialist publishers when dealing with institutional customers. The institution will not send cash with order but requires either a delivery note and invoice or a pro-forma invoice. The publisher will neither send the book without prepayment nor issue pro-forma invoices.

How then is mutual exclusion arranged? This depends to some extent on the language being employed. Some of the more recent languages specifically include concurrent programming constructs. If this is not the case then such constructs should be provided as library procedures. Early attempts at correct solutions to the mutual exclusion problem lead to fairly complicated solutions. Dijkstra introduced the semaphore which considerably simplifies the solution and consequently leads to better understanding. This was introduced in subsection 3.3.1. The essence of the semaphore is that in one primitive instruction both the testing and setting of the flag are carried out, thus avoiding the consequence of the flag being changed between testing and use. The semaphore s is a positive integer variable which after initialisation can only be operated on by the procedures *wait(s)* and *signal(s)*, defined as follows:

wait(s):   If $s > 0$ then $s := s - 1$ else the process that called *wait(s)* is suspended

signals(s):   If process p is suspended by a previous *wait(s)* on this s then wake up p else $s := s + 1$

A semaphore may be a binary semaphore (values 0 or 1) or a general semaphore (any positive integer) for the case where more than one resource may run parallel critical sections. The code illustrating the structure for two processes might look like:

```
program conprocesses;
var s: {binary} semaphore;
procedure process1;
begin
  repeat
    wait(s);
    critical1;
    signal(s);
    noncritical1;
  forever
end;
procedure process2;
begin
  repeat
    wait(s);
    critical2;
    signal(s);
    noncritical2;
  forever
end;
begin
  s := 1;
  cobegin
    process1;process2
  coend
end.
```

● The main program at the end employs the concurrency constructs **cobegin** and **coend** to start and terminate the two concurrent processes. A disadvantage of the semaphore system is the problem arising from a single omission of a *signal* releasing mutual exclusion and causing a lockout. A second disadvantage is the needless looping and re-testing associated with suspended processes. A safer, more-structured solution to the mutual exclusion problem is the monitor discussed earlier in section 3.5. Once a monitor is correct it will be correct for every instance used by every process. The users of the monitor only call a procedure and all monitor variables are only visible within that monitor.
● Remember that a monitor comprises three parts: a set of global declarations; a set of procedures; and a body which initialises the monitor variables. The latter is executed on entry, leaving the monitor as a static object whose procedures are called by processes as required. In this way exclusion is guaranteed, because all critical (shared) activity

has to be via the single controlling monitor. Consider again our
two-process system:

```
program monitor;
{monitor variable declarations}
procedure critical (x: integer)
  begin
    if {condition1} then "wait"
    {critical body}
    if {condition2} then "signal"
  end;
  begin {monitor body}
  {initial values of monitor variables}
  end.


program conprocesses;
procedure process1;
var x: integer
begin
  repeat
    critical (x)
    noncritical1;
  forever
end;
procedure process2;
var x: integer
begin
  repeat
    critical (x)
    noncritical2;
  forever
end;
begin
  cobegin
    process1;process2
  coend
end.
```

Note that we now have two programs, but only the second is active
and it is this that has two concurrent processes. The monitor program
has a pair of wait-signal commands and these are now embedded in
conditional statements. These are needed for synchronisation but are
not the same as semaphore commands, being defined for monitors:

c	a *condition* variable
wait (c)	The calling process is blocked and is put onto a FIFO queue with other processes blocked on this condition.
signal (c)	If the queue is not empty then wake the first process on the queue.

● To ensure that the signalling process leaves the monitor immediately after the signal, it is necessary to allow only one signal and to put this as the last statement in the procedure. Note that if a process is blocked waiting for c to occur, then wait(c) releases the mutual exclusion to allow c to occur as a result of some other process, thus avoiding deadlock. A further arrangement has to be made to ensure that, on signalling c, the first process on the queue is executed rather than a procedure call from a new process, which may itself change c. To complete the monitor, declarations of the conditions must be made.

9.1.2.2 The Rendezvous

● The above techniques provide a restricted but useful introduction to mutual exclusion and synchronisation. They are, however, only suitable for single processor systems or systems with a common store. Distributed systems *may* only be connected by means of messages sent one to another, and there may be no synchronisation between sending and receiving messages. The previous methods have co-operating sequential processes as distinct from communicating sequential processes. Hoare (1978) suggested the *rendezvous* technique. The basic idea is to achieve an information transfer at a pre-determined point in each process. It does not matter which process arrives at the rendezvous first, it simply has to wait until the other process arrives to complete the rendezvous. The alternative is to use a message system (subsection 7.3.4) with buffers at each site. The process calling for the rendezvous does so by executing an *entry* call statement (Ada terminology). The process providing service makes the rendezvous when it reaches an *accept* statement, indicating that it is ready for the rendezvous. The rendezvous is in operation when both processes reach their respective entry and accept statements, irrespective of which arrives first, and continues in operation until completion of the body of the accept construct. The calling process is blocked until the completion of the rendezvous, preventing if from changing the values of any parameters during this time. Thus the body of the accept construct is the mechanism within which information may be exchanged. More than one process may call the same entry; the first to arrive is accepted and since normally the accept process contains a loop, entry calls are dealt with in orders of their arrival. To avoid wasting time and/or to avoid failure, the *select* construct provides for alternative actions. The calling process may have, to avoid time-wasting, an alternative action while waiting for the rendezvous, and for failure recovery the entry call perhaps has a time-out alternative to avoid waiting indefinitely. Similarly, for the service process the select construct provides for conditional alternatives at rendezvous. It is clear that such a construct allows recovery from the situation where a process has been discontinued for some reason, usually because a fault has been detected, perhaps as the result of a particular exception being encountered. Aspects of concurrent programming are well presented by Ben-Ari (1982) and Pyle (1985).

9.1.3 Exception Handling

●   In spite of verifying and testing programs, there may be times when a program meets with unexpected situations. When these arise the system should cope with them in such a way as to allow normal operation to continue. Such exceptions to normal program execution usually occur in situations not intended to arise. Things which cannot happen have a surprising knack of occurring in slightly different circumstances to those envisaged. A good way of looking at what faults may occur and consequently how recovery may take place is the 'what-if?' approach. Some such exceptions are sometimes provided for in hardware — for example fixed point overflow having a limiting rather than end-around effect — and some may be provided for in the system software — for example, array bound checks. Some may have optional implementation via hardware flags — for example, V (overflow) and C (carry) flags in a status word. In embedded systems, exceptions may arise from external conditions requiring alternative programming or action. An interesting case was the hole which appeared in the star mapper of the GIOTTO satellite during its close encounter with Halley's comet. This allowed the sun to be seen and prevented re-acquisition of the correct attitude. Alternative star patterns had to be sought which avoided this problem and allowed experimental data to continue to be sent to earth. An exception must be detected and subsequently cause normal operation to be suspended in favour of executing an exception handler which allows return to normal operation.

Examples of types of exceptions which may arise and allow recovery are:

(1)   Pre-defined: storage error; numeric error;
                            communication error

(2) User-defined (internal):   range error; rate error; timing error
(3) User-defined (external):   no paper; low pressure; no movement

● Some operating systems automatically halt on, for example, a disc error or floating point overflow error, thus not allowing the software designer to implement error-recovery mechanisms without trapping these and/or modifying the operating system. In order to prevent a real-time system from stopping, it is desirable to adopt a fault-tolerant or defensive approach to design. Only Ada expressly includes facilities for implementing such an approach within the language, but this should not prevent measures being taken in any chosen implementation language. The basic principles are fairly straightforward. Implementing them in a way which guarantees uninterrupted functionality is less so. One has to think of all the possible ways in which a system may fail and defend the programs against all such eventualities. Clearly this is likely to result in unacceptably slow execution from an over-sized store. Nevertheless, some likely faults can both be detected and recovery guaranteed. An important feature is clearly to limit the effect of an error to the locality in which it occurred, to avoid affecting other processes. Secondly, temporary errors such as transient over-range can be accepted by employing a limit system and reporting the occurrence. Other errors, such as low supply level, can simply be reported and do not become serious until supply is actually exhausted. Optionally, alternative action may be taken to reduce the level of consumption until adequate supply is restored. Absence of supply does not necessarily imply a catastrophe if the process is not time-critical. For example, no paper can be signalled for a printer and the print job held until supply is restored. The same is not true for low fuel reported on an aircraft flight.
● Two mechanisms are required. The first is *raising* an exception when, for example, a module may attempt operation for a certain time, fail to receive a response, and consequently indicate that a fault has occurred. The second is *detection* of an exception such as a value out of range, and reporting it immediately. Then, as a result of an exception arising, an *exception handler* is called to carry out recovery action so that execution may continue. Detection of exceptions inevitably gives rise to an overhead. However, exception handlers do not, unless they are called, when an additional overhead is tolerable. This ensures that significant performance is only lost when necessary, that is under fault conditions.

9.1.4 Data Types and Data Abstraction

In subsection 6.1.7 we encountered the need for data abstraction and data structure design. In this section we look at the sort of provision desirable in high-level languages to support this. Early real-time languages such as CORAL were based on Algol 60 and continued the tradition of not having strong data typing. Pascal was the first to exhibit strong data typing and the later languages MODULA-2 and Ada, having Pascal in their ancestry, continue this trend. The consequence of strong data typing is that the types of all data values are checked for consistency with their use in the program, which gives a powerful means of detecting mistakes when programs are written and later modified. Strong data typing also implies a richness of available data types, each designed to fulfil a range of uses. Real-time languages have special needs in this respect because of their heavy involvement with the outside world. Historically, integers and reals have sufficed, leaving the user to struggle with many problems. More recently, additional types have been included, making life much more pleasant.

The *enumeration* type is used to represent data that otherwise needs to be coded as a set of numbers:

> **type**
>   days = (mon, tues, wed, thu, fri, sat, sun)
>   ScreenColours = (black, red, green, blue, cyan, magenta, yellow, white)

● The *subrange* type is used in preference to the standard type to improve the readability and security of programs. The reduction in cardinality may also save storage space and minimise the cost of run-time checks.

> **type**
>   Working Day = (mon .. fri)
>   ADCchannel = (0 .. 7)
>   RamPosition = (−1024 .. +1023)

● Note that such types are user defined and are an abstraction of the values used to represent them in the machine; the programmer need not be aware of the detail of the latter. Fixed point variables may be implemented in this way in some languages without explicitly assuming a particular word length or format. This flexibility is useful for input/output modules involving mixes of word lengths. Certain data structures are supported explicitly as types constructed from base types. It must be pointed out that provision varies from one language to another.

The *set* is a useful structure for storing and manipulating booleans and has associated operators such as union, difference, intersection, and inclusion and equality.

type
    colour = **set of** ScreenColours; {previously declared}
var
    colour, background, graphics, text

Allowing

    background := [yellow]
    graphics   := [red, cyan, green, magenta]
    text   := [blue, black]

The *array* is so well known that it is not presented, but the special case of an array of characters (the string) may be used as a string variable, but note that the string must be of finite maximum length to allow for storage allocation, and this may be inefficient in some applications.

The *record* is worth mentioning for its application, and records with variants. Consider a data acquisition record:

    samples =
      record
        Ch1PitchFinAngle : angle;
        Ch2YawFinAngle : angle;
        Ch3RollFinAngle : angle;
        Ch4Status : integer;
        Ch5Fuel : real;
        Ch6Alarm : char
      end.

Note the mix of types and the use of 'angle', which may be declared as a subrange type. Each sample period may not involve all channels. For example, fuel, alarm and status need not be sampled every time fin angles are measured. For this situation we need a structure with a variable number of records conditional on a variable — a record with variant parts:

    samples =
      record
        case sampling : rate of
        fast :
          (Ch1PitchFinAngle : angle;
           Ch2YawFinAngle : angle;
           Ch3RollFinAngle : angle);

```
slow :
    (Ch1PitchFinAngle : angle;
     Ch2YawFinAngle : angle;
     Ch3RollFinAngle : angle;
     Ch4Status : integer;
     Ch5Fuel : real;
     Ch6Alarm : char)
end.
```

The final data structure is the *sequence*, used extensively, but not exclusively, for serial files and I/O. It appears to have the structure of an array in that it comprises elements of the same type, but the essential difference is that the number of elements of an array is fixed by its declaration, whereas the sequence is left open, having a length which may vary up to a maximum length during execution.

The operations on a sequence are:

rewrite(s) or open(s) which defines an empty sequence.

write(s,x) which appends an element x to sequence s.

read (s,x) which assigns the value of the element at the current position to the variable x and increments the sequence pointer.

reset(s) which resets the pointer to the beginning of s.

Such a type is useful for distributed systems where serial transfer may be the only means of communication between processors.

9.1.5 Initialisation

Because embedded computer systems are controlling external hardware, it is essential to initialise data items properly, whether these are individual items or parts of larger structures. Failure to do this can, on commencement of live operation, cause at best unpleasant transients and at worst failure of the software and subsequently of the system. Consider, for example, an aircraft autopilot switched in from manual during a flight. A violent manoeuvre (transient) arising from incorrect initial conditions relative to the current state of the external system is both unnecessary and uncomfortable to the passengers and crew. Selection of a blind landing system close to an airport in poor weather conditions is a case where such transients are totally unacceptable!

● We need to consider several different aspects of initialisation. First, consider variables. Some should be initialised uniquely, perhaps to zero or some other constant. Others which are derived from a set of these do not require initial values as they are always calculated as required. Others may require calculation from external inputs or other data via additional expressions explicitly included in the code for this purpose. Still others may have keyboard input following screen requests, with default values. Second, consider data structures such as arrays and records. There are two points here: the data items themselves may require a set of initial values and the variables pointing to these structures must point at either a specific item or at least to some item in the structure. The latter are very important because the pointers are reference variables and incorrect initialisation can lead to catastrophic failure.

9.1.6 Low-level Input/Output

● Embedded computer systems are concerned not only with conventional peripherals, such as VDUs, printers and backing stores, but also with on-line instrumentation for control and monitoring and with communication links. Input/output for the latter classes is concerned with data buffer registers, status and control. Such input/output is necessarily machine-dependent. The aim is confine this dependency locally to allow the use of data structures and code modules from libraries as close as possible to the devices. Where possible, a module may have a high-level specification part and a low-level body, with the former having the common interface. The low-level body has to deal with several aspects of the hardware interface to the external system. Specifically, data items will often require type conversion, variables must be assigned specific addresses, and parameter passing may require implementation via a hardware stack in the hardware interface. Packing and unpacking of data, status and control words are often necessary. Many of these operations are difficult, tedious, inefficient or too slow when implemented in a high-level language, and are hence often coded in assembler which must then be linked to the specification part of the module. Earlier languages tended to ignore input/output on the basis that only conventional peripherals were envisaged and these would be interfaced by the operating system designer and not by application programmers. More recent languages exhibit features specifically designed to assist in this awkward area. Of some importance in this area is type conversion for basic data types, which allows conversion between internal values and the values used at the interface to external hardware.

9.1.7 Screen I/O and Graphics

First, consider normal text output to a screen. This facility has been in use for a long time and is achieved by using a standard serial channel directed to a screen or printer as specified by the user via the input/output part of the operating system. Only the screen and printer handlers require special code which is hardware-dependent. Similar arrangements apply to keyboard and mouse inputs. These arrangements, while making standard screen I/O easy to use, arise because most languages do not cater for special I/O, on the assumption that the operating system will fulfil all forseeable needs. Only a few modern languages recognise the need for such I/O, and make either specific provision or have additional language constructs which may be used for this (and other) purposes. Modern text representation includes several features which make it desirable for users to be able to define the display. First, the text has attributes associated with characters, words or lines. These include the traditional underline, inverse video and flashing attributes, but may also include foreground text colour. Second, the text may be formatted to highlight source code structure, such as indentation to emphasise control structure and colour to highlight keywords. This should be written in high-level code, but the language may not support interpretation to the text processor. Similar considerations apply to generation and use of windows and menus.

Graphics requires data representation that is inherently non-sequential. For example, consider a raster scan graphics system (that is one employing a television type screen) where a line is to be drawn at an angle to the horizontal. The data supplied to the screen requires splitting into pixels belonging to different lines, and must be supplied to the screen in an ordered but non-sequential way. Similar considerations apply to figures and pictures.

Several sequences of output data need to be sent to the screen independently and concurrently. The screen is used to display several overlaid pictures, each having its own positional information relative to the datum of the full screen. Both horizontal and vertical scrolling of text and graphics are required. Some subpictures may also be zoom written or read. Where support for such graphics is by means of a graphics display controller the language requirements are less demanding, but many existing small OEM (Original Equipment Manufacturer) machines likely to be used for local real-time controllers do not include these controllers, leaving any graphics facilities to be implemented in software. Basic procedures including dot, line, area fill, etc., can be written and subsequently called by modules defining more complex objects. Similarly, menu and window managers can be provided for user screen support.

9.2 SOME REAL-TIME HIGH-LEVEL LANGUAGES

It will be appreciated that it requires a book to define and describe a language, and several additional books of examples and applications to illustrate its use.

The purpose of this section is to briefly discuss three real-time high-level languages on the basis of their differences and special features. Many languages do not have comprehensive input/output facilities and these include several that have been specifically designed for real-time applications. Perhaps this indicates that input/output is not yet well-understood by language designers. Such an absence can be justified in general-purpose systems where these problems are relegated to the operating system designer, but it cannot be ignored in real-time systems where control and monitoring of external systems is required and in distributed systems where communication between distributed components is a central consideration.

9.2.1 CORAL 66

As its name suggests, this language has been around for sometime and derives from ALGOL 60. As a consequence it lacks strong data typing, now considered so important, especially for real-time work. It does, however, feature a FIXED type in which the programmer may declare the total number of bits and the number of fractional bits for fixed point non-integer representation. Where mixed types are used, Numbertype (Expression) can be used to define the form of the result of evaluating the mixed type expression inside the brackets. OCTAL may be used to represent bit patterns for masking or direct representation of bits or characters. String-handling facilities are poorly supported and are mainly intended for sending messages.

The only data structures specifically implemented in the language are the types ARRAY, which may only contain elements of the same type, and TABLE which is a special form of array in which the user specifies the number of words per entry and the total number of entries. Compilers are not required to check index values used when an array is addressed!

Control constructs include the now unpopular unconditional GOTO Label or Switch.

The conditional expressions include

IF Condition THEN Expression ELSE Expression;
FOR Expression WHILE Condition DO Statement (condition
    optional);
FOR Initial Value STEP Increment UNTIL Final Value.

The latter, if used with non-integer steps may have unpredictable results.

Separate compilation is permitted with communicators for different segments to use the same variables. The most frequently used is the COMMON communicator. This makes variables whose full definition is given somewhere in the program available to all segments. The scope of other variables is limited to the blocks (and sub-blocks) in which they are declared. LIBRARY communicators refer to objects whose definition is known to the compiler via the procedure library and objects fixed somewhere in the hardware, such as an interface, are referred to using ABSOLUTE or EXTERNAL. OVERLAY declarations are allowed which hint at storage being in short supply, a feature rarely required now.

Pre-setting is supported, but only within the scope rules. Thus it is possible to initialise constants, variables, pointers and arrays. Pre-setting is not dynamic, implying a restart if a program terminates and is then re-run. Machine code may be inserted (with care), but the only construct provided is

CODE BEGIN Codesequence END

and any storage used must be declared as EXTERNAL.

Bit manipulation may be done using BITS with parameters *Totalbits* to indicate a width from an (integer) word starting at a *Bitposition*. DIFFER, UNION and MASK are the logical operations allowed on integers. No specific provision is made for type conversion.

There is no specific support for concurrency, exception handling, input/output, screen I/O, graphics or distributed processing.

9.2.2 MODULA-2

MODULA emerged from experiments in multiprogramming (Wirth, 1977), and is descended from Pascal. MODULA-2 (Wirth, 1982), a derivative of MODULA, is a language which embraces all of the aspects of Pascal and is extended to include both the module concept and multiprogramming. We now briefly discuss the language's main additions with respect to Pascal.

The *module* concept encourages structure in program design. Programs are made up of modules which may contain subsidiary modules. Each module may contain constants, types, variables and procedures. Objects declared in modules may be local to that module and therefore invisible outside of that module. Objects may be *imported* from other modules or *exported* to other modules, thus supporting the concept of abstraction on a hierarchical basis, by removing the need to know details of the implementation of imported objects. The modules can be kept in a library of separately compiled modules which, upon loading, are linked via imported objects to those descriptions to which the compiler has access. This has a strong influence on the decoupling of modules, a feature which is further enhanced by separating the essentials from the implementation details which are to be hidden. Thus, a module comprises a *definition part* and an *implementation part*, and objects which are visible outside of the module are explicitly declared in an export list in the definition part.

The language is organised syntactically so that every keyword at the start of a structure has an associated keyword to end that structure. This assists with understanding source code and helps to support structure editors.

As with Pascal, strong data typing is a feature of MODULA-2. Simple types include enumeration and subrange types, as discussed above. Data structure is supported by ARRAY, SET and RECORD types, with the latter including variant parts. Arbitrary dynamic data structures may be implemented via the POINTER type, in which the type of variable pointed to is specified in the pointer type's declaration. Such variables may themselves contain pointers, which indicate the path to defining recursive data structures such as trees and lists. An advanced type found in the language is the PROCEDURE type, whose use is beyond the scope of this book, but its mention may provide food for thought!

Initialisation is achieved by assigning literals. Care must be taken with the scope of variables and to initialise appropriately by considering the import and export lists of the modules concerned.

Multiprogramming is specifically supported for loosely coupled processes — that is, concurrent processes that interact relatively infrequently, on a conventional single processor computer. This is achieved by time sharing the single processor, synchronised using WAIT and SIGNAL procedures on semaphores, implemented in a module *Processes*. The processes then communicate by shared variables and signals implemented in a monitor as the most likely option for guaranteeing mutual exclusion. Thus, such processes are coroutines executing quasi-concurrently, with the switching between processes by a call to a TRANSFER procedure.

To extend the concept to distributed processors requires the implementation of communications systems between these processors, perhaps using messages. In this way genuine concurrency will occur because of the parallel hardware, and quasi-parallel operation can occur by time sharing in each processor. Genuine concurrency may still occur in a 'single' processor system by employing parallel hardware as a peripheral operating under interrupt control, similar to conventional peripherals such as intelligent printers and terminals. Concurrent peripheral processes may be initialised from a normal module, and control transferred to other quasi-concurrent modules as described above. Such peripheral processes then communicate by interrupting the main processor using an IOTRANSFER procedure. The latter is necessarily machine-specific, relating to the particular interrupt vectoring system and device-specific registers and/or fixed storage addresses. The rendezvous technique is not supported in MODULA-2.

The remaining essential new features of MODULA-2 concern the low-level facilities. We have already recognised the need for software interfaces to specific peripherals — that is, data acquisition systems, fast signal processors, and general processors communicating with different forms of data structures to those found in MODULA-2. To achieve this, type indentifiers may be used as function identifiers to denote a type transfer function; for example, INTEGER(x) where the value of expression x, of type CARDINAL, is mapped into its corresponding value of type INTEGER. Such correspondence is defined from system-dependent information and not by the language. Two additional basic types exist. The first is WORD, used to assign a number of bits to a data representation. Data of type WORD may only be operated on after use of a type transfer function, as data of type WORD is not interpreted. The other basic type is ADDRESS, used to denote values used as addresses for words. Values of type ADDRESS are assigned as a *pointer type* — that is, used to establish dynamic relations between the static elements of data structures. Arithmetic operations are made on operands of type ADDRESS as though they were of type CARDINAL, thereby allowing pointers to external storage to be manipulated within the language. It must be emphasised that such facilities allow breaking of the strict type consistency rules of the language, which circumvents the compiler's type checking and the protection that this affords.

Screen I/O and graphics provision are described by Wirth (1982), assuming point plotting and raster scan display. This will be relatively slow but highly flexible. The concepts of advanced non-sequential data structures and multiple displays are discussed. It is probably true to say that this is an area of rapid change because of the appearance of sophisticated raster scan display controllers, thereby reducing the need to implement at this level. However, the powerful data structuring features of MODULA-2 are certainly a big advantage in supporting graphics at higher levels of abstraction than those discussed in the reference.

Finally, it must be said that MODULA-2 is a language that is easy to comprehend and requires a relatively small machine for its implementation, allowing for development on one or more constituent parts of a target system as an alternative to the host/target approach.

9.2.3 Ada

Ada (ANSI/MIL-STD 1815A 1983) is the first language to seriously tackle the problems of writing very large (and medium and small) programs for distributed, embedded computer systems. As such it is fairly complex, perhaps trying to be all powerful, but representing a significant move forward in language design. It specifically supports concurrency and the technical requirements associated with input/output, timing relationships and error recovery. Readability and structure are strongly featured. Consequently, reliability and maintenance were serious considerations in the design of the language. Ada requires a fairly large machine on which to run the compiler, leading to the host/target approach being the only option for most systems design. Subset/implementations of Ada are to be discouraged, as these will almost certainly give rise to an unwieldy tool with many of the original benefits lost. Those who move to Ada do so either to meet a contractual requirement or because of the powerful support for software engineering that the language provides. Because the language has so many facets, it is not possible to give more than a brief overview of some of these in this text, although this is not to suggest that Ada is difficult to learn. It is in some senses like a word processor where, after some basic introduction and practice, you can learn additional features as you need them. Pyle (1985) provides an excellent, well-illustrated introduction, presentation and detailed consideration of the language.

Ada programs are written in program units. The first is the *subprogram*, a unit for describing an action, which may be a function (produces a result) or a procedure (achieves an effect). Parameters are passed each having an identifier, mode, type and optional default value. The mode of a parameter is **in**, **out** or **in out** which is self-explanatory, as with many of the language features, which aids understanding. Blocks within a sub-program are enclosed within keywords; for example

> **begin---end**
> **case---end case**,
> **if---then---else---end if**,
> **procedure** FILTER---**begin------end** FILTER

which also aids understanding. Blocks in a program limit the visibility of identifiers declared in them. Subprograms comprise a specification part, having an identifier, all necessary information about its parameters and what effect it has, and an implementation part, the body, which gives details of what action is required when the subprogram is called.

The second type of program unit is the *package*, comprising a specification and a body. A package makes available a collection of entities for other parts of the program to use, and as such it may comprise only a specification part. For example, it may specify a collection of procedures for measuring and monitoring a control surface movement. Identifiers declared in the specification part are visible outside of the package in contrast to declarations in a subprogram or in a package body. The body of a package, which may also be written as a separate compilation unit, consists of a declarative part and an optional executable part. The declarative part contains all of the bodies of the subprograms of the specification part, including local variables or procedures. Anything declared in the body that was not declared in the specification is invisible outside of the body, thus hiding the implementation details. Packages may specify other program units and be specified by other program units, allowing a hierarchy of program units to facilitate structured design with associated scope and visibility rules for ease of understanding, limiting interaction, minimising coupling and aiding separate compilation.

● The third type of program unit is the task. Several tasks may run concurrently under one parent, either on a single processor as interleaved processes, or on several processors. Execution of the parent initiates all of the tasks declared in its declarative part. Each task is a sibling of the parent. Tasks may be active or passive, with the latter providing the means of communication between the former. To be useful, the communication must ensure mutual exclusion and be synchronised. The normal method of communication between tasks in Ada is the rendezvous discussed earlier. A novel construct in Ada is the *pragma*, used to give information to the compiler. Two are discussed here. The *pragma* SHARED(s) ensures that the variable s shared between tasks is updated for use at synchronisation points as a second means of communication between tasks. The *pragma* PRIORITY(level) ensures that a task including this among its entry declarations is never held up by a task with lower or unspecified priority. Interrupts in Ada are hardware-generated entry calls to a rendezvous. The programmer writes the interrupt handler as an accept statement in a handling task, thus allowing software and hardware interrupts with the same control structure.

● Exceptions are explicitly supported in Ada by

Declaration of exceptions:
ADC–OVERRANGE : **exception**
OVERDUE : **exception**

Raising exceptions:
raise OVERDUE --after receiving no response in a
reasonable time

Handling exceptions:
exception
when ADC_OVERRANGE
--set value to max
--log overrange

Ada, also deriving from Pascal, is a strongly typed language having all
the types previously discussed, but many are more flexible. For example

type ANGLE **is digits** 5 **range** − 180.00 .. 180.00;
(floating point)
type AMPS **is delta** .001 **range** 0.0 .. 10.0;
(fixed point)

Subtypes are equivalent to subrange types of MODULA-2. Derived
types allow the designer to make specific use of type checking to avoid,
for example, attempting to add dollars to pesetas, or metres to feet
(without conversion!). Private types allow for greater security.
Constraints may be applied to types in addition to the numeric
constraint above:

type hex **is** character **range** '0' .. 'F';

Accuracy constraints may be applied as above but note the
SHORT_FLOAT, FLOAT and LONG_FLOAT, predefined in Ada but
without corresponding fixed point types.

Index constraints may be applied to arrays whose size is not fixed in
the type declaration.

Access types are equivalent to pointers in MODULA-2.

● Initialisation may be included in the declaration of data item. The
syntax is name, type, and optional initial value or expression for this.

type length : float := 3.0E4;
type width : float := 5.0E2;
type area : length*width;

Such occurrences in packages should include expressions in the package
bodies.

● Low-level facilities are organised via a package containing
subprograms handling device-specific details including addresses, data

representations and code. The former are implemented with representation clauses:

> **for** ADC **use** 16#FF2E#;
> **for** ADC_DATA **use** VOLTS : **delta** .0001 **range** 0.0 .. 1.0

The latter may be implemented as a procedure body in a package in which the op-codes are declared, their values being given in representation clauses. Any operands must be declared with their ranges. Such a package may be available as a library package.

No specific support is given to screen I/O, but the language features are rich enough to allow development of suitable packages.

9.3 SUMMARY

In this chapter we have looked at the most important features of high-level languages as they are required for real-time systems. The concept of breaking down the problem into a hierarchy of modules and the consequent desire for separate compilation make a significant contribution to real-time program design. We have seen that this can be a considerable help in producing understandable and reliable software, especially where the program is large and designed by a team rather than one individual. The emphasis both on strong data typing, a rich variety of types capable of being used to construct complex data structures, and block structure support this at the other levels in the programs. Concurrency and the principal associated synchronisation and communication problems have been presented in a general way, with specific discussion of support for this in some high-level languages.

Problems especially associated with real-time systems, such as initialisation, exception handling and low-level input/output, have been discussed in general terms, and it is seen that the provision for these is rather different in the high-level languages presented. Although many languages have been and continue to be used for real-time applications, those presented in this chapter illustrate a move towards a more sympathetic approach than previously encountered, allowing the reader to compare other languages and perhaps see some of the difficulties and short-comings which might arise with their use in this respect.

Screen I/O is seen to be a developing area whose support at the lower levels is heavily dependent on specific hardware provision, but the improved ability to produce complex data structures for graphics remains an important issue.

Concepts

Subprograms; modules; processes and tasks; separate compilation; scope
and visibility; concurrency; mutual exclusion; synchronisation;
exceptions; rendezvous; initialisation; low-level constructs.

PART III: DESIGNING AND MEASURING THE SYSTEM

10 Design for Real-time Signal Processing

10.1 OVERVIEW

● Signal processing concerns the modification of signals to achieve one (or more) of a number of objectives. These include filtering, recovery of signals from noise, feature extraction, estimation, modelling and synthesis. The signals may be one or more dimensional, and may be functions of time or space. The processing may be carried out in continuous (analog) or sampled (digital) form. Some confusions of terms exist owing to the history of the subject. These are principally the use of the term 'linear' to mean 'not digital', and the use of the term 'digital' to mean 'sampled data'. A continuous system may, in fact, be non-linear and is clearly not digital. A sampled data system may also be non-linear. High-speed sampled data systems sometimes use analog processing (for example, charge coupled devices or CCDs). Our discussion is restricted to sampled data systems in which the signal processing is carried out using digital techniques, and in particular with software implementations or software control of hardware implementations.

● There are two fundamentally different ways in which signals may be represented, processed and understood. These are time domain and frequency domain representations. Figure 10.1 illustrates this by considering a 'black box' into which signals are input and from which modified signals are output, for each representation. There are (for linear, time-invariant systems) well-known mathematical formulae for describing the processes in each representation and also for transformation between representations, and the numerical form of these will be discussed. Digital signal processing is now an enormous subject, highly mathematical, and further complicated by numerical considerations. Having said this, it is possible to give an introductory discussion useful for real-time system designers. In particular, this chapter outlines some types of digital filters and controllers to be found in such systems and considers their software implementation. The associated processes of data acquisition and reconstruction are also presented. The real-time constraints of signal processing are sometimes

209

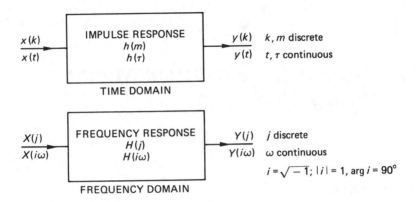

Figure 10.1 Time and frequency domain processing

severe, giving rise to the need for fixed point arithmetic, often with short word lengths, and the consequences both for implementation and for possible errors are outlined. Many aspects of digital signal processing are presented and illustrated in Lynn (1982) and Stanley *et al.* (1984).

10.2 PROCESSING FUNCTIONS

10.2.1 Data Acquisition and Sampling

Sensors may have analog or digital outputs, but both require to be sampled at an appropriate rate for any sampled data system. For analog sensors the sampling is carried out using a sample and hold circuit (SAH) which is switched at a rate determined by the system designer in relation to the maximum frequency component of the signal to be sampled. The held signal is then digitised using an analog-to-digital converter where it is held in a buffer register before being transferred to a pool or an activity via a channel. In many cases there are several inputs to be converted at a particular site, and in this case an analog multiplexor (MPX) precedes the sample and hold circuit. For this to work properly, the analog signals must be conditioned in two ways before they may be multiplexed. First, they must be scaled to match the fixed input range of the converter; this may be different for each channel and hence require amplification or attenuation. Second, they will generally require analog filtering to avoid any frequency aliasing associated with under-sampling. Digital sensors are sampled by updating buffer registers at a suitable rate and multiplexing digitally.

● A typical arrangement is shown in figure 10.2, in which four analog

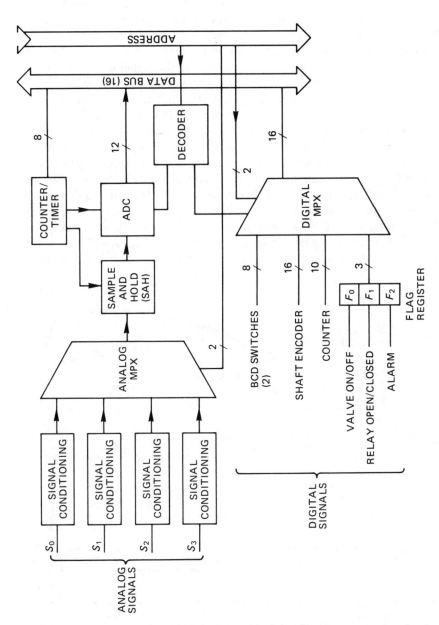

Figure 10.2 Analog and digital data acquisition

sensor signals are acquired along with two digital sensor signals and some digital flags. To avoid confusion let us first look at analog acquisition. The sensor may have a variety of output signals, usually electrical, such as voltage, current or resistance, and the amplitude of the maximum expected signal can be very low to very high — for example, $+10$ to -10 mV, 0 to 15 kV, 0 to 1000 A, 3 to 15 kΩ. The sensor signal must therefore be conditioned to the signal range of the ADC. Note that this may be bipolar or unipolar and have an offset. Before sampling at frequency F_s, an anti-aliasing filter is required to remove high-frequency components above $F_s/2$ in theory and $F_s/5$ or lower in practice, otherwise the under-sampled high frequencies appear as lower frequencies below $F_2/2$. After sampling, this problem cannot be rectified! The analog multiplexor requires an address from the processor to select a particular channel, and this is typically only a few bits (two in this case). After a change of MPX channel, the SAH must acquire the new voltage level before it can be switched to hold, and this includes the MPX settling time. Then a conversion is initiated and this also takes a finite time before conversion complete is signalled. It is useful to illustrate these actions in a timing diagram (figure 10.3). It is typical to

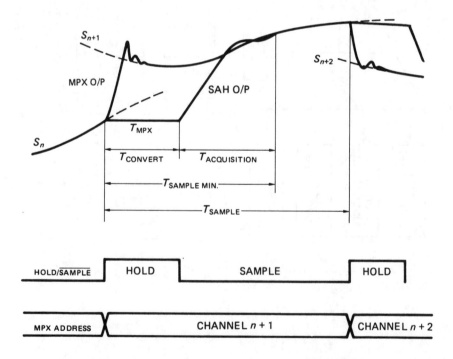

Figure 10.3 Multichannel analog data acquisition

find that sensor signals require different sampling rates. The ADC may be directly connected onto the processor bus or require connection via a parallel interface chip. Fundamental to the sampling process is the need to provide timing, and this may be done by program for slow rates or by a timer chip for faster systems. Inherent in the system illustrated is the hardware coupling via the shared resources, particularly the SAH, ADC and multiplexors. It should be noted that in many cases this could be avoided by duplicating, say, the ADC and SAH and thereby eliminating the analog MPX altogether, and for *some* systems this is economically attractive in addition to improving module isolation and reliability. If this is possible, low coupling between software modules is much easier to achieve.

Now let us consider the digital inputs. The sensor is also selected by the MPX address and the sampling rates are determined by this and subsequent reading of the buffer by the processor. Again, this could be organised by a decoded counter/timer to relieve the processor of this task. The bit inputs are rather like a CPU status register, except that some require to be looked at at regular intervals while others may generate an interrupt. Note that sampling of a particular signal must be regular, unless some form of time compression is employed with subsequent reconstruction.

● A point to consider is the word length from each of these inputs. They are commonly quite short, and frequently different. It is comparatively rare to find an ADC of more than 14 bits and typically they are 8 to 12 bits. Most employ 2's complement notation and are normally connected to the processor bus, left-justified with the unused least significant bits filled with logic zeros. Some processors have only 8-bit data buses and then the data must be transferred in two bytes with further multiplexing, for words greater than a single byte. The real world is rarely convenient!

● It is clear from this discussion that life for the programmer is difficult at this level. There are many fiddling details that will not go away. It is, however, very important to restrict this detail to the data acquisition code modules. The channels and pools associated with these sampled signals should have such details as ADC word length and, whether signals are unipolar or bipolar hidden from them, they should be seen as being of appropriate standard type whether fixed or floating point; however, it must be recognised that in some systems with severe real-time constraints that more than one type may be necessary. Central to the discusion is, however, the usually unavoidable proliferation of sampling rates. For example, in a missile system, roll rates are much higher than pitch or yaw rates because of the cigar shape of the body, and Pitôt pressure (altitude) changes are slower. Processor time cannot be squandered by having all systems sampled at the rate required for the fastest loop.

10.2.2 Time Domain Processing, Digital Filters and Controllers

● Time domain processing relates to an input sampled data stream of infinite length, of which only a finite contiguous length is stored. This may be seen as a rectangular window through which the infinite data stream is viewed. The processing, as will become apparent, involves significant amounts of arithmetic, particularly multiplication, and usually requires sets of coefficients either in pre-computed form or as parameters from other modules. The processing is applied to the finite length(s) of the input data stream(s) and produces output stream(s) to other module(s). This is most easily seen in the signal flow diagram for the FIR (Finite Impulse Response) digital filter (figure 10.4), which is an example of the general time domain system of the upper part of figure 10.1. Problems abound in real-time signal processing in respect of non-sequential addressing, fixed point arithmetic with associated overflow, truncation and rounding consequences, and of marching data sets, all usually in a context of trying to achieve as short a processing time as possible. This raises an important design issue. Should the processing be carried out by a single processor, distributed among several processors or be relegated to special-purpose programmable hardware under the control of a processor? A further point is to consider achieving the same result by using corresponding processes in the frequency domain. To attempt to throw some light on these questions, let us first consider where filtering occurs in our real-time systems.

Firstly, consider data acquired from one or more sensors. This is in raw form and often information must be extracted by a filtering process before it can be used — for example, to remove unwanted signals, improve signal-to-noise ratio or extract a feature from a picture.

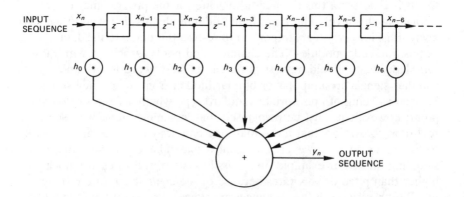

Figure 10.4 Finite impulse response (FIR) digital filter

Secondly, in simple systems stable feedback control is achieved by changing the open-loop frequency response by filtering the error signal. In more sophisticated systems this process is formalised into a module called a controller, as discussed in the next section. Let us now consider how digital filters may be constructed and what the implications and problems are for the designer. There are basically two types of filter, namely finite impulse response (FIR) and infinite impulse response (IIR) filters.

10.2.2.1 FIR Digital Filters

These are characterised by the relation

$$H(z) = \sum_{n=0}^{N-1} h(n)z^{-n} = h(0) + h(1)z^{-1} + h(2)z^{-2} + \ldots$$

$$+ h(N-1)z^{-(N-1)}$$

where $H(z)$ is the filter impulse response and the $h(n)$ are the set of filter coefficients comprising that response. The operator z^{-1} is a unit time delay of one sample period.

The operation of the filter may be seen from figure 10.4 in which a sequence of input samples is multiplied by the array of filter impulse response coefficients and the products summed to produce an output sample. The sequence of output samples is the filtered signal and is given by

$$y(n) = h(0).x(n) + h(1).x(n-1) + \ldots + h(n-1).x(n-(N-1))$$

● It is clear from the diagram that, although the input sequence is infinite, only the current sample and immediate past set of samples, numbering N in total and equal to the number of filter coefficients, is required to be stored to enable the output value to be calculated. This set is updated for every new input sample, a point we will return to later. The number of filter coefficients (taps) and their value determine the type and performance of the filter. The filter will be designed by a control/systems engineer using a filter design package, commonly based on the Remez exchange algorithm (Parkes and McClellan, 1973). The real-time programmer is then presented with a set of coefficients and a sampling rate which completely defines the filter. The arithmetic operations required are, by inspection, N multiplies and $N-1$ adds. The number of multiplications can be halved for symmetric filters, which have the advantage of a linear phase characteristic which is a common requirement. A further possibility for some applications is to cascade the filter with a decimator where the filter has a low pass characteristic. This eliminates the filter arithmetic associated with the stop band and also reduces the output sampling rate. The amount of arithmetic required is clearly an important factor in real-time systems. This type of filter, having a structure which is unconditionally stable, can also be used in systems where the filter characteristics are changed dynamically during system operation. The filter then becomes an adaptive filter.

The operation of the filter in the time domain is an example of a more general type of time relationship known as convolution. The numerical convolution equation is given by

$$y(n) = \sum_{m=0}^{n} h(m).x(n-m)$$

● The relation implies sequences of finite length, which results in two possible answers, both of which are valid in appropriate circumstances. If $x(m)$ and $h(m)$ are both of length N and are repetitive, then the result is a circular or periodic convolution, so called because the sequences are defined on a circle and may be evaluated over the restricted interval 0 to N instead of all n. However, in many cases the sequences are not repetitive — that is, they are aperiodic — and it must be arranged that the sequences are zero outside the required ranges. Consider $x(n)$ to be of length N_1 — that is, non-zero in the interval $0 < n \leqslant N_1-1$ — and $h(n)$ to be a sequence of length N_2 — that is non-zero in the interval $0 < n \leqslant N_2-1$. The resulting convolution will be a sequence of length $N_1 + N_2-1$. In order to achieve the correct result, the two input sequences must be padded out to this length by appending zeros. Where one of the input sequences is long, the overlap–add method may be used (Rabiner and Gold, 1975). Two useful special cases of the above are worth mentioning which are commonly employed to detect weak signals in the presence of noise and for many other purposes. These are auto-correlation where $h(m)$ is replaced by $x(m)$ — that is, the signal is compared with itself with varying time shifts, and cross correlation where a second signal replaces the impulse response $h(m)$.

10.2.2.2 IIR Digital Filters

These are characterised by the relation

$$H(z) = \frac{Y(z)}{X(z)} = \frac{\displaystyle\sum_{n=0}^{N-1} a_n \cdot z^{-n}}{\displaystyle\sum_{m=1}^{M} b_n \cdot z_m^{-m}}, \quad M > N$$

where $H(z)$ is the filter impulse response, and the coefficient sets a_n and b_n define the characteristics of the filter.

The operation of this type of filter may be appreciated by reference to figure 10.5. It is clear from this that, in addition to the output stream being a function of the input stream, the output stream is also dependent on the previous values of the output. Thus feedback is implied or, to give such a structure its more conventional term, it is a recursive structure. The diagram of figure 10.5 can be rearranged in several different ways. A canonical form (minimum number of delays, additions and subtractions) is shown in figure 10.6. As with all feedback schemes, the question of stability or convergence arises. This becomes

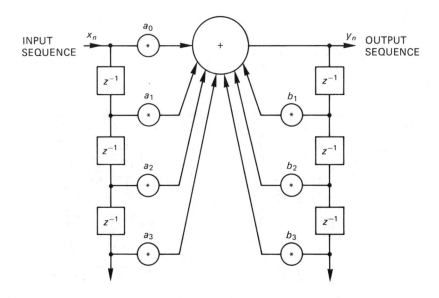

Figure 10.5 Infinite impulse response (IIR) digital filter

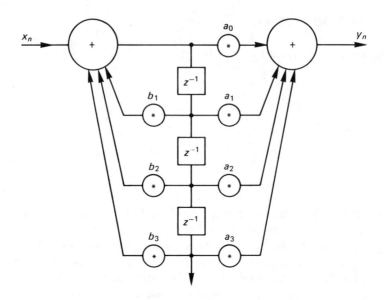

Figure 10.6 Canonical form of IIR filter

progressively more difficult as the number of terms in the feedback path
is increased. For this reason a popular rearrangement is the cascade
form of figure 10.7, usually in the form of second-order sections of the
form

$$H(z) = \frac{a_0 + a_1 z^{-1} + a_2 z^{-2}}{1 + b_1 z^{-1} + b_2 z^{-2}}$$

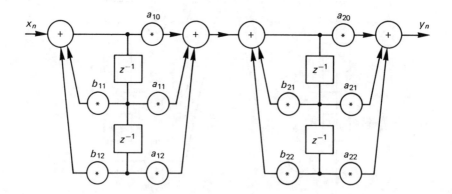

Figure 10.7 Cascaded bi-quad sections

known as a bi-quadratic section or bi-quad. This filter section can be easily designed without stability problems and a design package, often based on the Fletcher–Powell algorithm (Fletcher and Powell, 1963) is available to provide the coefficient sets for the minimum number of sections for an input overall filter specification.

The disadvantage of this approach is the group delay through a cascade of sections and this can be reduced by employing a parallel arrangement. These different arrangements are by no means exhaustive, but do give a feel for the most common realisations to be found both as hardware and software structures. The main performance variations between these structures are speed and the differing properties arising from the use of finite word lengths for arithmetic and coefficients, and this is discussed in section 10.4.

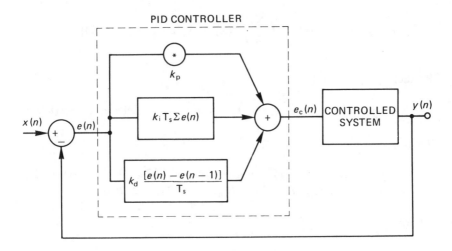

Figure 10.8 Digital PID-controller based closed-loop control system

10.2.2.3 Controllers

● A more formal approach to closing loops and achieving a satisfactory closed-loop performance is to employ a Proportional plus Integral plus Differential (PID) controller (figure 10.8). Obviously, many control systems are more complex than this but the single-variable, simple controller does illustrate some of the features of controllers. The three terms of the PID controller serve to contribute to the closed-loop performance in different ways. The proportional term in conjunction with the gain of the controlled system determine the bandwidth of the system. The integral term reduces the steady-state errors in position and velocity, and the differential term reduces the transient ringing and reduction in stability commonly acquired as a result of improving performance in the other two areas. In line with all closed-loop control systems in which digital processing is employed, the processing delay contributes to further instability caused by such delay appearing as additional phase shift at critical frequencies, and techniques are therefore employed to minimise this. The commonest is to use a predictor type of PID controller. In particular, examination of the PID equation shows that the differential term (which is supposed to confer stability) is formed necessarily by use of backward differences, and this means that this term is out of date. A solution is to modify the controller to predict the required output on the basis of the previous values. The initial equation from figure 10.8 is

$$e_c(n) = K_p e(n) + K_i T_s \sum_{k=1}^{n} e(k) + K_d[e(n) - e(n-1)]/T_s$$

Predict

$$e(n) = e(n-1) + [e(n-1) - e(n-2)] = 2e(n-1) - e(n-2)$$

Then

$$e_c(n) = K_p[2e(n-1) - e(n-2)] + K_i T_s[2e(n-1) - e(n-2)]$$
$$+ K_i T_s e_{sum}(n-1) + K_d[e(n-1) - e(n-2)]/T_s$$

where

$$e_{sum}(n-1) = \sum_{k=1}^{n-1} e(k)$$

Hence

$$e_c(n) = [2K_p + 2K_i T_s + K_d/T_s]e(n-1)$$
$$- [K_p + K_i T_s + K_d/T_s]e(n-2) + K_d T_s e_{sum}(n-1)$$

$$= K_1 e(n-1) + K_2 e(n-2) + K_3 e_{sum}$$

where

$$K_1 = 2K_p + 2K_i T_s + K_d/T_s$$

$$K_2 = -K_p - K_iT_s - K_d/T_s$$

$$K_3 = K_iT_s, \qquad e_{sum}(n - 1) = \sum_{k = 1}^{n - 1} e(k)$$

● Further improvements are to pre-compute K_1, K_2, K_3 and to accumulate $e_{sum}(n - 1)$ recursively as $e_{sum}(n - 2) + e(n - 1)$. These techniques provide for a more up to date calculation of $e_c(n)$ without increasing the arithmetic required. In many applications K_p, K_i, K_d are fixed, but it is possible to surround this with a closed-loop system which modifies the constants to achieve a desired performance by comparison with a reference system to make it adaptive. Further arithmetic is required for this since the constants can no longer be pre-computed.

10.2.3 Frequency Domain Processing and Transforms

Filtering can be regarded as modification of the amplitude and phase of various frequencies, and is more easily understood in the frequency domain. If one considers the convolution executed in the time domain by an FIR digital filter, by Fourier-transforming the convolution equation one arrives at the equivalent operation in the frequency domain which turns out to be the much simpler complex conjugate multiplication

$$Y(i) = X(j) \, . \, H(j), \quad i = 0,1,..N/2 - 1$$

in complex form, where $X(j)$ is the input spectrum, $H(j)$ is the filter frequency response and $Y(j)$ is the output spectrum with j being the frequency index, and N is the number of time domain data samples. Or

$$Y_r(j) = X_r(j) \, . \, H_r(j) - X_i(j) \, . \, H_i(j),$$
$$Y_i(j) = X_i(j) \, . \, H_r(j) + X_r(j) \, . \, H_i(j)$$

in real arithmetic, where suffices r and i indicate real and imaginary components.

This operation requires much less arithmetic than the time domain equivalent. Unfortunately, signals usually arise in the time domain and the filtered signal is also required in this form. Therefore, to implement filtering in the frequency domain implies Fourier transformations of both input and result, as in figure 10.9. The discrete Fourier transform is given by

$$X(j) = \sum_{k=0}^{N-1} x(k)\exp[-i(2\pi/N)jk], \qquad 0 > j \geq N - 1$$

where $x(k)$ is a sequence of N input samples of a time domain signal, k and j are time and frequency indices and $X(j)$ is the spectrum of $x(k)$.

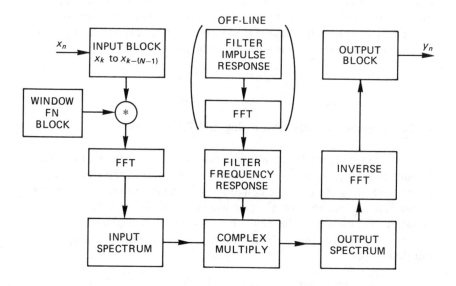

Figure 10.9 Filtering in the frequency domain

The arithmetic for this is massive, requiring N^2 complex multiplies and adds. Fortunately, there is a fast way of achieving both forward and inverse discrete Fourier transforms called the fast Fourier transform (FFT). The signal flow graph for such a transform is shown in figure 10.10. This figure, which is one of a number of variants, exhibits several interesting features. Firstly, the total transformation is the result of several iterations in which each iteration requires an identical set of arithmetic operations, with the data and coefficients and the addressing of these being different. The basic arithmetic operation is called a butterfly on account of the characteristic shape of its signal flow graph, of which one is shown in bold for each iteration. The arithmetic for this is given by

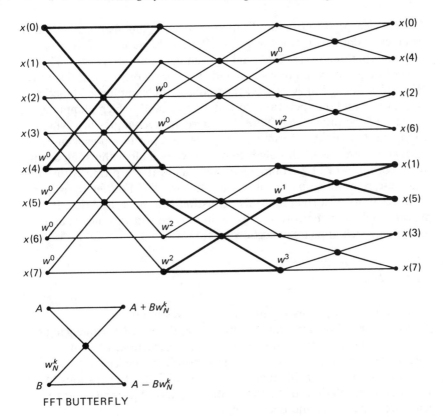

FFT BUTTERFLY

Figure 10.10 Eight-point decimation in time FFT signal flow graph

$$X = A + W^k \cdot B$$

$$Y = A - W^k \cdot B$$

in complex form where $W^k = \exp[-j(2\pi/N)k]$
$$= \cos(2\pi k/N) - j\sin(2\pi k/N)$$
$$= C_k - jS_k$$

In real arithmetic form this is

$$X_r = A_r + (C_k B_r - S_k B_i); \qquad X_i = A_i + (C_k B_i + S_k B_r)$$

$$Y_r = A_r - (C_k B_r - S_k B_i); \qquad Y_i = A_i - (C_k B_i + S_k B_r)$$

where suffices r and i indicate real and imaginary parts.

● It is clear that four multiplications and six additions are required. If the block of data being transformed is 2^m, then the number of butterflies per iteration is 2^{m-1} and the number of iterations is m. The number of complex multiples and adds for this algorithm is reduced to $2N\log_2 N = 2mN$. For $N = 1024$ this reduces the complex arithmetic from over 2 million operations to just 20 thousand, which eliminates 98 per cent of the processing! Note that there are techniques involving arranging the number of samples to be padded out to a power of 2, alternative versions of this algorithm, real-valued algorithms, algorithms for N not a power of 2, zoom algorithms, and the chirp transform, all of which are relevant to particular circumstances. The Fourier transform is a subject in its own right and this discussion is necessarily brief. It provides only a framework for discussion of the software needs and problems which appears in section 10.4.

10.3   CONTROL

Control of signal-processing functions involves a number of considerations. For time domain processing there is the sequencing of sample acquisition, processing and data reconstruction, and for frequency domain processing there is a more complex sequence of operations. On top of this there may be multichannel operations to be considered in relation to hardware coupling and sequencing and to software sequencing and decoupling.

10.3.1 Continuous and Block Operations

● The previous discussion illustrates two modes of operation: continuous operation and block operation. Continuous operation is characterised by the addition of a new sample, resulting, after some processing delay, in an output sample. This is typical of time domain functions such as FIR and IIR digital filtering, PID controllers and convolution. The amount of storage required for input and output data streams is minimal. Processing in the frequency domain *can* be organised in a similar fashion but the penalty is very severe. The frequency response is modified every time a new input (time domain) sample is added and an old one discarded. A complete Fourier transform is required for each new sample, which is in most circumstances unacceptable. This arises since inputs are normally in the time domain and every frequency is affected by every sample; it is an example of maximum coupling, which cannot be avoided. It is usual, therefore, to resort to block operations to reduce the processing overhead. A typical example of this is in speech processing where the input is a continuously sampled speech waveform, split into perhaps 10 ms lengths for processing. The result is re-sampling of the data into sections at a lower sample rate, and assumes that components in the spectra do not change significantly between sections. There is the further complication of inappropriate choice of division between adjacent sections where events occur bridging the join. The latter problem is minimised by using overlapped sections as, for example, in the case of the convolution of long data sequences mentioned earlier. There are two significant consequences of employing block operations. First more storage is required for the complete block(s), and second there is a time delay associated with the processing. The latter is of great significance, especially for Fourier transforms, where all of the input data is required before processing can start. Hence the delay is the time to acquire the complete block ($N.T_s$) plus the time to process the block. This can be greater than the equivalent time domain operation but is very dependent on the block lengths employed and the application.

Algorithm control is straightforward for time domain processing, normally requiring one cycle of the process per input sample and generating one output sample. Frequency domain processing normally requires identical arithmetic to be performed on all corresponding elements of the input and output blocks. A simple loop to process all elements is all that is necessary. The Fourier transform, however, requires processing on pairs of complex operands within a block and associated loop control for all pairs within the block. Outside of this, iteration control is required to complete all iterations for the size of block being transformed. Between iterations, modification is required to the operand and coefficient address sequence modules to re-initialise them for the next iteration.

Of course, Fourier transforms are only part of the processing required in the frequency domain, and as a consequence form a part of an outer control loop of a sequence of functions. Typically, this might be

(1) acquisition
(2) windowing
(3) formatting
(4) forward transformation
(5) complex multiplication
(6) inverse transformation
(7) data reconstruction

● Let us consider the need for all of these operations. Acquisition we have covered already. Windowing arises because the data is a continuous stream of samples, and taking a section of this infinite sequence is equivalent to multiplying by a rectangular window such that all values outside of the window are zero and all values inside the window are scaled by unity. Unfortunately, this gives rise to end effects when the transform is carried out. This is due to the fact that what is being computed is a Fourier series and not a transform.To achieve a more correct result it is necessary to have data whose start and finish values and slopes are either equivalent to a repetitive situation or zero. Since this can rarely be guaranteed, an artificial means is required. Window functions, of which there are many, taper the ends of an implied rectangular window so that the conditions for linear rather than circular transformation are achieved. Formatting is necessary because unless a real-valued algorithm is employed, the data input to the transform program module must be converted to complex form by appending an additional set of zero-valued imaginary components. These may be interleaved if complex number storage organisation is alternate real and imaginary components; or more usually an additional block, initialised to zero, is allocated. Either organisation can be transformed but the latter is often more convenient. Of course, most, but not all of the data are real rather than complex, the latter arising from the sidebands of carrier-based transmission systems. If N real samples are transformed to the frequency domain, the sampling theorem dictates only $N/2$ frequencies. Complex transform algorithms give rise to N frequencies, which is apparently an anomaly. However, the results include both the expected $N/2$ frequency values plus their complex conjugates, giving rise to inefficiency amounting to twice as much computation as is necessary and requiring twice the storage space. The usual way round this problem is to divide the data into two equal parts and regard these as real and imaginary orthogonal sets. This is treated as complex data and transformed using the complex algorithm. An extra iteration on completion yields the correct and expected $N/2$ frequencies.

Some awkward consequences of using the fast Fourier transform are the non-sequential addressing of both data and complex sine coefficients, and the requirement for re-ordering the frequency data upon completion, as it usually ends up in bit-reversed order. These are discussed later in this chapter. The next operation is complex multiplication, and is equivalent to filtering (convolution) in the frequency domain. It is worth noting that specifying an 'ideal' cut-off filter in the frequency domain does not achieve the expected result because of the limitations of a sampled representation of the filter frequency response. Inverse transformation converts the filtered data back to the time domain, usually using the same code as the forward transformation but with complex conjugate sine coefficients. The final operation is to reconstruct the equivalent output analog signal if an analog output is required; this is also discussed later.

10.3.2 Multichannel Systems

Naturally the above only covers the situation where one variable is being sampled, filtered and output. In a feedback situation one normally finds that both input (demand) and output are sampled and differenced to produce an error signal, and it is this which requires filtering or processing in some way. Some systems are made up of several feedback loops which, although not completely independent, comprise independent subsystems such as this with a higher-level control system superimposed. Such an arrangement is typical of an aircraft flight control system in which aileron, elevator and rudder control systems are under the overall control of the auto-pilot and altitude controllers. This arrangement fits nicely into our concept of loosely coupled modules, giving reduced complexity, increased reliability and the highly desirable possibility of a fail-soft capability!

Not all systems are organised like this, although it must be said that this structure is desirable. Many modern systems are multivariable and this requires an understanding of such systems which is really the province of the control engineer. However, there are examples of systems where multichannel capability is required at a relatively low level. Consider an array of aerials or aerial elements each receiving the same signal. If we assume that each element has an identical characteristic, then the only difference between the signals is a time delay. If the signals are shifted in time to eliminate this delay and added together, the resultant is a larger signal if the original arrives along the axis of the array. If the applied time shift is progressively reduced, then this is equivalent to the signal arriving at an angle to the array, and thus by processing the signals in this way the aerial main lobe can be steered electronically over some (limited) angle. This is potentially both faster and more reliable than a mechanically steered array. The technique is also useful for transmitting as well as receiving and is used for sonar as well as radio and radar signals. The consequence for the software is first a requirement to simultaneously gather the data from each element. Timing is very important here and can be precisely achieved by simultaneously switching analog samplers to hold and subsequently digitising these sequentially. The second is to perform the required shifting. This is, of course, achieved by the use of pointers rather than actual movement of stored data arrays. Finally, the arithmetic proceeds on a set of parallel samples for each sample period.

10.4　PROCESSING CONSIDERATIONS

From the preceding discussion it is clear that implementing various
signal-processing functions efficiently involves solving several problems.
Some of these are inherent in the nature of the task and some are
specific to performance requirements in terms of speed and accuracy.
Real-time systems often demand high processing speeds and signal
processing, as we have seen, involves a lot of arithmetic. There are
several approaches to solving these problems and appropriate solutions
are necessarily application-dependent. The problems are associated with
addressing data for accessing operands in ways demanded by processing
algorithms, the use and consequences of fixed point arithmetic, and the
special problems associated with the need to employ special-purpose
arithmetic processors for which usually only assembly languages are
available.

10.4.1 The Moving Data Set and Addressing Mechanisms

● The fundamental problem is illustrated in figure 10.11 where, from
an infinite set of input samples only a finite set, relative to the current
sample, needs to be stored. This is illustrated for a pair of adjacent
sample sets, from which it is seen that the finite set marches along the
address space. The data structure required is clearly a hopper. However,
as pieces of data are put into the hopper endlessly, the hopper must be
organised to be of finite length by making the pointer modulo N, where
N is either the number of samples required (for example, equal to the
number of taps of an FIR filter) or more conveniently a power of 2
greater than or equal to N. An obvious consequence of this structure is
that the pointer rotates around the memory segment allocated, pointing

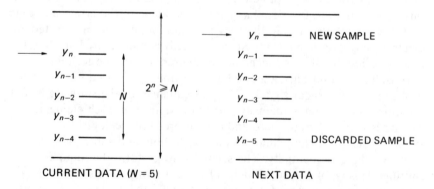

Figure 10.11　The moving data set

at the current sample. Access to other samples in the recent past is then by offset from this pointer which must, of course, also be modulo N.

● Some algorithms require a more complex access mechanism. This is especially true for symmetric FIR filters where, for speed, it is common to translate the structure of figure 10.4 to that of figure 10.12. The symmetry allows pre-addition of data samples before multiplication by a common coefficient, thereby almost halving the number of multiplications required. The access mechanism now must include two offsets from the current sample pointer which, modulo N, enables reading of the relevant pair of operands. A further mechanism is required for supplying the coefficients. These could be included as constants, but although fast this is not flexible. A small table or one-dimensional array suffices, and leaves the option of easy modification without disturbing the code, plus the possibility of dynamic modification for adaptive applications. IIR filters require far fewer data items per section, but need a derived intermediate set, and this is required for each section of a cascade.

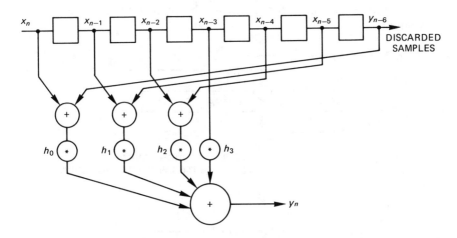

Figure 10.12 More efficient structure for symmetrical FIR filter

● A very important algorithm is the fast Fourier transform and, as previously indicated, addressing is a problem since simple sequential access is inadequate. Although there are many different forms of the algorithm, all suffer from this problem and discussion of one suffices to illustrate the points. The problem breaks down into two parts. The first is data access. The signal flow graph of figure 10.10 shows that the time domain operands are supplied in normal sequential order and the resulting frequencies are produced in bit-reversed order. Intermediate

interations require an address word, which can be generated by
concatenating a normally ordered counter and a bit-reversed counte.
with the boundary moving along one place for each iteration, and the
overall word length appropriate to the address space of the block to be
transformed. There can be a significant time involved in implementing
bit-manipulation processing using high-level code. A further
complication is the need to address and process pairs of complex
operands. The resulting counter has the structure of figure 10.13a. The
second problem is associated with the complex sine coefficients
(sometimes called twiddle factors). These are also required in
bit-reversed order but they have an associated problem of detecting
when this counter should be updated. A further normal counter can be
used for this with a variable length mask whose length is increased by
one bit for each iteration, as in figure 10.13b. It is clear from the signal
flow graph given that the data, once used, may safely be over-written,
and this form of FFT is then called 'in-place'. The re-ordering of the
frequencies to put them in normal order can be done in-place, but
algorithms for copying to another array while re-ordering are usually
simpler and faster. Since store is cheap, this method tends to be
favoured.

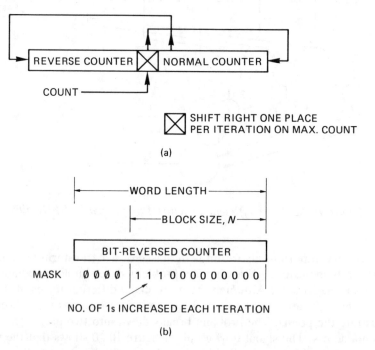

*Figure 10.13 (a) FFT operand address counter. (b) FFT coefficient
address counter*

10.4.2 Data Types, Resolution, Errors and Processing Speed

10.4.2.1 Data Types

● Traditionally, number representation is of two basic types, namely integers and reals. The first is commonly four bytes and the second is full floating point. As we have seen, digital signal processing is arithmetic-intensive and time-critical in the environment of real-time systems. The consequence of employing the most desirable type — that is, reals — is slow execution time compared with fixed point arithmetic. But this is an over-simplification. In any particular application reals, or types derived from this basic type, should be used wherever possible to avoid the necessity of scaling and the problems of overflow and resolution (dynamic range). Some smaller systems have real arithmetic implemented as software routines rather than by hardware. This can cause a very significant lack of performance. If floating point representation is too slow, then perhaps the faster integer arithmetic can be used. Integers, however, are often inappropriate in signal-processing applications for a number of reasons. First, there is the problem of number range. To maintain resolution it is desirable to scale an integer variable as high as possible, but then there may be occasional overflow occurrences. Clearly, these could be dealt with as exceptions, but this can be avoided without catastrophic results in many cases. Figure 10.14 shows a correctly scaled signal and the same signal with overflow. It is assumed that 2's notation is used (this is essential to avoid the highly undesirable case of two zero codes implicit to one's complement and sign and magnitude representation). The wrap around effect is clearly disastrous. However, if arithmetic checks are built in, then a limiting characteristic can be achieved, which is typical of some real-life situations, is usually acceptable, and if flagged can be eliminated for subsequent operations by later rescaling. This is also illustrated in figure 10.14. Fixed point arithmetic has a second problem associated with multiplication. Integer multiply of, say, 32-bit words results in a 64-bit result. If this is to be rounded to 32 bits, which 32 do we keep? The answer usually is that integer arithmetic is unsuitable for many signal-processing applications and it is common to use a fractional representation. Clearly, only the most significant half is then required.

● The next consideration is rounding or truncation. This is application-dependent, but a useful guide is to employ a rounding technique that does not have an offset which produces accumulating errors — for example, use conditional forced one rounding. Even addition has overflow problems, and it is undoubtedly true that testing for and recovering from arithmetic overflow is significantly slower than designing for no overflow to occur. The latter is not always possible, but

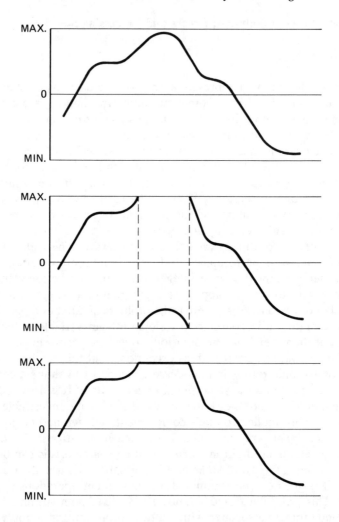

Figure 10.14 Normal, overflow and limiting characteristics

for some cases it is easy. Consider the arithmetic for the FFT butterfly. Multiplication is by sine or cosine which have maxima of unity. Hence the product has the same scaling as the multiplicand. Two additions are always required, hence the results can only grow by 2 bits. If the data is initially scaled down by 2 bits (that is, with two extra copies of the sign bit) then overflow cannot occur. Of course, underflow may cause a problem for successive iterations. This can also be avoided by monitoring the minimum number of result sign bits and conditionally shifting all of the data block down by zero, one or two places before commencing the next iteration. This example serves to illustrate the avoidance of overflow and of consequent time penalties, and introduces the concept of block floating point. For some systems 16-bit or 24-bit representation is sufficient. As we have seen, some modern real-time languages allow user declaration of data types. This has several applications. Number ranges may be restricted as discussed above. Further, some operands may be only positive or only negative, and extra resolution can be gained within a given word length. Perhaps one of the most useful is restriction of the integer range of loop counters to speed up control of loops. Similar considerations apply to pointers. All of these features can be helpful in time-critical areas.

Time domain processing normally involves real numbers, whereas frequency domain variables are invariably complex — for example, real and imaginary (cartesian) or radius and angle (polar). This arises because each frequency component must be specified as having a phase relative to some reference as well as a magnitude. Sometimes it is useful to define a complex data type for frequency domain data, but for many applications it is sufficient and desirable to use different but related names for the two component parts.

10.4.2.2 Resolution

● For floating point representation, resolution is seldom an issue except where conversion to fixed point representation is required for output to a limited-resolution device such as a graphics screen or digital-to-analog converter. Fixed point arithmetic, however, can give rise to resolution problems if processes are cascaded and care is not taken to avoid underflow resulting from precautions against overflow. Another way of expressing resolution is in terms of dynamic range, commonly on a logarithmic scale. Consider a low pass FIR digital filter implemented in 16-bit fixed point arithmetic. Stop band attenuations of greater than 60 db (0.001) are sometimes specified. Avoidance of overflow and multiple add and multiply operations results in a limit of around 70 db for 16-bit arithmetic, as illustrated in figure 10.15. A further example is found in fixed point implementations of FFTs. A ball-park figure for loss of resolution is half a bit per iteration. For a 16-bit implementation of a 1024-point FFT, the results are only accurate to about 11 bits after the required 10 iterations. Although faster, fixed point arithmetic has its limitations and problems.

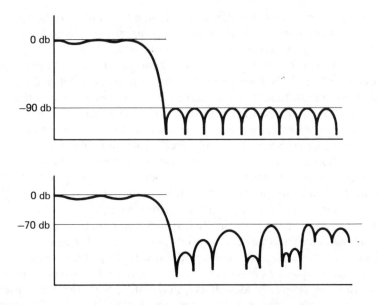

Figure 10.15 90-db stop band low-pass filters with floating point and 16-bit fixed point arithmetic

10.4.2.3 Errors

● Errors, as distinct from faults, may be classified under two major headings: catastrophic and minor. Let us first consider the most important type, the catastrophic errors. These must clearly be avoided by use of good design and by monitoring, detection and taking corrective action. We have already seen that implementation of a limiting characteristic avoids the end around folding inherent in 2's complement overflow. This is a general requirement for many systems, but there are cases which are more restrictive and depend on scaling. Take, for example, a control fin on a cruciform missile. It is clear that the maximum fin angle must be less than 90 degrees and typically this might be only 25 degrees. The variable representing fin angle demand to the fin servo must not exceed, say, 20 degrees if the servo exhibits transient overshoot, to avoid hitting the mechanical limits. In practice, this limit may be variable, having a lower limit at low altitude to avoid the fin breaking off as a result of excessive force in thicker air. There are general checks which can be made to detect errors in variable values. These include the maxima and minima already discussed, discontinuities between successive samples, and maximum rate of change of a variable. Appropriate actions taken if such anomalous behaviour is detected can prevent excessive force, motion and travel in the external system. This is particularly important in the early stages of testing, but is also relevant to fault detection and fail-soft in normal use. Other techniques include the detection of control in an incorrect direction, producing progressively larger error signals or signals out of range, as a result of sign errors or instability in feedback loops. An example of a catastrophic failure of this nature occurred in an early rocket system in which destruction was necessary shortly after launch, which upon investigation proved to be an incorrect sign in a guidance equation — an expensive mistake. Would you like to try a blind landing for the first time, based on your software? This topic is also relevant to modelling and simulation, considered in the next chapter.

10.4.2.4 Processing Speed

● There are many factors which determine processing speed. For some systems, and probably for parts of all systems, processing speed is not critical and therefore other considerations such as simplicity, reliability, correspondence, etc., already discussed, can have their desirable priorities. However, some parts of systems require special treatment if critical timing targets are to be met. An important principle is to isolate the time-critical areas within processes, restrict any special treatment to these areas, and then minimise such treatment by careful design.
● There are several approaches to solving time-critical problems. Perhaps after ascertaining where the problems are, the first technique is to question the necessity of achieving the relevant performance requirements, particularly with regard to complexity and detail. Sometimes it transpires that there is a difference between essential and desired performance. Assuming that the required performance is essential, the next level is to consider whether the chosen algorithms are efficient. The third level is to consider the structure of the chosen algorithm. Many algorithms in signal processing involve nested loops. By replacing the inner loop with a more carefully designed, more efficient version, it is often the case that substantial speed improvements are possible. Consider two examples. The first is a return to the FFT algorithm where the inner loop is the so-called butterfly. Implementing this loop in an efficient way, by using, say, fractional fixed point arithmetic or replacing the compiled code by a more efficient assembler object, can have a dramatic effect on the execution time, since most of the time is spent in this loop. The outer loops for control within the block being processed and for iteration control have little effect on overall execution speed. A second example is the acquisition of a data sample into a pool, which again is a frequently occurring event. Of

course, all of these techniques may still not achieve the desired speed, in which case one has to resort to some hardware assistance which we now consider.

10.4.3 Local Processors, Coprocessors

● The ready availability and low cost of microprocessors, memory and support chips make distributed processing both feasible and in many circumstances desirable. Control systems often have a hierarchy of control loops, and local control not only avoids the problems of long communication channels to a central shared processor, unnecessary coupling and sharing of facilities, but gives the positive advantages of redundancy and increased reliability, additional performance due to parallel processing, and the possibility of local user monitoring and interaction via displays and terminals on the local system, as discussed in subsection 6.1.1.

● It is desirable but not necessarily essential for processors to be of the same type or be code-compatible to allow development on a single host. Some microprocessor families have 8-bit and 16-bit members that are completely code-compatible, which can be used to advantage (see section 7.7). Such families are amenable to running objects under versions of the same operating system, independent of processor. A relatively recent development is the appearance of special-purpose processors tailored to specific application areas. This trend is likely to continue as the cost of VLSI design reduces. Substantial improvements in speed are made possible by the existence of such devices, but unfortunately there are significant consequences for the software designer. Let us consider several different configurations of such systems of processors. First, let us look at the requirements in signal processing. There appear to be four major general needs. The most obvious is arithmetic processing, where the specific needs are for multiplication, double length accumulation, barrel shifting, scaling and limiting, and local storage for operands and coefficients. Usually the arithmetic is pipelined, and control is organised for overlapped fetch and execute cycles in a Harvard architecture. A further feature may be independent load and store of operands from external memory. Such a processor chip is illustrated in figure 10.16 in block diagram form. Not surprisingly, compilers are not usually available for such processors. Consequently, only assembler support is provided. However, restricting the functions to a module body with suitable software interfaces isolates this problem and confines it locally. The second problem is addressing operands and coefficients. Here again special address processors exist to match arithmetic speeds with the supply of operands and disposal of

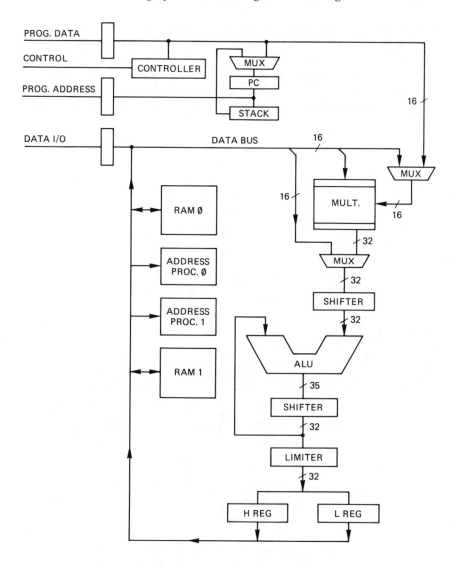

Figure 10.16 Signal-processing microprocessor

results. The third area is control of loops and iterations and this, as has already been discussed, because it has a lower speed requirement, can be carried out with a conventional general-purpose processor — as can the last area, which is communication. It is not always necessary, fortunately, to go to such lengths. Standard microprocessors implement floating point arithmetic by sequences of internal microcode instructions and this is necessarily slow, although adequate for some applications.

Powerful arithmetic coprocessors and accelerators can speed up arithmetic very considerably, but note that compilation speeds are largely unaffected. The code is exactly the same but executes faster; the hardware traps the appropriate instructions and passes them to the coprocessor. Some possible configurations are shown in figure 10.17. It is perhaps worth mentioning some specific chips for reference, but note

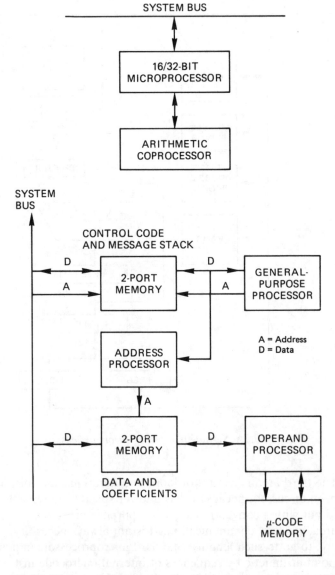

Figure 10.17 Higher-performance signal processing system architectures

that new chips are appearing very rapidly and consequently specific types quickly date. Floating point coprocessors are typified by the Intel 8087 series which accelerates the 8086 series of general-purpose microprocessors. Intel also produce the 2920 which includes multichannel ADC and DAC functions on chip, in addition to a signal processor. Texas Instruments' TMS320 series includes on-board multiplier and barrel shifter, in addition to local RAM in a Harvard architecture, allowing execution speeds of 5 to 10 MHz. Alternative arrangements are exhibited by chip sets having individual functions such as multiply–accumulate, barrel shift, arithmetic logic unit (ALU) and program sequencers from manufacturers such as AMD, TRW and Analog Devices. This approach allows faster operation up to about 20 MHz. Of great interest to the programmer is the appearance of full floating point processors operating at similar speeds — for example, AMD's Am 29325 and TRW's TMC3032 and TMC3033, which eliminate most of the problems associated with fixed point arithmetic, but at a cost.

10.5 OUTPUT AND DATA RECONSTRUCTION

● Output can take many forms, but first let us consider conventional output to printer or screen. Text presents no problems but numbers do. Representation as reals requires conversion to alphanumeric form of floating point notation, and this is usually available as a library routine with the operating system instructed to direct the resulting file to printer, screen or other display device. Graphical representation of output requires conversion to fixed point notation, perhaps after conversion to a logarithmic scale if a large number range is to be displayed. The latter is a common requirement in the frequency domain.
● Often output is to control devices and required in analog form. Here the digital data must be reconstructed to produce an equivalent 'continuous' analog signal. Again, fixed point notation is required and as for analog-to-digital conversion the word length of digital-to-analog converters (DACs) is restricted typically to 10 or 12 bits and occasionally to 16 bits. The level of analog signal produced is dependent on the scaling arranged by the conversion from floating to fixed point representation, and particularly by the reduction from standard fixed point to the short form required by the DAC. It is also dependent on the reference voltage supplied to the DAC and to the associated amplifier gain and offset. Usually, either 2's complement or pure binary notation is employed. This is again the hard end of the software design and should be restricted to the reconstruction module. Figure 10.18a illustrates the process, from which it is seen that a stepped reconstruction is achieved unless additional techniques are employed.

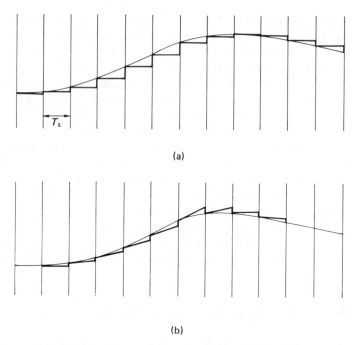

(a)

(b)

Figure 10.18   (a) Zero-order hold data reconstruction. (b) First-order hold data reconstruction

This form of reconstruction is called zero-order hold (ZOH) and has the important feature of an inherent delay of half a sample period. This can be compensated to some extent by including this delay with the processing delay, and employing prediction to reduce its effect if necessary. There are several ways to improve the stepped waveform. One is to increase the output sample rate, the second is to interpolate or use a digital filter to correct the frequency response. Both imply an additional processing load. A linear interpolation leads to first-order hold (figure 10.18b). Analog filters are sometimes employed for final smoothing. Another consideration is how near to the Nyquist rate it is necessary to go. At the Nyquist rate there are only two samples per sinewave cycle, and obviously reconstruction becomes progressively more difficult as the number of samples per cycle decreases. The problem is a compromise between additional processing required to minimise the effects of a low sample rate and additional processing required at a higher sampling rate. It is necessary to be aware of such problems as they invariably have significant consequences for software design in this area, and such detailed problems cannot be avoided at this level.

10.6 SUMMARY

We have seen that signal processing has two basic forms. Time domain processing concerns evaluating expressions in the z operator, where z^{-1} is a delay of one sample period. Such processing includes FIR and IIR digital filters, PID and other controllers, and general operations such as correlation and convolution. An essential feature of time domain processing is that it operates with infinite length input data sample streams, producing infinite length output streams but without requiring much storage. Usually, each input sample or set of samples produces one output sample or set of samples. Frequency domain signal processing, on the other hand, essentially concerns block operations which incur a greater delay between input and output, but frequency domain processing has significant advantages for some applications. The relationship between time and frequency domains is the Fourier transform, usually implemented in its fast form (FFT). Frequency domain data is always in complex form, whereas time domain is normally in real form.

Associated with the signal processing itself is data acquisition involving sampling at regular time intervals and sometimes conversion from analog form. Data output from processing is again necessarily in sampled form and may require conversion to analog form. It is apparent that all of these activities are very much concerned with time intervals and clocks on a strict timing basis.

A consequence of signal processing requiring a great deal of arithmetic processing operations, especially add and multiply, is the use of fixed point arithmetic, often with short word lengths. This gives rise to programming difficulties when using high-level languages and is associated with dynamic range and rounding error problems.

Concepts

Sampling; conversion; time domain; frequency domain; digital filters; controllers; dynamic range; fixed point errors; signal processors; reconstruction.

11 Performance Measurement

● During all phases of the production of a real-time sytem, it is necessary to be able to measure the performance of those parts of the system already constructed, and to predict the behaviour of parts of the system yet to be built. Without these measurements, it is difficult or impossible for the designer to gauge whether the system is going to meet its performance requirements. In order to *predict* the behaviour of part or all of the system, the designer uses *system models*. To gauge the performance characteristics of existing parts of the system, he uses *performance monitors*.

Before discussing techniques of performance measurement we have to define what we mean by performance. An obvious definition might be how well the system performs, but this is too general. Different groups involved in the design may well have differing and conflicting views on performance. For instance, the overall system designer is interested in the performance of the system as a whole and how well the requirements specification is met. The software designer is interested in how the software system uses resources, how it interacts with the external world, how it reacts to exceptions, how reliable and robust the code is under various conditions, and so on. The control system designer is interested in measuring the effectiveness of his control strategies, and the financial controller is interested in the cost of down-time and whether the cost could be reduced for the next model.

● A designer constructs models of aspects of the projected system so that he may gain an insight into how different design decisions will affect the final performance of the system. He either builds a mathematical or *analytical* model or he simulates the performance of the system using a computer-based *simulation* model. By manipulating these models, he can gauge the effects of alterations or extensions to the system design.

● At some point during system development, a decision must be made as to what computing hardware will be used in the final system. It is necessary to compare the performance of different hardware systems in the light of the requirements of the system being constructed. To do this it is necessary to model hardware performance as a set of meaningful parameters that can be used to compare competing hardware systems.

242

● Once the system is constructed, it is possible to obtain an accurate measure of system performance. From this it is possible to ensure that the system meets its requirements and to highlight any areas needing further optimisation or testing. Performance-measuring tools, both in hardware and software, are used to derive these measurements.

This chapter will discuss the modelling techniques used to predict system behaviour and the monitoring techniques that can be used to measure the performance of an existing system.

11.1 MODELLING TECHNIQUES

The two modelling techniques, analytical and simulation, apply a simulated workload to a model of the system in order to derive performance parameters.

11.1.1 An Analytical Model — The Queue

The queueing model consists of a system of *servers* interconnected by queues of *customers* or jobs to be done. Figure 11.1 shows four servers interconnected by four queues of customers. In a real-time environment, the customers will normally take the form of interprocess messages which must be processed by the system processes acting as servers. Examples of customers include individual transactions waiting to be processed by the input process of an on-line transaction system, or records waiting to be written to disc. We can also consider processes which share a serially re-usable piece of code to be customers. The processes must queue up to be served by the code element (this may be undesirable in certain circumstances, see subsection 8.2.1).

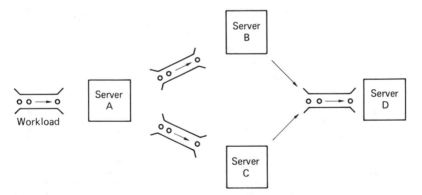

Figure 11.1 Typical analytical–statistical model structure

● In order to specify fully an analytical queue model of a system, it is necessary to define the arrival pattern and service distribution of the workload, the capacity of the servers and the scheduling discipline used by the servers.

Customer-arrival pattern A customer is drawn from a set of possible customers, called a *population* or *input source*. For simple analyses, this population is assumed to be infinite. This assumption makes for a more tractable model, since the number of customers in the queue will not reduce the size of the population. A second simplifying assumption is that the pattern of customer arrival is completely random. It is assumed that the time of arrival of a customer is totally independent of the time of arrival of the previous customer, and that a mean arrival can be specified. This pattern is conventionally termed a Poisson arrival pattern.

For a Poisson arrival pattern, the probability that a customer will arrive within a time x after the arrival of the last customer can be expressed as

$$F(x) = 1 - \exp(-x\lambda) \tag{11.1}$$

where λ is the average arrival rate of customers and where the function takes the value unity for 100 per cent probability. Figure 11.2 plots this function. Note that the probability of a customer arriving gradually approaches unity as the inter-arrival time is extended. We state that a

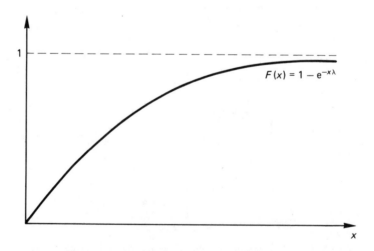

Figure 11.2 Exponential cumulative distribution function

Poisson process has inter-arrival times that are *exponentially distributed* with a mean of $1/\lambda$.

Workload distribution   Once a customer arrives at a server, it will require a certain amount of service. What constitutes this service demand will, of course, depend on the system being modelled. It could consist of a number of CPU instructions to be executed, a number of disc accesses or perhaps an amount of information to be transferred down a communication channel. For most simple analyses, it is assumed that the service demand is the same for all customers and that it can be described as a simple probability distribution of service demands. Most simple solutions use an exponential distribution of service times.

The server   Next, the nature of the server must be modelled. The rate at which it is expected to service customers must be defined. The average service time can readily be derived

$$\text{average expected service time} = \frac{\text{average service demand}}{\text{server's capacity}}$$

or in conventional symbols

$$\bar{x} = \frac{S}{C} \tag{11.2}$$

The *capacity*, C, depends on the system being modelled. For example, a server modelling a CPU would have its capacity expressed in units of million instructions per second (mips).

The inverse of the service time, the completion rate, is given the symbol μ.

● *Scheduling discipline*   Usually, the first customer in the queue is the first to be served: a FIFO scheduling discipline. However, others, such as the round-robin and pre-emptive disciplines discussed in chapter 4, are used if applicable to the system being modelled.

11.1.1.1 Measures of Performance

Before proceeding to discuss a specific queueing model, it will be useful to express a number of important relationships. These relationships are regularly used in the description of real-time computer system performance.

First, we can define the *utilisation factor* as the product of the average arrival rate and the average service time per customer.

$$\rho = \lambda \bar{x} \tag{11.3}$$

Clearly, this provides us with a figure which expresses the fraction of the system's capacity that is now in use. Obviously, the figure cannot exceed unity. In fact, as we shall see below (equation 11.9), it cannot even approach it.

● The system *throughput*, or average number of customers completed per unit time, is another important parameter. The throughput is equal to the arrival rate for as long as this is less than the maximum servicing rate, $\rho\mu$. The maximum throughput is equal to the maximum servicing rate.

● Perhaps the most important measure of the performance of a real-time system is its *response time*. For some systems, we can regard the response time as the total time that a customer is in the system. For other systems it could be argued that the response time is the time that a customer must wait before commencing to be serviced. We can state that the average time that a customer is in the system is equal to the average service time plus the average time spent waiting in the queue.

$$T = \bar{x} + W \tag{11.4}$$

Further, we can relate the average number of customers in the system, $\overline{N}$, to the average arrival rate and the average time spent in the system:

$$\overline{N} = \lambda \overline{T} \tag{11.5}$$

● This result can be extended to show that the number and time in the queue are related by

$$\overline{N}_q = \lambda \overline{W} \tag{11.6}$$

11.1.1.2 A Simple Queueing System — The M/M/1 Queue

Conventionally, queueing systems are described using the shorthand notation *A/B/m*. *A* describes the customer arrival pattern, the inter-arrival time distribution; *B* describes the service time distribution; and *m* defines the number of servers serving the queue. The symbol M represents an exponential distribution, and thus an M/M/1 queueing system is one with a single server, where the arrival pattern is a Poisson process and the server times are exponentially distributed.

● The M/M/1 queue is a simple model that is readily amenable to analytical solution. More complex models may more closely parallel the system being modelled; however, they require a more complicated mathematical analysis. This is especially true with distributed systems, as mentioned below in subsection 11.1.1.4. Fortunately, the M/M/1 model behaves in a very similar manner to the more complex models. It can therefore often be used in place of more complex models to provide solutions that are normally within an acceptable degree of accuracy. We shall not attempt to analyse the M/M/1 system rigorously, but simply state some useful results. The first result is as follows

● average number in the system $= \dfrac{\text{utilisation factor}}{1 - \text{utilisation factor}}$

or

● $\overline{N} = \dfrac{\rho}{1 - \rho}$ (11.7)

Applying equation 11.5 to this equation we get

● average time spent waiting in the system

$= \dfrac{\text{utilisation factor} \times \text{average service time}}{1 - \text{utilisation factor}}$

or

$\overline{W} = \dfrac{\rho\overline{x}}{1 - \rho}$ (11.8)

● *The average total time in the system, $\overline{T}$, is*

$\overline{T} = \dfrac{\overline{x}}{1 - \rho}$ (11.9)

● Depending on how we define response time — either as total time in the system or as time waiting for service — equations 11.8 and 11.9 relate response time to the utilisation factor. Note that these quantities are inversely proportional to $(1 - \rho)$. Thus as ρ approaches unity, that is, as the utilisation approaches the server's full capacity, these quantities approach infinity. Figure 11.3 shows the effect. We can only maintain high utilisation of the server at the expense of

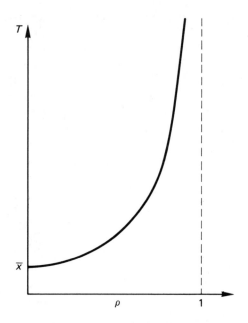

Figure 11.3 Average delay vs ρ for M/M/1 queue

greatly increased queue lengths. This implies that we cannot maintain a utilisation factor close to one over an extended period. However, in the short term, if the queue length is greater than zero, utilisation must be unity as a customer will currently be being served. Hence, in the long term average queue lengths must either be less than one or else infinity. A queue is purely a technique for handling short peaks in demand.

11.1.1.3 Example

An an example, consider a simple M/M/1 queueing situation (figure 11.4). Assume that the average service time per customer is 1 s and, initially, that one customer arrives every 2 s. Now

$$\text{Average service time} = \bar{x} = 1 \text{ s}$$

$$\text{Average arrival rate} = \lambda = \tfrac{1}{2} = 0.5 \text{ s}^{-1}$$

Therefore, the utilisation factor $\rho = \bar{x}\lambda = 0.5$, that is, the server is 50 per cent utilised.

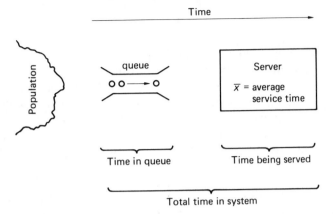

Figure 11.4 Queueing model

Furthermore, throughput = arrival rate = 0.5 s⁻¹, and the average total time in the system, the response time is

$$\overline{T} = \frac{\overline{x}}{1 - \rho} = \frac{0.5}{1 - 0.5} = 1 \text{ s}$$

Now, as we increase the arrival rate, the utilisation factor and the response time increase. Note in table 11.1 the price, in response time, paid for increasing utilisation of the server.

TABLE 11.1

Average arrival rate (customer/s)	Utilisation factor	Average response time (s)
0.50	0.50	1.00
0.60	0.60	1.25
0.70	0.70	1.67
0.80	0.80	2.50
0.90	0.90	5.00
1.00	1.00	∞

11.1.1.4 Limitations of Queueing Theory

● As with any modelling technique, simplifications and assumptions have been made in order to produce results that can be treated mathematically. For example, it is assumed that for a short period it is possible to maintain an infinitely long queue. This is impossible in a real system since the queue must be held in a finite memory. It is for this very reason that a designer is often interested not in the average queue length (the measure provided by queueing theory), but in the maximum queue length, about which queueing theory has little to say.

● Furthermore, consider figure 11.1. Whereas for server A we can perhaps assume that the arrival rate follows a Poisson distribution, the arrival rates for servers and C will be distorted by the behaviour of A. Also, if the servers are processes sharing a single processor, their individual capacities will be influenced by the processor scheduling strategy.

Distributed systems add another dimension to the problem, resulting in the requirement to model complex queueing networks. This, coupled with features of systems behaviour such as concurrency, synchronisation and mutual exclusion, results in the simple view of queueing theory, as presented here, being inadequate. It would appear that no one solution is available for all such systems. Some may be modelled using product form queueing networks, PFQNs (Baskett *et al.*, 1975) but this technique suffers from the imposition of restrictive assumptions on the workload. More recently, generalised stochastic Petri nets (GSPNs) have been used as a tool to model queueing systems involving concurrency (Ajmone-Marsan *et al.*, 1984). Unfortunately, this technique requires substantial resources to implement the model. A combination of these techniques can minimise these limitations. Discussion of such techniques is beyond the scope of this book, but it is as well to appreciate both the difficulties and possible solutions to the problems of modelling complex queueing systems.

11.1.2 Simulation

● Unfortunately, the results obtained from the analytical modelling of a particular system may not be open to convenient mathematical solution. Many systems are not readily amenable to this form of modelling. In these situations it becomes necessary to build a *simulation model* of the proposed system. This takes the form of a computer program that models the system under study. While running, the program is closely monitored in order to extract data as to the dynamic behaviour of the system being modelled. Note the distinction between an analytical and a simulation model: an analytical model is a static mathematical approximation, whereas a simulation is a dynamic, operating replica. Setting up and running a useful simulation model is a time-consuming and expensive process. For this reason an analytical approach should be used wherever possible. Simulation is, none the less, an extremely useful technique, and it is worthwhile to take a brief look at the methods used.

The Model

A simulation model consists of *elements* and *events*. The elements model the various items in the system: processes, pools, memory, file areas and the like. In the model, these elements take the form of data structures which contain information as to the nature and behaviour of the system item being represented. The data structures are linked together in such a way as to model the interrelationships between the system items.

The events reflect the changes in the environment of the elements as time goes by. Events include such things as the arrival of jobs to be done, memory allocation demands and interrupts.

Time

● The model simulates the events that occur as a result of the passing of time. Two methods are used to simulate time passing: synchronous and asynchronous (event advance) timing. In the first case the simulated time is advanced by a fixed increment. The system is then updated by determining what events will have occurred in that time increment and manipulating the elements accordingly. In the simulation of a queueing system, for example, the events occurring during a time increment could be the arrival of a customer on the queue and the completion of a job being serviced. Simulated time is then advanced a further increment and the process repeated for as often as needed to expose the operational behaviour of the model.

The event advance technique does not advance time by fixed increments. Instead, the model is advanced by the amount of time necessary for the next event to occur. The model maintains an event list or 'calendar' which lists the events and the time at which they will occur. The simulation moves through this list, manipulating the system elements as necessary.

The Workload

● Two different approaches are taken in providing a simulation model with a workload. Either a statistical approximation of the workload is derived and applied to the model — called a *self-driven* simulation — or actual workload data, derived from a working system, is applied to the model — a *trace-driven* simulation.

In a self-driven simulation, the workload is characterised as a set of probability distribution functions that describe the arrival rate of jobs to be done, and the probable service times required by the jobs. If the arrival rate and service times are assumed to be Poisson processes, then a stream of jobs can be created by applying to the distribution functions random numbers representing probabilities, thus generating an arrival rate and service demand for each job. These simulated jobs are then applied to the simulated 'servers' in the model.

● The use of self-driven simulation implies that the designer can derive the necessary probability functions. This may not always be possible because of the nature of the system being modelled. An alternative scheme is to carefully monitor — or trace (see subsection 11.3.2) — the workload on an existing system or part of a system, building up a set of arrival and service time values corresponding to real jobs in the observed system. This set of values is then applied to the server model. Of course, this method implies that there exists a running system that can be monitored. The technique is clearly of greatest use when attempting to predict the effect of changes to an existing system whose workload can be readily characterised.

● Sometimes it is necessary to simulate the external system to provide a realistic workload. It may be unnecessary to make such a simulation complex; often a considerably reduced and simplified model will suffice and exhibit the major characteristics of the external system and be more realistic than a simple stochastic model.

Languages

As mentioned above, the construction of a computer simulation model can be a time-consuming activity. However, it is possible to facilitate the production of such programs by the use of special-purpose programming languages. These languages, which include SIMSCRIPT, SIMULA, CSL, and GPSS, provide a convenient way to represent the elements and their interrelationships, handle the internal timing mechanisms, generate random numbers and collect and output performance data. This is discussed in detail in subsection 8.2.3.

11.1.3 Simplification

There are some problems inherent in any modelling technique. We accept that the model is a simplification of the real system. However, in order to provide any meaningful results, the model's behaviour must closely parallel that of the real system. The problem arises in balancing this simplification. The model must be manageable, yet not so oversimplified that it loses its usefulness. There must always be a tradeoff between realism and manageability.

Another problem is that of verifying the accuracy of the model. At the early stages of production, when no parts of the system are yet built, the designer will attempt to verify the accuracy of his model by comparing its performance against similar systems. Once parts of his system are constructed, he is in a position to compare his model against these, and adjust the model if necessary.

11.2 HARDWARE ASSESSMENT MODELS

Hardware performance is usually modelled as a set of parameters; these include clock cycle rates, instruction execution times, store access time, bus speeds and direct memory access speeds. The magnitude of these parameters will have a fundamental effect on the ultimate performance of the system. The problem with this parameter model is that great care must be taken when using any given parameters to compare the efficiency of two different pieces of hardware. The parameters cannot be taken in isolation; they must be viewed in the light of overall system behaviour.

● Take instruction speeds as an example. It is not enough to compare the power of two CPUs purely on the basis of their relative instruction cycle times. Clearly, a fast, powerful instruction rarely used by the system software has little positive effect on the desirability of a particular CPU. CPU performance is a function of cycle time, instruction power *and* the relative execution frequency of the different instructions.

● Store access time is another parameter that is meaningless when taken in isolation. A more realistic measure would be the amount of information made available to the processor by a single memory access. This is often referred to as memory bandwidth, and is a function of width of word accessed, bus speed and the existence of cache memories and interleaving. Again, any inference drawn from these parameters must be kept in perspective. Obviously, a fast high-volume link between the CPU and memory will be of minimal use to a system where most data transfers occur between backing store and memory via a direct memory access channel.

Because of the difficulties in comparing the performance of computer hardware on the basis of parameters alone, a number of other techniques are used to model system hardware, including the following.

11.2.1 Instruction Execution Times

● Sometimes it is known, often from previous experience, that certain problem areas, usually those associated with the use of low-level code and special-purpose processors, are likely to be critical with regard to execution speed. For most if not all processors, execution times are available for every instruction type. Prior to implementation and measurement it is useful to be able to assess the expected time to execute particular pieces of code, especially in the time-critical areas. By associating each instruction with its execution time it is possible to accumulate execution times for both simple and nested loops, for example, to estimate the processing time for a Fourier transform of a block of given size. For other modules with variable loop times, maximum and typical loop counts can be substituted to obtain the execution time estimates. Although the results will not necessarily be accurate to the last detail, the information so obtained will indicate if the times are likely to be acceptable and hence highlight possible problem areas at an early stage. Of course, such activity can be done by hand, but automating the process makes for a useful tool.

11.2.2 Instruction Mixes

● These consist of models of programs that are thought to be typical of those expected in the running system. They are mathematical models formed by calculating a figure of merit. This figure is determined by adding together the execution times of each instruction, weighted by the relative frequency with which the particular instruction is expected to appear in the system's software. It is worth noting the importance of the first sentence of this subsection. Often the necessary information is available for a general mix rather than for that expected of the particular system being designed. If the weighting differs significantly from the general mix, then a means of estimating the correct weights is required. Signal processing is an area where we have seen a substantial difference in the use of add and multiply operations compared with general applications. Suitable weights for particular applications can usefully be obtained by evaluating existing systems.

11.2.3 Synthetic Programs

● Rather than making assumptions as to the expected instruction mix, a program can be written to emulate the behaviour expected of typical programs in the final system. This is called a synthetic program. It is an invented program that does not necessarily perform a meaningful function, but simply exercises the hardware in a way thought to be typical of the future system software. Again, a figure of merit is calculated by summing the instruction execution times. When comparing machines of widely variant instruction set design, it is most valuable to base comparison on figures of merit derived from synthetic programs.

11.2.4 Benchmarks

● A benchmark is a complete program, written to be representative of a class of programs in the completed system. Usually it will be a program that will eventually form part of the system. The program is actually run on the hardware and the performance measured. For this reason it provides a more realistic workload than is possible using synthetic programs. The use of benchmarks is, of course, limited to existing systems; the hardware must be available and the program written.
● As well as being used to compare competing systems, benchmarks are widely used as acceptance tests. In these cases a benchmark will consist of a workload which the system must handle within a pre-defined time span.
● Again the use of benchmarks must be carefully considered. A benchmark suitable in one application area may be quite inappropriate in another. This can be especially true for manufacturers' benchmarks aimed at highlighting the performance in the areas for which the system was originally designed. Many existing universal benchmarks relate to general program mixes and, although a useful guide should be treated with some care.

11.3   MONITORING TECHNIQUES

Modelling techniques are used during the preliminary stages of system design and development, when the system and its facilities are not yet in operation. However, once the system reaches the construction stage, performance information can be obtained by observing the actual system. This can be done in two ways — by monitoring the hardware or by monitoring the software.

11.3.1 Hardware Monitors

● These consist of hardware devices designed to collect performance data. Manufacturers of these devices usually provide an analysis program which summarises the data collected. The hardware comprises a large number of probes which are attached to pins in the circuitry. These probes monitor the logic levels of selected pins at times dictated by events in the system, for example, every hardware clock cycle. The information collected is stored on a magnetic tape which is later processed by the analysis program. Hardware monitors have the great advantage of being totally independent of the system under examination. At a binary logic level, the hardware need have no knowledge of the fact that it is being measured. The resolution of the hardware monitor can be extended to a level below that of an individual clock cycle. It can measure values in any part of the hardware, as well as events occurring simultaneously in different parts of the system.

● The major disadvantage inherent in this style of monitor stems from the difficulty of associating the measured electrical data with logical items or events within the software system. Conventionally, the system designer sees the system as a collection of processes, channels, pools, procedures, variables and other logical entities. The hardware monitor can only provide information as to data bus and address bus values, register values, etc. To attempt to translate information derived from a hardware monitor into meaningful behavioural system data can prove a difficult task.

● However, trapping particular instructions can be a useful way of achieving a meaningful relationship between the system aspects and the hardware monitoring. This is common practice with the logic analyser, a measuring instrument which can be used to great effect. It is important to realise that performance measurement should be included as a fundamental aspect of system design. Although omission is an undesirable but rectifiable situation in the software, hardware modification to retrofit performance monitoring facilities is even more undesirable.

11.3.2 Software Monitors

A software monitor is a program whose job it is to collect and store data concerning the state of the system at pre-determined times. The major advantage of a software monitor is that it can be given a knowledge of the variable names, procedure names, processes and other logical items in the system. It can monitor the system as it is seen by the designer. But software monitors also have inherent disadvantages. Running a software performance monitor can disturb and may even bias the behaviour of the system under observation. This is especially true in a real-time environment where the timing of process activity is so important. Heisenberg's uncertainty principle has far-reaching implications.

Software monitors are of two types.

11.3.2.1 Free-standing Monitors

● Free-standing monitoring processes are activated as a result of certain events in the system. They are usually specified as clock level processes, and are activated when required. Deciding the rate of activation requires a careful balance. The more often the monitor is activated, the finer the detail of performance analysis gained. But the frequency of activation will itself affect the system. The more often it is activated, the greater the perturbation to the system under evaluation.
● The monitor process, when activated, stores system status information such as queue lengths and dynamic process priorities in a known location, frequently on backing store. The information can then be processed at leisure by an analysis program, which supplies performance information statistics. The monitor process builds an overall picture of system behaviour. For this reason, as well as providing the designer with information, it could well be used to supply information to the high-level scheduling process and, possibly, to the recovery system.

Snapshot dumps As its name suggests, this monitor produces a 'snapshot' of the system or program state at the time it is executed. Typically, register values, variable values, sections of main memory and the status of peripheral devices are dumped to a peripheral (line printer, tape or disc). The information provides a comprehensive picture of the system state at that time. These monitors may be activated on a regular basis, but more usually on the occurrence of a pre-determined event of interest to the designer. They are often activated when the system recognises that a failure is imminent.

Such dumps are often in hexadecimal form and require considerable skill for interpretation. A better scheme is to print the information in terms of variable names and data structures, which makes for much quicker and easier comprehension.

11.3.2.2 Embedded Monitors

The second form of monitor is embedded into the measured code by means of a pre-processor or a compiler. These monitors are often included with assertion mechanisms in software development packages.

The monitor runs contiguously with the measured code, and is called into action when certain events occur. These events include calls to the executive, function calls or even the execution of branch or jump instructions.

This style of monitor provides a more detailed and accurate picture of the code behaviour being measured but, since it is part of the code itself, certain characteristics may be masked. Embedded monitors fall under two general headings.

● *Traces*   Traces generate a continuous record of events as they occur during program execution. This execution history is particularly helpful at the program debugging stage, when it can be used to highlight the point at which the program commenced incorrect action. Moreover, as mentioned in subsection 11.1.2, the output from a trace monitor can be used as input data for simulation models. Unfortunately, this output does not provide an aid for performance evaluation unless it is drastically reduced and summarised.

● *Profilers*   Profilers gather summaries of the events as they occur. These summaries take the form of cumulative tables and provide a useful insight into the overall behaviour of the program. After the program is run, the profiler produces a source listing of the program, stating the frequency of execution of each statement, displayed beside each statement. This information is particularly valuable because most programs spend a large amount of their time executing a small amount of the total code and the information can be used to highlight these areas for possible later optimisation. Profilers can also help detail the thoroughness of program 'exercise' at the testing stage. After a test run a profiler will pinpoint those statements which have not been executed, and presumably these statements will be the target of further testing.

Profilers provide further information in the form of execution summaries. PET is a typical software measurement system, created for FORTRAN programs, whose assertion mechanisms we discussed in chapter 5. PET produces the following information for a subroutine:

Subroutine name
Number of executable statements that were actually executed
Percentage of total executable statements that were actually executed
Number of subsidiary subroutine calls that were actually executed
Percentage of subroutine calls that were actually executed
Number of decision branches that were actually taken
Percentage of possible branches that were actually taken
Number of times the subroutine was called
Amount of time spent executing the subroutine

Finally, it produces, for the whole program, an indication of the relative time spent executing each subroutine. Experience with the PET system has shown that these relative execution time figures are only marginally distorted by the presence of the profiler.

11.3.3 Properties of Performance Monitors

● As the prime requirement, the monitor must be able to extract the necessary performance characteristics from the system it is measuring. This implies that the monitor is in a position to access information associated with the status of the various system entities. It further implies that the sampling rate is sufficiently rapid to recognise every occurrence of all significant events, and that some timing effect is not masking any events.

Secondly, the monitor must cause minimum interference to the system being measured. This criterion tends to clash with the first requirement. The monitor must use the minimum of processing time and take up as small an area of main memory as possible. Clearly a compromise must be made between the above two requirements.

● Finally, the monitor must be convenient to use. Unless this is the case, the effort expended in creating it will not be justified. The monitor must be easily incorporated in the system; the user must be able to adjust the fineness of observation and the events which trigger the measurements. Most importantly, the output must be meaningful. The output of traces, profilers and dumps must refer to the logical entities in the system, and not to physical entities such as the octal values stored at particular physical locations.

11.3.4 Levels of Measurement

● It is vital that the designer knows exactly what aspect of system performance he is seeking to measure, and what relationship the results of his measurement will have to the overall system performance. Monitoring tools are capable of supplying a large and cumbersome amount of information. When measuring objects as complex as real-time systems it is often difficult to keep the results in true perspective. In order to maintain this perspective, it is essential for the designer to keep in mind which level in the virtual machine hierarchy is being measured.

Hardware level Here instruction mixes, synthetic programs and benchmarks are used to measure the performance of the basic hardware under a specific workload. When using these measurements it is important to remember that the amount of parallelism, present in the form of multiprocessing software and direct memory access hardware, may have a greater effect on system performance than raw hardware speed and power.

Executive level   Since the executive level processes are a necessary system overhead, it is desirable to make them as efficient as possible. Suitable measurement will point the way toward areas of possible improvement. The processes themselves can be profiled to highlight much-used code modules. These can then be rewritten with a view to efficiency, possibly in assembler code.

● It is also valuable to maintain a free-standing performance monitor within the executive to observe possible inefficiencies in the allocation of process memory, system freespace handling, interrupt handling and so on.

● *System level*   Measurements at this level are directed at improving the overall efficiency of the system. Again, it is important to be clear on exactly what aspect of efficiency is being measured. A measure of efficiency for an air-defence system could be response time; for a batch-based operating system it could be the maximum usage of resources; and for an on-line transaction system some compromise between response time and processing throughput. Generally, most measurements of performance at this level are directed towards deciding on a correct scheduling algorithm.

11.3.5 Processing Time Estimation and Measurement

● We have seen that techniques are available for estimating the execution times for specific assembler code modules and to give a general indication of high-level language instruction mixes. In many cases this is insufficient information for estimating processing time for a number of reasons. Firstly, for each process there is abnormal behaviour under fault conditions to be modelled. Fault-tolerant programming is highly desirable for reliability, but the extent to which performance is degraded not only in the module concerned but in others directly affected by association or by consequent scheduling difficulties must be estimated in order to establish the allowable complexities and procedures for exception handlers. Secondly, we are dealing with quite complex systems in which both genuine and quasi-concurrency are featured. As a consequence we need to separate the module processing times from the interprocess communication times. The latter is very much concerned with the efficiency of communication. We have the problem of deciding how much information to send and how often. We also have the associated problem of how to code the information. Highly coded information reduces the requirement for high communication bandwidth but adds an overhead for encoding and decoding. In additon, there is the communications protocol overhead. This can be reduced only by recourse to specialised protocols and simpler error detection and recovery procedures, which are then less reliable and maintainable. Estimating separately the processing times for the modules and that of the communication channels allows us to apply our queueing models to the overall system. Subsequently we may measure the performance of the actual system using the techniques already described, and compare this to the estimates. The comparisons will show up the strengths and weaknesses in the estimation and modelling techniques. This is an area receiving considerable attention as distributed real-time systems become ever more sophisticated.

11.4 PERFORMANCE EVALUATION

We have seen some of the possible techniques and problems associated with performance measurement, now we address the problem of assessing the results, which may appear in a variety of forms, many of which will require processing in order to extract and present the information we are seeking in a meaningful way.

11.4.1 Meeting the Specification

● We set out to achieve a top-down design, starting with the requirements specification. We need to consider performance measurements in the light of these requirements. Such consideration is necessary at various stages of the project in order to have confidence in proceeding — armed with the knowledge that at each stage the best estimates of performance remain in line with the requirements. Failure to do this can be catastrophic and is usually caused by becoming involved with the detail while losing sight of the objective. As the design proceeds the more detailed specification of hardware, software and interfaces becomes available, permitting the required performance to be considered at a lower and more detailed level within a framework of the performance of the overall system. Progressively the combination of actual code and simulation of other modules and external processes produces more accurate estimates of performance.
● When the system becomes fully constructed, the actual performance can then be measured and compared with the original specification.

This, of course, must be measured under various conditions, these also being part of the specification. Finally the system is handed over, and the performance monitoring continues to obtain more information about the system in operation, including the occurrence of errors, faults, and unusual operating conditions. This may give rise to modifications to the system to reduce faults and improve performance.

11.4.2 Fault Testing

● Testing, monitoring and performance assessment are usually associated with normal operation. Because of the necessity of non-stop operation in real-time systems, even if under degraded operation, it is essential that response to faults and consequential performance are measured and assessed. We have seen that software can be written to be fault tolerant with defence against predicted error conditions. If these errors are generated within the software, such as an overflow, then testing the response to such faults is relatively easy to arrange by flagging. External faults will normally be signalled by an interrupt or a time-out. It is usually a simpler process to insert a software interrupt to a specific exception handler or recovery block at the point in the code where time-out or external interrupt might have occurred than to arrange for a real fault to occur. Of some interest in the assessment is how such errors propagate, particularly in terms of faults in other modules consequent upon the original error, in relation to the time it takes for systems to recover completely or, if this does not happen, to determine the cause of the resulting failure and hence institute revisions to avoid this. It is sometimes useful to complete this exercise by simulation prior to connecting the external system.

11.4.3 Fail-soft and Error Recovery

● Elsewhere we have discussed specific provision for raising and handling exceptions of both hardware and software origin. We have seen in subsection 5.3.5 that a hierarchy of fault detection and correction procedures is both desirable and implementable, but at a cost. Recovery mechanisms have been discussed in general terms; assessing their performance is a system level activity. Let us assume the schema of figure 5.4. We need to exercise the major pathways in this schema to assess the consequences at various levels of faults. It is clear that as we progress down the figure the detected errors become less specific and the recovery action takes longer. In a distributed system the situation is more complex. We may have the possibility of redundant processors and hence can move a process with a fault to a processor in which this fault does not occur. This is not always possible, especially where a particular processor is connected to a particular external system. Sometimes recovery is not immediately possible, in which case system reconfiguration to a lower performance level is necessary. Exit from the bottom of the diagram should be avoided if at all possible. Consider an aircraft in which a network of engines, electrical and hydraulic generators, local and central computer systems, and control constitute the automatic system. Performance assessment will include failure in any or all of these systems. Progressive down-grading of performance is both essential and possible, perhaps leaving the pilot with a standby computer supporting only the essential functions to maintain the safety of the aircraft. Failure of a particular subsystem may require alternative software and hardware to be activated; for example, automatic navigation may be substituted by manual navigation via instruments previously only used for monitoring, but leaving the lower-level software/hardware systems, such as elevator and aileron closed loop systems, intact and operative. Such provision must be thoroughly tested at all levels of faults and degradation, with automatic or human intervention as is necessary, and the resulting system performance assessed at each stage.

11.5 SUMMARY

● Without accurate quantitative performance data the designer must make purely subjective projections as to how very complex systems will perform or are performing. This is an activity fraught with risk. Performance measurement provides the designer with firm quantitative information on which to base his decisions. It is applicable at all stages of software development.

At the preliminary design stages, when no actual system exists, analytical and simulation modelling techniques can be used to gauge the effect on system performance of different design possibilities. These models, in conjunction with hardware assessment models, provide an initial guide to hardware selection. Once parts of the system have been built, performance monitors highlight areas of coding and scheduling inefficiencies, and provide an indication as to the thoroughness of testing. Performance monitors can provide data for simulation models, used at this stage to predict the effect on system performance of design changes and extensions and alterations in scheduling strategy.

Concepts

Analytical models; simulation models; workload; queueing theory; synthetic programs; benchmarks; hardware monitors; traces; profilers.

12   *Current Trends*

We have described a number of design techniques and construction tools that will be of general use in the production of real-time software. The ideas discussed are generally independent of application, environment, size or speed of the system being built. Nevertheless, any design must be brought to the point where it is implemented as software executed by hardware. Therefore, in closing, we briefly examine just a few new trends in hardware and software development.

Hardware

The reduction of time-scale and cost of VLSI design continues to produce a plethora of hardware devices, many of which are distinctly useful in real-time systems. New processors provide higher speed, more powerful facilities and mechanisms to assist with distributed architectures, particularly in respect of access to buses and memories, and for interprocessor synchronisation primitives. Instructions sets are seen to be more appropriate to handling high-level language constructs and parallelism, which leads the way to more systems being constructed in modern high-level languages. The ability to directly address the large and cheap memories now available removes many of the objections to the use of such languages, and implies that channels and pools can be implemented to reside purely in main storage, giving increased speed and simplicity. Many new designs include memory management hardware, making it possible to implement firewalls between user and executive space and even between individual processes. Large EPROMS allow further protection in that much of the executive can reside in read-only memory which does not allow corruption.

Dedicated processors for signal processing employ novel architectures for processing at high data sampling rates with instruction sets related to the application area. This permits architectures more related to the structure of the problem, and which are consequently faster and easier to relate to the data structures required. Such processors require programming in assembly language, but only for local modules, and the newer high-level languages allow support of the required low-level code but with reduced protection. Some new existing and proposed devices implement the 32-bit floating point standard at speeds equal to current fixed point devices, thereby removing many of the problems of finite word length and dynamic range. Although at the time of writing these are rather expensive, they point to the way forward. For ultra high-speed (and cost), gallium arsenide LSI devices achieving the ultimate performance are becoming available and indicate the way to further speed improvement in certain areas.

Of great interest are the reduced instruction set computers (RISC) which implement only the small set of often used instructions very efficiently, achieving a high-speed performance with a consequently reduced silicon area for control functions, and thereby allowing longer word lengths and more general-purpose registers. It will be interesting to see how such an approach compares with the currently popular 'highly-featured' architectures.

Reliability is a key issue in real-time systems. It may come as a surprise to learn that some existing processors have hardware bugs consequent upon their complexity and the difficulty of complete testing. The VIPER microprocessor (Dettmer, 1986) addresses this problem, being the first processor to be designed using formal methods to specify the behavioural description rigorously, and to verify the correctness of the design. This is a synchronous logic RISC design, with polling replacing interrupts for closer control of process swapping.

Cheap disc drives, including Winchesters, allow for distributed file stores, which give potential advantages of improved access and reliability.

Software

Perhaps the most significant recent trend in real-time software implementation has been the acceptance of high-level languages. Initially this was spurred on by the acceptance of a temporary *de facto* standard, namely PASCAL. However, from this have developed Modula-2 and Ada, both of which are gaining a considerable following. They are designed to support the development of complex real-time systems using distributed processing, and specifically for supporting the areas of concurrency, mutual exclusion, synchronisation, exceptions, and the low-level needs of such systems. Thus they will give a major thrust to better design, improved reliability and performance. In particular, recent developments in Modula-2+ in the areas of exceptions, storage management and concurrency for multiprocessor systems (IEEE, 1986) look promising. In the meantime, the language C is rising fast in popularity. It is in C that the operating system UNIX and its variants have been written. The interface between a language and an operating system is seen to have some importance. C exhibits many of the desirable features required for real-time applications. UNIX unfortunately lacks a number of features essential for real-time use. Real-time UNIX versions are currently under development by several manufacturers (Rauch-Hindin, 1986), which should alleviate these problems.

To support the design of real-time systems, the recent development of MASCOT 3 and its application as a design methodology provide a major step forward in controlling the complexity, and of improving both the speed of implementation and the reliability, of the end product. The general emergence of integrated project support environments (IPSEs) is a recognition of the importance of integrating the individual tools employed previously for the development of complex software systems.

Modern knowledge engineering techniques are being used to maintain fact and rule bases concerning system specification so that complex specifications can be checked for consistency, and effective testing programmes developed.

Today, developments in both software and hardware are easing the designer's job by facilitating simple, well structured designs. However, tools are of little value unless used intelligently. No tool can guarantee good design. The designer must continually strive to reduce complexity and enforce structure. At all times the catch phrase should be 'keep it simple'!

References

Ajmone-Marsan, Balbo and Contre (1984). 'A class of generalised stochastic Petri nets for the performance evaluation of multiprocessor systems', *ACM Trans. Computer Systems*, Vol. 2, pp. 93–122.

Baskett *et al.* (1975). 'Open, closed and mixed networks of queues with different classes of customers', *ACM*, Vol. 22, No. 2, pp. 248–60.

Belady, L. A. and Lehman, M. M. (1976). 'A model of large program development', *IBM Syst. J.*, Vol. 15, pp. 549–57.

Ben-Ari, M. (1982). *Principles of Concurrent Programming*, Prentice-Hall International, Englewood Cliffs, NJ.

Bergland, G. D. (1978). 'Structured design methodologies', *Proceedings of the 15th Conference on Design Automation (IEEE)*, pp. 475–93.

CCITT (1976). SDL Functional Specification and Description Language in *Series Z Recommendations (Z101–104) of CCITT Sixth Plenary Assembly, Geneva*, October.

Cole, R. (1985). *Computer Communications*, 2nd edn, Macmillan.

Constantine, L. L., Myers, G. J. and Stevens, W. P. (1974). 'Structured design', *IBM Syst. J.*, Vol. 13, pp. 115–39.

Dettmer, R. (1986). 'The Viper microprocessor', *IEE Electronics and Power*, September pp. 61–78.

Dijkstra, E. W. (1968). In F. Genuys (ed.) 'Co-operating sequential processes', in *Programming Languages*, Academic Press, London.

Fletcher and Powell (1963). 'A rapidly convergent descent method for minimisation', *Computer Journal*, Vol. 6, No. 2, pp. 163–8.

Gee, K. C. E. (1983). *Introduction to Local Area Computer Networks*, Macmillan.

Hoare, C. A. R. (1974). 'Monitors: an operating system structuring concept', *Commun. ACM*, Vol. 17, pp. 549–57.

Hoare, C. A. R. (1978). 'Communicating sequential processes', *CACM*, Vol. 21, No. 8, pp. 666–77.

Hopgood *et al.* (1983). *Introduction to the Graphic Kernel System G. K. S.*, Academic Press.

IEEE (1986). *Software*, November.

Jackson, M. A. (1975). *Principles of Program Design*, Academic Press, New York.

Katz, P. (1981). *Digital Control Using Microprocessors*, Prentice-Hall International, Englewood Cliffs, NJ.

Loughry, D. C. (1983). *Standard Digital Interface for Programmable Instrumentation*, IEEE, New York.

Lynn, P. A. (1982). *An Introduction to the Analysis and Processing of Signals*, 2nd edn, Macmillan.

Marsden, B. W. (1985). *Communication Network Protocols*, 2nd edn, Chartwell-Bratt.

MASCOT 3 (1979 and 1986). MASCOT Suppliers Association, RSRE, Great Malvern, Worcs., UK.

McDermid, J. (1985). *Integrated Project Support Environments* (IEE Software Engineering Series 1), Peter Peregrinus.

Ornstein, S. M., Crowther, W. R., Kraley, M. F., Bressler, R. D., Michel, A. and Heart, F. E. (1975). 'Pluribus — a reliable multiprocessor', *AFIPS Conference Proceedings*, Vol. 44, pp. 55–9.

Parks, T. W. and McClellan, J. H. (1973). 'A computer program for designing optimal FIR digital filters, *(IEEE) Trans. Audio and Electroacoustics*, December.

Pyle, I. C. (1985). *The ADA Programming Language*, 2nd edn, Prentice-Hall International, Englewood Cliffs, NJ.

Rabiner, L. R. and Gold, B. (1975). *Theory and Application of Digital Signal Processing*, Prentice-Hall, Englewood Cliffs, NJ, pp. 63–5.

Randell, B. (1977). 'System structure for software fault tolerance', *Current Trends in Programming Methodology, Vol. 1*, Prentice-Hall, Englewood Cliffs, NJ, pp. 195–219.

Randell, B., Lee, P. A. and Treleaven, M. B. C. (1978). 'Reliable computing systems', in *Springer Lecture Notes in Computer Science No. 60, Advanced Course on Operating Systems*, Springer-Verlag, pp. 282–391.

Rauch-Hindin, W. (1986). 'Real-time UNIX seizes new products' markets', *Mini-Micro Systems*, September, pp. 61–78.

Ritchie, D. M. and Thompson, K. (1978). 'The UNIX time sharing system', *Bell Syst. Tech. J.*, Vol. 57, No. 6, pp. 1905–29.

Ross, D. T. (1977). 'Structured Analysis (SA): a language for communicating ideas', *Trans. IEEE Software Eng.*, Vol. SE-3, pp. 16–33.

SDL Functional Specification and Description Language in Series Z Recommendations (Z101–Z104) of CCITT Sixth Plenary Assembly, Geneva (1976). October.

Stanley *et al.* (1984). *Digital Signal Processing*, Reston.

Stuki, L. G. (1978). *New Directions in Automated Tools for Improving*

Software Quality, Current Trends in Programming Methodology, Vol. 2, Prentice-Hall, Englewood Cliffs, NJ, pp. 80–111.

Tanenbaum, A. S. (1981). *Computer Networks*, Prentice-Hall Software Series, Englewood Cliffs, NJ.

Thomasian (1986). 'Queueing network models for parallel processing of task systems', *IEEE*, Vol. C-35, No. 12, pp. 1045–54.

Wilson, I.R. and Addyman, A. M. (1982). *A Practical Introduction to PASCAL — with BS 6192*, 2nd edn, Macmillan.

Wirth, N. (1977). 'MODULA — a language for modular multiprogramming', *Software Pract. Experience*, No. 7, pp. 3–35.

Wirth, N. (1982). *Programming in Modula-2*, Springer-Verlag.

Selected Bibliography

Aho, A. V., Hopcroft, J. E. and Ullman, J. D., *The Design and Analysis of Computer Algorithms*, Addison-Wesley, 1974.

Alagic, S. and Arbib, M. A., *The Design of Well-Structured and Correct Programs*, 2nd edn, Springer-Verlag, 1979.

Apt, K. R., *Logic and Models of Concurrent Systems*, Springer-Verlag, 1985.

Barnes, J. G. P., *Programming in Ada*, Addison-Wesley, 1981.

Barringer, H., *A Survey of Verification Techniques for Parallel Programs*, Springer-Verlag, 1985.

Beizer, B., *Micro Analysis of Computer System Performance*, Van Nostrand Reinhold, New York, 1978.

Berry, R. E. and Meekings, B. A. E., *A Book on C*, Macmillan, 1984.

Bjorner, D. (ed.), *Abstract Software Specifications*, Springer-Verlag, 1986.

Bjorner, D. and Jones, C. B., *Formal Specification and Software Development*, Prentice-Hall, Englewood Cliffs, NJ, 1982.

Bourne, S. B., *The UNIX System*, Addison-Wesley, 1984.

Brachman, R. J. and Levesque, H. J., *Readings in Knowledge Representation*, Freeman, 1985.

Brinch Hanson, P., *Operating System Principles*, Prentice-Hall, Englewood Cliffs, NJ, 1973.

Brown, D. C. and Chandrasekaran, B., *Design Problem Solving: Knowledge Structures and Control Strategies*, Pitman/Morgan-Kaufman, 1986.

Buchanan, B. G. and Shortliffe, E. H., *Rule Based Expert Systems*, Addison-Wesley, 1984.

Demarco, T., *Structured Analysis and System Specification*, Yourdon/Prentice-Hall, 1980.

Gane, C. and Sarson, T., *Structured Systems Analysis: Tools and Techniques*, Prentice-Hall, Englewood Cliffs, NJ, 1979.

Hamming, R. W., *Digital Filters*, 2nd edn, Prentice-Hall, Englewood Cliffs, NJ, 1983.

Hart, A., *Knowledge Acquisition for Expert Systems*, Kogan Page, 1986.

Hearn, D. and Baker, M. P., *Computer Graphics*, Prentice-Hall, Englewood Cliffs, NJ, 1986.

Holt, R. C., Graham, G. S., Lazowska, E. D. and Scott, M. A., *Structured Concurrent Programming with Operating System Applications*, Addison-Wesley, 1978.

Houpis, C. H. and Lamont, G. B., *Digital Control Systems — Theory, Hardware, Software*, McGraw-Hill, 1985.

Irvine, C. A. and Brackett, J. W., 'Automated software engineering through structured data management', *IEEE Trans. Software Eng.*, Vol. SE-3 (1977), pp. 34–40.

Jenson, K. and Wirth, N., *Pascal User Manual and Report*, 3rd edn, Springer-Verlag, 1985.

Jones, C. B., *Software Development: A Rigorous Approach*, Prentice-Hall International, Englewood Cliffs, NJ, 1980.

Jones, C. B., *Systematic Software Development Using VDM*, Prentice-Hall, Englewood Cliffs, NJ, 1986.

Keravanou, E. T. and Johnson, L., *Competent Expert Systems*, Kogan Page, 1986.

Kernighan, B. W. and Plauger, P. J., *Software Tools in Pascal*, Addison-Wesley, 1981.

King, M. J. and Pardoe, J. P., *Program Design Using JSP: A Practical Introduction*, Macmillan, 1985.

Kopetz, H., *Software Reliability*, Macmillan 1979.

Kuo, F. F., *Digital Control Systems*, Holt-Saunders, 1981.

Liskov, B. and Guttay, J., *Abstraction and Specification in Program Development*, MIT Press, 1986.

Lister, A. M., *Fundamentals of Operating Systems*, 3rd edn, Macmillan, 1984.

MacLennan, B. J., *Principles of Programming Languages: Design Evaluation and Implementation*, Holt, Rinehart and Winston, 1983.

Mansford, E. and Drummond, J. R., *Evaluation and Measurement Techniques for Computer Systems*, Prentice-Hall, Englewood Cliffs, NJ, 1973.

Myers, G. J., *Reliable Software Through Composite Design*, Petrochelli-Charter, New York, 1975.

Myers, W., 'The need for software engineering', *Computer*, No. 11 (1978) pp. 12–24.

Naylor, C., *Build Your Own Expert Systems*, Sigma/Wiley, 1983.

Owen, G. J., 'Rollback — a method for process and system recovery', *Proc. IEE Software Eng. Telecom. Switching Syst.*, (1973) pp. 118–24.

Rich, E., *Introduction to Artificial Intelligence*, McGraw-Hill, 1983.

Richie, D. M. and Thompson, K., 'The UNIX time-sharing system', *Commun. ACM*, Vol. 17 (1974), pp. 365–75.

Sommerville, I., *Software Engineering*, Addison-Wesley, 1982.

Takamura, S., Kawashima, H. and Nakajima, H., *Software Design for Electronic Switching Systems*, Peter Peregrinus, 1979.

Theaker, C. J. and Brookes, G. R., *A Practical Course on Operating Systems*, 2nd edn, Macmillan, 1983.

Webb, J. T., *CORAL 66 Programming*, N.C.C. Publications, Manchester, 1978.

Welsh, J. and McKeag, R. M., *Structured Systems Programming*, Prentice-Hall, Englewood Cliffs, NJ, 1980.

Williams, C. S., *Designing Digital Filters*, Prentice-Hall, Englewood Cliffs, NJ, 1985.

Wirth, N., *Programming in Modula-2*, 2nd edn, Springer-Verlag, 1983.

Wirth, N., *Algorithms and Data Structures*, Prentice-Hall, Englewood Cliffs, NJ, 1986.

Young, S. B., *Real-Time Languages — Design and Development*, Ellis Horwood, 1982.

Yourdan, E., *Techniques for Program Structure and Design*, Prentice-Hall, Englewood Cliffs, NJ, 1975.

Glossary

Ada   A programming language developed under the sponsorship of the United States Department of Defense.

Addressing mode   The manner in which the address forming part of a machine instruction is interpreted as an actual store location.

Analog-to-digital convertor   A peripheral device for converting a sampled data analog signal to short-word-length fixed-point digital form.

Analytical model   A mathematical approximation of an aspect of a system's performance.

ANSI/IEEE Std 488/GPIB Interface   A general-purpose hardware interface standard for connection of (programmable) measuring instruments to computers.

Arrival pattern   A statistical description of the arrival times of customers queueing for service.

Assertion   A logical statement describing the expected behaviour of a module at a particular point during the execution of its code.

Asynchronous operation   Information transfer and system operation by means of exchange of tokens (handshake) rather than clocking at regular time intervals.

Audit process   A process designed to check a system for errors or inconsistent behaviour. It compares the current system state with its own in-built view of correct operation.

Backing store   High-capacity storage not directly accessible by the CPU, for example, discs and drums.

Batch   Mode of computer operation where programs are run in groups. The programs making up each group are selected so as to optimise the use of the system resources while each group is run.

Baud rate   The rate in bits per second at which digital data is transmitted on a serial line. Preferred rates are commonly used, such as 110, 2400, 9600 baud.

BCD (Binary Coded Decimal)   A four-bit binary code used to represent a single decimal digit.

Benchmark   A program or set of programs designed to be representative of the expected workload on a system; used to derive information about system performance.

273

Bit map   An array of binary digits, each representing the state of a system item, for example on/off, activated/not activated, allocated/not allocated; or a pixel in a bit mapped graphics display.

Bootstrap   A small program (often resident in non-erasable read-only memory) designed to load a larger program into main memory. This larger program is, in turn, designed to load the remainder of the system software.

Builder (system builder)   A program designed to load code elements of user processes and to include their process descriptors in the process descriptor pool.

Bus   A set of wires on which data, address and control information can be distributed from one of a number of sources to one or more destinations.

Cache memory   A random access storage element of smaller capacity than main storage, but with faster access.

CCITT   International Telegraph and Telephone Consultative Committee.

Change Manager   Part of an IPSE which tracks source code changes anywhere in a system and reports affected modules.

Channel   Pathway down which information can flow.

Checkpoint   A stage at which a program is known to be operating correctly.

Checksum   A numerical value which is a function of the binary patterns making up a data file or the code element of a process.

Circular buffer   List of memory elements linked or accessed in a circular chain.

Clock (logic)   A logic signal which latches data into a flip-flop or register.

Clock (real-time clock)   A hardware device which generates an interrupt at regular intervals.

Closed loop system   A system involving software or hardware or some combination of these in which the output is a function of both the input and the previous output, implying negative feedback or recursion.

Code element   That part of a process which consists of executable instructions and data.

Code sharing   Technique whereby two or more processes use the same section of code as part of their code element.

Cohesion   A measure of the strength of the internal structure of a module.

Concurrent programming   Writing code for processes that are to execute in parallel.

Conditional compilation   Technique whereby a compiler either includes or ignores sections of program code; dependent on parameters provided to the compiler when activated.

Configuration manager   Part of an IPSE which builds programs from desired source versions, and detects the need to rebuild programs when sources are modified.

Control register   A hardware register containing a collection of bits used for control purposes.

Controlled system   Set of devices which interfaces to the environment, whose functioning is controlled by a real-time system.

Controlling system   The software component of a real-time system, together with its necessary processing hardware.

Conversation   A recovery block containing part of the progress of more than one process. All the processes must pass their acceptance tests before any of the processes can exit the recovery block.

Conversion   Changing the representation of a variable, commonly associated with analog and digital forms of variables.

Coprocessor   An additional processor enhancing the performance and/or instruction set of an existing processor.

CORAL   High-level language developed for real-time applications by the UK Ministry of Defence.

Coupling   Measure of the closeness and complexity of interrelationships between modules.

Cyclic redundancy check (CRC)   An error-detection scheme for serial data transmission.

Data abstraction   Design technique whereby processes and modules are given restricted knowledge of the layout of system data structures.

Data structure design technique (Michael Jackson technique)   Design technique whereby the form of the data structures in a design define the structure of the code which acts on them.

Deadlock (deadly embrace)   Situation wherein a process (or set of processes) cannot continue operation because another process (or set of processes) holds a resource required by the first process. At the same time the second process is halted because it requires resources held by the first process.

Digital filter   Selective amplification and attenuation of signals at various frequencies using sampled data representation, implemented digitally with hardware and/or software.

Digital multiplexer   Hardware mechanism which gates one of several sources on to a bus.

Digital-to-analog convertor   A peripheral device for converting short fixed-length digital numbers to scaled sampled data analog form, usually as a voltage.

Dispatcher   Hardware or software mechanism which carries out actions necessary to swap a processor from execution of one process to the execution of another.

Dynamic range   Number range over which a signal is usefully represented.

Enumeration type   A data type wherein the values or names of the type are declared, such as TYPE DAY = (MON, TUES, WED, THURS, FRI).

Error seeding   Method of assessing the success of a testing scheme. Known errors are introduced into a system and the percentage of 'seeded' errors detected is related to the probable percentage of unknown errors that have been detected.

Event (significant event)   An occurrence which results in a change in the state of a system.

Event scanner   Process which scans a system and compares the present status of the system with that found by a previous scan and reports the discrepancies as events.

Executive (kernel)   That part of a real-time system which supports the existence of, and controls the activities of, the process in the system.

Fault tolerant systems   Systems which can continue in operation in spite of the occurrence of faults.

FIFO   First in first out.

Finite state machine   A machine or system which exists in one of a finite number of possible states at any particular time.

Frame   One block in a block structured data transmission system, usually containing address, control, data and check fields. In a graphics system a frame is a single picture from a set or sequence.

Frame buffer   Temporary storage for one or more frames in a data transmission system. Random access storage containing the data for each pixel of a frame in a graphics system.

Frame check sequence   Cyclic polynomial sequence for error checking in frame-oriented serial data transmission.

Frame refresh rate   Rate at which the screen is rewritten in a graphics system.

Freespace   A pool of memory elements (in main storage or backing store) which is available for temporary use by any of the system processes.

Frequency domain   The domain in which a signal has frequency as an independent variable.

Gate   Device for keeping cattle in and people out! Alternatively, low-level hardware for implementing basic logic functions such as AND, NOR, Exclusive OR.

Generic library   A library composed of compile-time subprograms, packages or modules written in generic, parametric or pure code form, from which instances may be created for local use.

Graphics display controller   VLSI chip for controlling a raster scan graphics screen, commonly also providing low-level facilities such as line, circle, graphics character, area fill, pan and zoom.

Hardware accelerator   A hardware device or subsystem to speed up execution (a subset) of a processor's instruction set.

Hardware lock/unlock   A method which ensures that process swapping cannot occur while the 'lock' is on. For example, the temporary disablement of interrupts in a single processor system.

High-level scheduler   A process which is capable of altering the priority of processes in a system.

Hopper   *See* **Circular buffer**.

Implementation part   That part of a procedure, task or module containing the implementation details of the facilities provided, including any local declarations invisible outside that part. *See also* Specification part.

Interpreter   Program which reads, interprets and acts on a sequence of coded instructions.

Interrupt handler   Process which is executed immediately on the occurrence of an interrupt.

IPSE   Integrated Project Support Environment.

Kernel   Protection domain wherein processes have access to all available machine instructions.

Latching   Staticising transient data into a flip-flop or register.

Life cycle costs   The cost of a product as measured over its lifetime.

LIFO   Last in first out.

Low-level construct   A simple language construct (commonly assembly language) associated with low-level code, as distinct from the more powerful constructs available in most high-level languages.

Main memory, main storage   That part of a computer system's storage which is directly accessible by the CPU.

MASCOT   Modular Approach to Software Construction, Operation and Test.

Memory bandwidth   The amount of information made available to the processor by a single memory access.

Memory management hardware   Hardware mechanism, residing between the CPU and main memory, which maps the address field of a processor instruction on to an actual physical location. Also usually implements protection domains.

MODULA-2   A high-level language, descendant of Pascal and Modula, suitable for use in a multi-processing environment, incorporating facilities to support asynchronous processes. The language also strongly supports modular programming and low-level processes.

Monitor   A collection of routines which controls and protects a particular resource.

Monitor manager   Part of an IPSE which provides a mechanism for users to be notified when particular elements or modules of a system are changed. This may be for information only or because there are implications for other modules.

Motor controller   Interface chip for control of electric motor, commonly a stepper motor.

MTBF   Mean Time Between Failures.

MTTR   Mean Time To Repair.

Multiplexing   The sharing of a system resource, for example, the processor or section of storage, by more than one process. The simultaneous transmission of more than one message or data item down a communication channel.

Negative edge   Hardware term for the high-low transition of a logic signal.

On-line system   System which actions each transaction or event in the controlled system, to ensure that the device and file status is continuously up to date.

Package (Ada)   A logical piece of a program covering one aspect of the problem.

PASCAL   Structured high-level language originally developed by Niklaus Wirth in 1968.

Performance monitor   Tool implemented in software or hardware, used to gauge performance characteristics of existing parts of the system.

Pixel   A picture element in a bit-mapped graphics display system.

Poisson arrival pattern   A pattern of customer arrival where the time of arrival of one customer is totally independent of the time of arrival of the previous customer.

Poll mechanism   Schema for polling (see below) — for example, serial poll, circular poll.

Polling   Technique of monitoring device status by regular inspection of the values of register(s) associated with the device.

Pool   Collection of data items which are available to more than one process in the system.

Positive edge   Hardware term for the low–high transition of a logic signal.

Positive edge-triggered   Hardware term for action following the low–high transmission of the trigger signal.

Pre-emptive scheduling   Technique whereby the running process may be stopped in order that a higher-priority process may continue.

Priority   A measure of the relative importance of processes in a real-time system. A process's priority may be fixed or may vary with changing environmental conditions.

Process control systems   Real-time systems which control industrial processes, especially chemical, aerospace and manufacturing.

Process descriptor   Part of a process, consisting of a data structure in which the volatile environment of the process can be stored should the process be temporarily suspended.

Profiler   A software utility which summarises the results of a program trace to provide information on the frequency of execution of different parts of the subject program.

Program counter   CPU register containing the storage address of the next instruction to be executed.

Protection domain   Combination of a process's memory area and its privileges.

Protective redundancy   Technique which guarantees continued performance of the module's functions by including at least one or more identical, but functionally redundant, modules in the system.

Protocol   A formal method for defining format and control, particularly for communication systems.

Queue   A list or ordered linked set of memory elements. In queueing theory, a line of customers waiting for service.

Queueing theory   Mathematical discipline concerned with the analytical model of systems that are made up of queues.

Raster scan graphics   Graphics system based on a television type monitor or display device wherein the picture is constructed on a set of horizontal scan lines or raster.

Real-time system   A control system which responds virtually instantaneously to change in the environment it is controlling. 'Instantaneous' is a relative measure, dependent on the system being controlled.

Reconstruction   Term used to indicate the effective reproduction of an analog (continuous) signal equivalent to its sampled data form.

Record type   A data structure for associating elements of arbitrary types.

Recovery block   A number of alternative code blocks, headed by an acceptance test. All the code blocks form the same function, but in different ways. If, when executed, one code block fails the acceptance test, then another code block is tried.

Recovery monitor   Process which instigates recovery action when signalled that a fault has occurred.

Re-entrant code   Code segment which can be executed by more than one process at a time without the action of one process affecting the action of the other processes.

Relocatable code   Code which can be executed successfully irrespective of its position in main store.

Relocation pointer   Base address of a relocatable code segment. During code segment execution, the value of the relocation pointer is added to all address references before they are applied to the main store.

Rendezvous   A symmetrical synchronisation mechanism in Ada, in which two tasks coincide for a period of time to exchange information, after which they continue parallel execution. The rendezvous connects a task calling for service with a task providing the service, the latter usually being passive. Whichever task arrives first at the rendezvous waits for the other.

Response time   Time that a system will take to react to a change in, or stimulus from, its environment.

Rollback   A recovery technique. On detection of an error, the system is returned to the state that existed prior to the fault, and then restarted.

SADT   Structured Analysis and Design Technique.

Sample and hold amplifier   Hardware device for converting continuous signals to sampled data form, usually preceding an ADC.

Sampling   The act of freezing an analog (continuous) variable at particular instants of time in order to obtain a sampled data representation of the variable.

Scheduling   The allocation of resources (especially the CPU) to a number of competing processes.

Scope of visibility   Those parts of a program where a declaration is visible — that is, where its identifier may be used.

SDL   Specification and Design Language.

Self-driven simulation   Simulation technique wherein a statistical approximation of the workload is applied to the model. *Compare* **Trace-driven simulation.**

Semaphore   Non-negative integer value used as a synchronisation primitive.

Sequence type   A data structure designed for serial access having elements of the same type, and having a length which is left open (as distinct from an array whose length is defined during its declaration).

Serially re-usable   Provided that no two processes execute the code simultaneously, serially re-usable code may be used by more than one process without causing mutual disruption.

Server   Parts of a queueing system which process customers and therefore process the workload. In MASCOT 3 the module that interfaces an external device.

Service time   The rate at which a server is expected to service customers.

Set   A collection of elements, not necessarily of the same type, sometimes ordered.

Shuffler   Process designed to coalesce resident code segments into a contiguous system freespace.

SIGNAL   Synchronisation mechanism. When executed it allows a process to pass a corresponding WAIT operation.

Signal   An external input or output, commonly a voltage proportional to an external variable such as position or pressure.

Significant event   *See* **Event.**

Simulation model   Software based model of part or all of a system, or aspect of system performance.

Single pulse   One of a set of (clock) pulses.

Snapshot dump   Summary of the state of the system at one instant. Typically the value of the contents of all registers and all or part of the main storage.

Software trap (software interrupt)   A machine instruction which, when executed, causes an interrupt.

Specification part   That part of a procedure, task or module which contains the specification of the facilities provided within, and in which declarations are made of identifiers which are externally visible. *See also* **Implementation part**.

Stack   A last in first out (LIFO) list of memory elements. Commonly used to hold temporary variables during process execution, especially during interrupts and process swapping. System software commonly implements a system stack via a hardware stack pointer register; users may also employ stacks via software pointers.

State transition diagram   A graphical representation of a finite state machine, showing the interrelationships between states, events and actions.

Structured walkthrough   A formal meeting between persons concerned with a software module during which the design document, program code and testing scheme are discussed, step by step, in an attempt to highlight inconsistencies and inaccuracies.

Subrange type   A data type wherein the range is a subset of the range of the standard type. For example, TYPE OCTAL = (0 .. 7) is a subrange of the type INTEGER.

Synchronous operation   Information transfer and system operation by means of clocking at regular time intervals.

Synthetic programs   Programs which emulate the behaviour expected of typical programs in the final system.

System throughput   Queueing theory parameter. The average number of customers serviced per unit time.

Table-driven software   Programs which define their actions by reading control data from tables rather than following fixed algorithms.

Test data generator   A tool which analyses a program and uses this analysis to produce a set of data which, when input to the subject program, will cause execution of all, or a specific subset, of the control paths in the program.

Test harness   A set of hardware and/or software mechanisms which provides an environment in which the system, or parts of a system, may be tested and observed.

Test probe   A hardware or software mechanism which enables observation of the detailed operation of a system (especially data flow).

Time domain   The domain in which a signal has time as an independent variable.

Time-out   Occurs when a device or subsystem ceases operation and flags at the end of a pre-determined time.

Timeslicing   Method of sharing the processor by systematically allocating each process in the system fixed amounts of time for use of the processor.

Top-down functional design   Design technique wherein a problem is broken down into smaller and smaller parts.

Trace   A record or history of events that have occurred during a program's execution.

Trace-driven simulation   Simulation technique whereby actual workload data, derived by observation of a working system, are applied to the model. *Compare* **Self-driven simulation.**

Transducer   Hardware device for transferring power between systems, usually having different forms, such as pressure-to-voltage, current-to-torque.

Trap   *See* **Software trap**.

Tri-state   Hardware term for logic with three output states, namely high (active), low (active) and high impedance (passive). Used to construct bus systems efficiently.

UNIX   Operating system produced by Bell Laboratories for the Digital Equipment Corporation PDP11 processor. Is fast becoming a world standard, having been ported to many other processors.

User space   Protection domain wherein processes have limited access to processor instructions and cannot transfer control outside their memory area.

Utilisation factor   That fraction of the system's workload currently in use. The product of the average arrival rate and the average service time per customer.

Vectored interrupt   Interrupt mechanism whereby enabled device signals a vector pointing to its service routine.

Virtual machine   A machine comprising software and hardware whose attributes and functions are tailored to a particular application.

Volatile environment   The information which, if lost, would mean that a process could not continue operation from the point at which it last executed an instruction.

WAIT   Synchronisation primitive. When executed by a process it causes the process to suspend its operation until a particular event occurs.

Watchdog timer   A hardware or software mechanism which generates a signal (or interrupt) if not reset within a given timespan.

Workload   The service demanded of a system by its environment.

Index

283